About the authors

D1418640

Anna Feigenbaum is a lecturer in media University and has held fellow positions at the Rutgers Center for Histori- cal Analysis and the London School of Economics and Political Science. She completed her PhD at McGill University, Montreal, in 2008, where her project was funded by a Mellon Pre-dissertation Fellowship, the Institute of Historical Research, University of London, and the Social Sciences and Humanities Research Council of Canada. She has published in a range of outlets, including *South Atlantic Quarterly*, *ephemera*, *Feminist Media Studies*, *Fuse* magazine and Corpwatch.org. She is an associate of the Higher Education Academy and is a trained facilitator and community educator, running group development workshops for academics, non-governmental organisations and local initiatives. She can be found on Twitter at @drfigtree.

Fabian Frenzel is lecturer in organisation at the School of Management, University of Leicester, and Marie Curie post-doctoral fellow at the Depart- ment of Geography, University of Potsdam, Germany. He has worked on democratic politics in Europe, Africa and Brazil, looking at issues such as alternative media, international development and climate change. His PhD thesis is from the Centre of Tourism and Cultural Change, Leeds Metro- politan University. He is currently working on a two-year research project funded by the EU to investigate the valorisation of areas of deprivation and poverty in tourism. His work has been published in journals such as *Environment and Planning A*, *Tourism Geographies* and *Parallax*. He has edited (with Ko Koens and Malte Steinbrink) *Slum Tourism: Poverty, power, ethics*, published in 2012.

Patrick McCurdy is assistant professor in the Department of Communica- tion at the University of Ottawa, Canada and holds a PhD from the London School of Economics and Political Science. His thesis on how radical social movement actors interact with media at the site of protest was selected as part of the LSE History of Thought theses. His work has been published in several journals, including the *International Journal of Communication* and *Critical Discourse Studies*. He has published two co-edited books: *Mediation and Social Movements* (with Bart Cammaerts and Alice Mattoni), 2013; and *Beyond WikiLeaks: Implications for the future of communications, journalism and society* (with Benedetta Brevini and Arne Hintz), 2013. He can be found on Twitter at @pmmcc.

PROTEST CAMPS

*Anna Feigenbaum, Fabian Frenzel
and Patrick McCurdy*

Zed Books
LONDON | NEW YORK

Protest Camps was first published in 2013 by Zed Books Ltd, 7 Cynthia Street, London N1 9JF, UK and Room 400, 175 Fifth Avenue, New York, NY 10010, USA

www.zedbooks.co.uk

Copyright © Anna Feigenbaum, Fabian Frenzel and Patrick McCurdy 2013

The rights of Anna Feigenbaum, Fabian Frenzel and Patrick McCurdy to be identified as the authors of this work have been asserted by them in accordance with the Copyright, Designs and Patents Act, 1988

Set in Monotype Plantin and FFKievit by Ewan Smith
Index: ed.emery@thefreeuniversity.net
Cover design: www.roguefour.co.uk
Original cover image © Janine Wiedel Photolibrary/Alamy
Printed and bound in Great Britain by CPI Group (UK) Ltd, Croydon, CRO 4YY

Distributed in the USA exclusively by Palgrave Macmillan, a division of St Martin's Press, LLC, 175 Fifth Avenue, New York, NY 10010, USA

All rights reserved. No part of this publication may be reproduced, stored in a retrieval system or transmitted in any form or by any means, electronic, mechanical, photocopying or otherwise, without the prior permission of Zed Books Ltd.

A catalogue record for this book is available from the British Library
Library of Congress Cataloging in Publication Data available

ISBN 978 1 78032 356 5 hb
ISBN 978 1 78032 355 8 pb

CONTENTS

ILLUSTRATIONS

ACKNOWLEDGEMENTS

Some say it takes a village to write a book. Perhaps in this case you could say it took a protest camp. This project was made possible by all those who have shared their stories of protest camping. In particular, we are grateful to Moustafa Ayad, Claire English, Wolfgang Frenzel, Mayriam Ishani, Christiane Leidinger, Andrew Offenburger, Ramy Raoof, Kevin Smith, Victoria Sobel and multiple Occupy livestreamers as well as participants in the Ottawa and Montreal 'Campfire Chats' sessions for detailing their experiences with us. We also thank the photographers, artists and zinesters who generously shared the images that appear in this book.

Much appreciation goes to our editors Ken Barlow and Kika Sroka-Miller at Zed Books, our peer reviewers, and the impeccable work of our patient copyeditor Judith Forshaw. For thoughtful insight on early drafts, we thank Adam Bobbette, Gavin Brown, Stephen Dunne, Paolo Gerbaudo, Anastasia Kavada, Keir Milburn, Julie Uldam, the Feminist Media Studies Writing Group in New York and members of the Networks of Exchange Seminar at Rutgers University. We are grateful for the enrichment and nourishment throughout this process that came from the Protest Camp Research Collective and to all those who participated in our workshops and conference discussions. For financial and research support we thank Emory University's African American Collections, the Rutgers Center for Historical Analysis and the University of Leicester.

As book writing requires our own re-creation, it would not have been possible without the nurturing and care we are so fortunate to receive from our families and friends. Anna would like to especially thank her family of passionate writers and teachers, Susan, Bernard, Andrew and Alex, as well as Kheya Bag and Anja Kanngiesser for their constant gifts of confidence and clarity. Anna owes much of her productivity to Daniel Buchan for his delicious cooking and daily awesomeness. Fabian would like to especially thank his parents Dorothea and Siegfried for endless love and support, his brothers Sebastian and Korbinian for the many things we share, and

Merry Crowson for all the good times. Patrick would like to thank his parents Allan and Diane for their love and guidance and for encouraging him to apply for a job in Ottawa in the first place, and his brother Scott for always being prepared to help. He would also like to thank his wife Katrina and two wonderful children Lachlan and Beatrice for their love, patience and laughter. And finally, we would like to thank each other. This book was an experiment in horizontal decision-making, and like all consensus processes, it took time, critical discussion and the strength of affinity to build it together.

The illustrations in the book are from photographs taken by the authors except for: 1.2, reproduced by courtesy of Peter Kuper from his book *Diario De Oaxaca* (PM Press); 1.3, reproduced by courtesy of Occupy Portland; 2.3, reproduced by courtesy of Coal Action Scotland, http://coalactionscotland.org.uk/; 2.4, reproduced from the Southern Christian Leadership Conference records by courtesy of Manuscript, Archives, and Rare Book Library, Emory University; 2.5, reproduced by courtesy of the Women's Library, Archive Collection 5GCW/E London, UK; 2.6, reproduced by courtesy of *The Occupied Wall Street Journal*; 2.7, reproduced by courtesy of Ramy Raoof; 3.1, reproduced by courtesy of Clive J. Maclennan; 3.3, reproduced from *Spare Rib*, May 1984 by courtesy of the Women's Library, London, UK; 3.4, reproduced from *Copse, the Cartoon Book of Tree Protesting* by Kate Evans (currently out of print but an ebook version is forthcoming from cartoonkate.co.uk); 4.1, reproduced by courtesy of Ape Lad; 5.2, reproduced by courtesy of Jubilee Journey; 5.10, reproduced by courtesy of Nanky Rai.

You can follow the Protest Camps project on Twitter at @protestcamps and learn more about the broader Protest Camps Research Collective at http://protestcamps.org.

For those who camp to protest injustice.

When we are asked how we are going to build a new world, our answer is, 'We don't know, but let's build it together.' (John Jordan)

INTRODUCTION

From Tahrir Square to Syntagma Square, from the Puerto del Sol to the streets of Tel Aviv, from Wall Street to the London Stock Exchange, in 2011 protest camps became a global phenomenon. Indeed, for many it was through these movements that the practice of protest camping entered the public imagination. Yet, if our understanding of protest camps was left to the wild and often violent imagination of the mainstream media, protest camps would likely be seen as obstructive and illegal nests chock-full of 'die-hard' activists. However, behind the news headlines of struggles between 'folk devil' campers and authorities, beneath the undercover exposés of protest camp life, there is a rich and varied history of protest camps.

While the protest camp as a tactic of political contention has certainly garnered more attention recently, it is not a new phenomenon. Its origins are multiple and can be traced back to nomadic cultures, to the seventeenth-century Diggers movement, to indigenous peoples' resistances to colonial land grabs, to the birth of the Boy Scouts and summer camps, and even to ancient military practices of setting up encampments for battle. From this long, rich history, protest camps emerged in the late 1960s as a distinct political practice, often deployed intentionally. Protest camps proliferated alongside the rise of what have been termed 'new social movements'. Championed by researchers such as Alain Touraine and Alberto Melucci (1989; 1996), new social movement scholars were interested in how 'large-scale structural and cultural changes' brought about the rise of solidarity and collective identity and the formation of social movements that went beyond the realm of traditional politics calling for social change (Diani 1992). As we show in this book, within many of these new social movements, protest camps have been set up as part of protests relating to migrant rights, labour rights, land claims, ecological conservation and nuclear warfare, to name only a few.

Not only do protest camps encompass a diversity of demands for social change, they are also spaces where people come together to imagine alternative worlds and articulate contentious politics, often in confrontation with the state. What makes protest camps different from other place-based or space-based social movement gatherings and actions is the sustained physical and emotional labour that goes into building and maintaining the site as simultaneously a base for political action and a space for daily life. At a protest camp, people's perspectives towards others, as well as towards objects and ideas, are shaped through communal efforts to create sustainable (if ephemeral) infrastructures for daily life. Camps are frequently home to do-it-yourself (DIY) sanitation systems, communal kitchens, educational spaces, cultural festivals and performances, as well as media, legal and medical facilities. These alternative infrastructures facilitate the consumption and production of goods, the distribution of resources, and modes of labour and leisure that occur in and around protest camps.

Yet despite the increasing frequency of protest camps as an organisational form of protest over the past 50 years, and while much has been published on individual protest camps and movements that include protest camps, rarely has the camp itself been considered as something that is at once a very local and specific strategy, and a transnational or global practice. There are, of course, many wonderful activist books, alternative media articles and beautifully handcrafted zines that document, discuss and critically reflect on protest camps. These documents are cited in, and have shaped, much of this book. As for academic work, scholarly books and peer-reviewed journal articles have come out sporadically, dotted across a range of disciplines from social movement studies, media and communication studies to political science and organisation studies. Most of this existing scholarship regards camps as just one form of protest among many; they are grouped together with other strategies such as street parties, demonstrations, assemblies and direct actions (Epstein 2002; Klandermans 1994; McKay 1998; Duncombe 2002; Pickerill and Chatterton 2006; Brodkin 2007; della Porta et al. 2006; Crossley 2003; Jasper 1998; Chesters and Welsh 2004). However, as recent world events reveal, protest camps are not just a passing tactic. They can be the focal point of a movement both organisationally and symbolically and are both a contemporary and an historical practice.

In June 2010, before the protest camps of the Arab Spring and the Occupy movement, the three of us began a conversation about what a research project on protest camps might look like. And so, in much the same spirit of the DIY ethos our movements inspire, we began this protest camp book project together. The idea for such a book came from our personal and academic involvement with protest camps since the early 2000s, but in this book we pick up on a conversation that dates back much further and extends much wider than our own discussions. Our role here is to give this conversation focus, to zoom in on it, to find the connections and points of conflict that have emerged as patterns within it. Like good facilitators (of a protest camp meeting perhaps), our job is as much to find out what discussions already exist as it is to help guide the conversation as it moves forward.

In a way, this book is published in the midst of an ongoing conversation, since the act of protest camping is now being given more attention than ever before. While we could not have anticipated the wave of protests that swept the globe in January 2011, when these events took place we attempted to gather information about these new protest camps. That said, in studying this upsurge in protest camps – and indeed protest camps of the past – we were limited by the resources to which we had access. Indeed, there is much rich documentation about many protest camps stored in faraway archives that we did not have funding to visit. And there are even more stories and histories about protest camps written in languages we do not speak. In fact, any attempt to cover the actual range of protest camps across the world would require a large multinational and multilingual research team. Our global ambitions for this project have been kept in check by the availability of resources at hand; as such, readers will note that our primary vantage point lies in studying protest camps from North America, the United Kingdom and mainland Europe, although we made a conscious effort to diversify our discussion of camps beyond these areas. We too are aware of this limitation and believe it highlights the need for further research into the similarities and differences between protest camps across time, space and culture. At the same time, we did not think that this limitation should prevent us from opening up a wider conversation about the need to study protest camps. If anything, the empirical or theoretical holes or deficiencies that the reader may spot in our modest contribution point to the need for more scholarship from a diverse array of methodological and theoretical perspectives.

Just as we refrain from speaking universally of the protest camp across cultures and contexts, we also explicitly avoid treating the protest camp as a quantifiable or measurable social movement strategy. For a number of reasons this book does not seek to answer the question 'Does a protest camp help a movement succeed?' This question cannot capture the complexity or dynamics of the diversity of protest camps. While camps sometimes emerge in movements, at other times they are spaces where movements converge, and sometimes they are places where new movements are fostered and grow. Of course, the tactical successes and failures, the potentials and pitfalls of a protest camp can be examined in relation to specific, contextualised movement experiences, yet any overarching or universal answer to this question is both impossible and undesirable. In short, we feel it is the wrong question to ask about protest camps. Rather than a definitive tome, we see this book as the beginning of an area of inquiry and hope it can serve as a springboard for the study of future protest camps.

The multiple origins of organised camping

The word 'camp' originates in the language of the Roman military and its use of the Latin word *campus,* meaning 'an open field' or 'open space for military exercise'. Its original use was in the Campus Martius, a flood plain just outside the ancient city of Rome, where the Roman armies practised. From there it continued to be used in both the Roman and Germanic language families. In Old English, *camp* is a word for contest and emerged around a ball game that is considered to be a forerunner of modern football. The term 'champion' is derived from this use. A linguistic link to leisure culture is observable, as is the more obvious relation to the original military use.

In medieval times, in English, 'camp' comes to be used as a term to describe temporal accommodation of the army, a usage taken from the French at the time. The verb 'encamp' also comes into use around this time. The military meaning, as much as the word's use in the context of contest and game, points to the development of the modern political metaphor of the camp that is broadly used to describe political alignment and faction. There is evidence that this usage started in the sixteenth century in English (Booth 1999). From the early nineteenth century, 'camp' is used to describe both meetings and gatherings (for example of the Methodists) and also individual alignment to particular religious, and subsequently political, groups with the term camp follower.

In English, there is also a second, more recent, meaning of camp as an aesthetic category. Popularised by Susan Sontag in 'Notes on "camp"' (1964), this term has drawn significant attention in postmodern and queer aesthetics. It derives from the French verb *se camper*, meaning to plant oneself or stand squarely in front of something, and is therefore closely related to the more spatial meaning of the original term and constitutes another early metaphor of the territorial camp (Booth 1999). These linguistic and etymological traces reflect, to some extent, the social practices of camps and camping as they develop historically.

In France, the noun and verb 'campaign' (*campagne*) comes into use in the seventeenth century for military advance and to suggest the army taking to the 'open field' in the summer after it has spent the winter resting. This adds a mobile notion to the previously more localised meaning of a military camp and also signifies aspects of the European colonial mobility at the time. The Vikings had already been described as 'camp people', but with the European 'discovery' of the American continent and the subsequent practice of colonisation, the necessity to travel and to live for long periods of time in temporary housing (in camps) prompted the development of new meanings for the military term (ibid.).

The fact that people on the move camp, and that their architecture is temporal, links the camp with nomadic societies. The act of camping was something people engaged in long before it had a 'proper' name. Before and beyond their Roman military origins, camps are probably the oldest form of human settlement (Cowan 2002). In the modern development of the meaning of the word 'camp', important inspiration derives from encounters between mobile settlers and semi-nomadic indigenous tribes. These encounters propelled exchanges and cross-fertilisations of diverse mobile infrastructures, as in North America. The settlers camped because it was a pragmatic way to master the colonisation process; however, some native Americans' technological knowledge, which was linked to their partly nomadic lifestyles, proved highly useful for the settlers moving westward, for example regarding tipis that allowed for open fires inside them. Similarly, European technologies that were useful to temporary housing and mobile lifestyles, such as the horse and carriage, quickly became absorbed by native American nomadic cultures (Leed 1991).

It might be no surprise that this process of cross-cultural 'camping' influenced the development of the word 'camp' in a variety of ways. As politics developed in new settler republics in North America, the word 'campaign' was used for the first time in its contemporary political meaning. 'Campaign' was taken from the French and their use of the term in the military, but was equally inspired by the experiences of mobile 'campaigning' in the colonial experiment (Booth 1999). However, in the colonial conquest of North America, 'camp' also developed a darker meaning. In the whole of the British Empire, the word came to signify the tools of population control and forced migration. The regime of transportation, a colonial technique to populate overseas territories with criminals from the homeland, established the camps of the state of Georgia and the country of Australia. It is estimated that in the eighteenth century 60,000 prisoners were sent to penal colonies in North America, amounting to a quarter of the total number of settlers from Britain (ibid.). In the early years, members of religious minorities and political prisoners were transported. In the Australian case, prisoner-settlers were Irish nationalists as well as trade unionists. Over this whole period, the majority of transported prisoners were the poor. Their practices of subsistence hunting and farming on common land were strategically made illegal by the process of privatisation of the previously common land in the seventeenth to nineteenth centuries, the so-called 'enclosure of the commons' (Leed 1991). During the conflict with rebellious Boer settlers in South Africa in the early twentieth century, the British Empire used concentration camps to imprison whole populations in an effort to cut supply lines for Boer guerrilla fighters. The inmates consisted mainly of children and women from both Boer and African backgrounds who were held in dismal conditions that led to the death of about 28,000 Boers and about 14,000 Africans, most of them children. The Boer concentration camps prefigure the well documented use of concentration camps by fascist and totalitarian states in the twentieth century to control, punish, terrorise and extinguish populations and peoples.

Another thread or genealogy that can be teased out of the entangled history of protest camping is the rise of Scout camping and political youth movements. These developed first in Europe and the USA, but have been picked up widely around the world ever since. In the context of the American summer camp, as well as in the later Wandervoegel and Scouts movements, camps were consciously employed to create (or rather re-create) the infrastructures of daily life. The purpose of the exercise for the young people involved was the development of certain characteristics, and the foundations of these movements were seen as deeply educational. For educators at the time, the simplification of life that the camp provided was supposed to reconnect participants to nature and simplicity. Untangling social reproduction was seen as a valuable learning experience, allowing the participants to reconsider life in 'civilisation'.

One of the earliest examples of this modern organised camping was the Wandervoegel movement, the initiative of Berlin schoolteachers who considered the experience of nature as central to children's development. The Wandervoegel movement developed organised camping in Germany (Hetherington 1998; Giesecke 1981) and reflected an explicitly negative view of city life, to which it was opposed. Concurrently, organised camping appeared in the American summer camp movement. As Smith (2006) explains, US camps were often 'counter-modern' in spirit, reflecting ideals of nature, authenticity and simplicity against the perceived problems of cities and civilisation. The young campers were supposed to learn to live autonomously, and organised camping expressed a critique of the ways in which modern life was organised. The camps were meant to provide a contrasting experience to modernity, especially for the youth, for whom such experience was deemed important. Smith argues in respect of the American summer camps:

> The people who operated these camps understood ... that it was the contrast between the everyday world of a child's life and the camp world that had the potential to help children develop (ibid.: 71).

Movements such as the Wandervoegel have been described as an early counterculture (Cresswell 1996; Hetherington 1998). However, they were not of the left-leaning tendencies we associate with countercultures today; if these early movements had political orientations, they tended to the right. Summer camps and Scout movements were infused with authoritarian ideologies (Kneights 2004), and the German Wandervoegel, despite some anti-authoritarian underpinnings in its foundation period, was fully integrated into the German Empire's nationalistic frenzy in the build-up to the First World War. The movement merged with the Hitler Youth organisation in the

1930s (Giesecke 1981). In Britain, Lieutenant-General Lord Robert Baden-Powell, the inventor of Scout camping, called to his Scouts to overcome class boundaries in the defence of the British Empire in proto-fascist rhetoric:

> Remember, whether rich or poor, from castle or from slum, you are all Britons in the first place, and you've got to keep Britain up against outside enemies, you have to stand shoulder to shoulder (quoted in Rojek 1993: 40).

Incidentally, Baden-Powell was a veteran of the Boer wars and would have been aware of the concentration camps erected in the conflict.

In the United States, the origins of organised camping rested upon a range of foundation myths of unity and camaraderie. For some camp founders, the aim was to bring nature and practical outdoors skills to city boys; for others it was to strengthen religious bonds or generate a sense of community virtue. Many early organised camps explicitly referenced tribal practices and inheritances from Native Americans. Boy Scout tents were often emblazoned with images of Native American men in headdresses (Snyder 2006), and camps such as Ernest Thompson Seton's Woodcraft Indians 'emphasized the Indian virtues of honesty and forthrightness, outdoor living, council fires, and Indian dances' (Carlson 1986: vi). Seton's approach to camping influenced Scouting movements in both the US and Britain.

What emerges across these origin stories of organised camping is the relationship their founders saw between the act of living outdoors together and the formation of a community of understanding. The content of this understanding varied greatly and points to a key feature of the organised camp as unique structural, spatial and temporal form that shapes those who live, work, play and create within it. These acts of daily living and exchange are often laden with ideology, at the same time as they exceed and at times resist the political goals of their founders. As Eells documents with regard to the origins of organised camping:

> Because the camp was recognized as a powerful influence on behaviour and ideological thinking, many religious and political groups turned to it as a unique means of propagating their special points of view (Eells 1986: 57).

This recognition led to a proliferation of different forms of organised camps, as camping proved too popular to be politically instrumentalised for one particular set of ideologies. Scout camping was 'infiltrated' by girls who managed to overcome its exclusive designation 'for boys' that its founders had envisioned (Mills 2011). Despite concerns that 'camp work' might make women's hearts too weak and that ladies would be exposed to the informal dress and table etiquette required for living outdoors, camps for girls spread across the United States in the 1910s and 1920s (Eells 1986). In Britain, by 1925, a Woodcraft Folk splinter group separated from the Scout movement because of its excessive militarism. Harking back to the 'tribal virtues' of Seton's Woodcraft Indians, the Woodcraft Folk in the UK went on to develop into a socialist alternative to the right-wing orientation of the Scout movement (Davis 2000). The Woodcraft Folk's educational ideals were partly inspired by the early socialist Robert Owen, who envisioned an education based on ideals of community and the experience of nature as early as the late eighteenth/early nineteenth century. Owen, who in 1823 founded the utopian community of New Harmony in Indiana, also stands at the beginning of a history of intentional communities that begin to spring up in the nineteenth century in the UK and US. As utopian projects they prefigure and relate closely to ideas expressed in the late nineteenth-century camping movement; however, there is the caveat that the camping movement established alternative communities in an exceptional, holiday-like time period, integrated into and not alternative to the status quo. In the later socialist orientations of the Woodcraft Folk and similar camping movements linked to left-wing political groups, the prefigurative and perhaps antagonistic positioning of the camp towards the status quo returned. The consequences of this can be seen today, as some key organisers of UK protest camps recall their Woodcraft Folk experiences in their childhood as sites where they acquired the skills and ethos now used in operating protest camps such as the communal squat 'Grow Heathrow'. Another example of the role these camping traditions play in contemporary protest camps is the German socialist-oriented Die Falken (The Falcons), who on more than one occasion provided their large tents and marquees to support protest camps across Germany, for example to construct a refugee rights protest camp in Berlin in autumn 2012.

From the first half of the twentieth century, two more significant forerunners of today's protest camps need mentioning. These are the

Bonus Army camps of 1932 and 1933 and the Hoovervilles, springing up both as a result of, and a response to, the great depression in the United States. Hoovervilles were 'shanty towns' set up to provide basic infrastructure for those left homeless by the economic collapse. While they served primarily as a place to sleep and eat, many took on aspects of alternative villages, some even naming streets and electing a mayor. Moreover, as we will discuss in the next chapter, the Hoovervilles were often established in central city spaces, such as New York's Central Park. This exposed the crisis by making its effect visible to the public. Taking on a similar form to the Hoovervilles, but mixed with elements of military base sites, the Bonus Army camps sustained World War One veterans also struggling through the recession. These camps, situated near the capitol buildings, served as planning bases and sites for the reproduction of daily life during the Bonus Army's months-long protests in Washington DC, as veterans demanded payment of promised benefits for their time served. As in the other instances, there is not enough space here to discuss these predecessors of protest camping in great detail, but the ways in which they inspired activists, particularly in North America, must be acknowledged. Immediately before the Occupy Wall Street protests, anti-austerity activists had created 'Bloombergville' in protest against cuts in New York's city budget in the preceding months. Bloombergville, which was also inspired by anti-austerity protests in Greece and Spain, referenced in its name the 1930s Hooverville camps. What is interesting here, and a question we will return to, is that the Hoovervilles were not set up as protest camps as such; they were camps of necessity, expressions of poverty or want, rather than conscious protests in many instances. However, they form an example of the sometimes fleeting boundaries between different kinds of camps that we will discuss in more detail below.

Protest camps, in their contemporary form, only seem to become a popular and explicit social movement strategy, alongside the developments of broader emancipatory movements, in the late 1960s and 1970s. It is in this period that we begin to see encampments built not just to provide a base or a symbol for dissent, but to allow for social reproduction and the re-creation of everyday life in ways that contest the status quo. In this way, protest camps follow on from organised forms of camping and intentional communities – often picking up on architectural structures, camp work practices, and community

0.1 Global protest camps prior to 2011

organisation principles from earlier camps – but now frequently with an explicit emancipatory idea(l).

What makes a 'protest camp'?

The intersections and overlaps in these origin stories of camping – which have been only partially sketched out here – make it tempting to place protest camps as direct descendants of those other camp forms. Attempting to make links between varied camping practices, Loefgren (1999) argues that recreational camping and penal camps share certain features of architecture and planning, and that they do so to such an extent that Loefgren finds it 'tempting to name the 20th century the era of the camp' (ibid.: 256). Hailey (2009) has suggested differentiating between three kinds of camps: camps of *control*, of *necessity* and of *autonomy*. Camps of *control* describe those camps that are erected by states to confine populations, like the example of camps in the British transportation regime, the Nazi concentration camps or those of the migration control regimes of the European Union (EU), but also in the military, where they serve to control and organise mobile troops. Here, camps are characterised by strong levels of order and discipline. Camps of *necessity* are those erected in response to emergencies and catastrophes, but perhaps also those that are linked to colonial adventures and the forced dispersal that resulted from them. Hailey lists refugee camps (following natural disaster or political upheaval and war) as the most obvious examples. Finally, Hailey discusses camps of *autonomy* as those camps that campers set up themselves and voluntarily, in order to pursue a variety of aims – education, leisure, protests or fun. What is particularly interesting about Hailey's divide between camps of control, necessity and autonomy is that he seems to base his definition on the character of entry into and exit from the camp and differences between enforced entry and prevented exit (covering both camps of control and camps of necessity) and voluntary entry and exit (camps of autonomy). We find it useful and necessary to differentiate between the variety of camps, not least because there is obviously a world of difference between a state-controlled camp in which people are incarcerated and a camp that people set up voluntarily to protest. The clear typology Hailey suggests, however, has its limits. As we discussed earlier, both migrant camps and other, more emergency-oriented camps have been shown to develop some strong elements of autonomy within their organisation, with their inhabitants using the space of the camp to start to formulate political demands and to frustrate the attempts of the sovereign power to control them (Solnit 2005). Sometimes refugee camps can become protest camps, as in the case of the Western Saharouri protesters or Palestinian refugee camps. These boundaries also become fuzzy in instances where solidarity camps are set up adjacent to or within existing refugee camps (Calais and Woomera, for example). Once they are established and to some extent become independent of the levels of control, necessity or force used in their creation, do camps potentially share a logic of internal organisation? A logic that tends to provide space for autonomy? In studying protest camps such an internal view of the camp as a space that enables or enhances certain forms of communal organisation is of course particularly interesting. We discuss the role of the camp in the politics of organisation in more detail in Chapter 5.

Overall, we use a flexible and, in part, strategic definition of what counts as a protest camp. Put simply, we define a protest camp as *a place-based social movement strategy that involves both acts of ongoing protest and acts of social reproduction needed to sustain daily life.* While we draw mostly from movements and campaigns that explicitly articulated a strategy or practice of 'protest camping', we occasionally cast our net wider. Some of the place-based social movement actions we pull under this heading were labelled as 'protest camps' by mainstream media or movement discourses, even if they did not, at the time, articulate their practices in these words. In a few cases we have also applied this term to occupations that shared the social reproduction practices and nomadic architecture of protest camps, although they took place largely indoors (the Alcatraz Occupation, Wisconsin Capitol occupation, and the Claremont Road protests).

As we are concerned with questions of social justice and emancipation, we specifically focus on those protest camps that articulate, at least in part, an emancipatory politics. Just as wider forms of organised camping can be mobilised to propagate and enshrine a variety of ideologies, so too can an organised camp be set up to 'protest'. Oppositional and dissenting politics are not the exclusive arena of the left, as histories of fascism and camping make clear. Thus while a history of what could equally be called the 'protest camps' of right-leaning, conservative or even fascist politics could be written, our unequivocal focus on emancipatory politics means that we have consciously decided not to include such camps. In addition, not all protest camps are created intentionally as protest camps, which poses a challenge when thinking about the relationship between 'intention' and 'action'. This is seen in the cases where camps of necessity transform into and become camps of protest politics.

For these reasons, rather than equate or classify protest camps as camps of autonomy following Hailey (2009), we instead turn 'autonomy' from a feature or motivation of a camp into a set of questions about a camp. Throughout this book, and particularly in its final chapters, we ask: what are the (im)possibilities of autonomy for the protest camp? In what ways do protest camps enact a contentious or antagonistic politics against the status quo, and often against the repressive state? How and when do protest campers attempt to build alternative worlds together – and what stands in their way?

The link between protest camps and (new) social movements

Protest camps do not emerge as social movement practices out of nowhere. Rather, they arise out of and in relation to specific cultures, movements and struggles. As T. V. Reed argues, movement cultures are generally formed from 'existing cultural structures' to support a new movement's 'goals, ideas, and strategies' (Reed 2005: 14). Likewise, Eyerman and Jamison write that social movements are 'emergent spaces which are carved out of existent contexts' (Eyerman and Jamison 1998: 21). This is what Meyer and Whittier termed 'social movement spillover' to describe how the 'innovations of one movement may diffuse into others' (Meyer and Whittier 1994: 291).

Our decision to focus on the encampment aspect of social movement protest means that a number of other issues and areas of study must remain out of focus. There are stories and contexts that cannot be captured in the frame of our protesters' lens. We cannot offer, for example, detailed histories of the movements from which these camps arose, nor long commentaries on the many factors that went into the formation of particular movements. There are already a number of good books that do just this, and we have drawn ideas from them and done our best to point to them as further resources. Nor do we focus on long-standing debates between various political factions and organisations. This too is covered at length elsewhere and is intentionally de-emphasised here, since part of our project is to make room to consider the significance of the protest camp itself, along with the many ways in which protesters become entangled in much more than just each other's ideas and ideologies. From the protest camper's perspective, we are also concerned with the ways in which our politics grow through, around and in between the structures, objects and environments in which people find themselves camping together. To do this, we need some tools, or concepts, for reflective thinking.

Concept soup

In her book examining what a 'methodology of the oppressed' might look like, Chela Sandoval argued for a transdisciplinary approach to research, and a transversal approach to politics, that seeks to combine concepts and ideas from different periods and perspectives that can help us better understand and navigate political struggles under the conditions of global capitalism. Discussing what she termed an 'apartheid' of academic knowledge, she wrote:

> There is as yet no agreed-upon interdisciplinary approach for bringing these languages together in the shared project that underlies their many articulations: a theory and method of

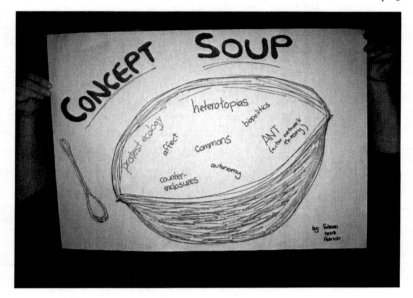

0.2 The concept soup

consciousness-in-opposition that focuses on the citation and deployment of a differential form. Nevertheless, this 'differential' mode of oppositional consciousness is being manifested in the academic world under varying terminologies, concomitantly and symptomatically from across disciplines (Sandoval 2000: 77).

It is often the case with studies of social movements that researchers and writers must shift and move between different perspectives. The dynamic and multifaceted nature of protest means that debates around it are often taking place in slightly different registers and languages. Yet, whether geographers, architects, art historians or sociologists, many of us doing academic work on social movements are concerned with similar ideas. There are, of course, nuanced, and often important, political differences to draw out from the terms with which we speak and write. Yet, as Sandoval urges, there is as much an art – or a method – that must be cultivated for making connections as there is a sophistry in squabbling over the exact meaning of 'historical materialism' (or any other key term, for that matter).

Theories and their associated concepts act as lenses to help make sense of the social world. In order to study protest camps, we took an interdisciplinary approach to social theory that combined our various backgrounds and expertise with existing debates about social movements and protest camps within the literature. In doing this, our goal has been to forge links between scholarship and debates within sociology, political science and communication in order to develop an approach that is capable of studying protest camps in a robust way. In what follows, we present the core concepts that inform and underwrite our approach and that have helped us think about protest camps and have oriented our analysis of their various aspects and characteristics.

Spatiality and temporality Spatiality, in its various material, imagined and representational forms, is at the heart of all protest camps. Notions of space are key to understanding the physicality and dynamics of the protest camp. Discussions about the concept of space have proliferated in both academic and activist discourse and are captured in ideas and terms such as 'open spaces' (Shukaitis et al. 2007), 'temporary autonomous zones' (Bey 1991), 'convergence spaces' (Routledge 2000) and 'convergence centres' (Juris 2008), urban social centres (Montagna 2007; Hodkinson and Chatterton 2007; Leontidou 2007), picket lines (Brown and Yaffe 2013) and, in respect of student activism, 'campus connections' (Crossley 2008; Zhao 2001). Protest camps are often defined by their physical location. In geographical literature we also find rich discussions about the links between space, place and protest. This is directly relevant to the study of protest camps as it concerns the interactions of framing and place (Heaney and Rojas 2006) when protest campers choose certain locations for their camps, as happened recently with Occupy Wall Street or by the protesters in Tahrir Square. Hakim Bey (1991) put forward the idea of 'temporary autonomous zones' to describe the creation of revolutionary spaces free from state control. Paul Routledge's (2000) writings on 'convergence spaces' captures both the imagined space – the space created around an issue or idea, and around which diverse networks coalesce and form relations – and the material form of this space, which physic-ally manifests itself in an occupation, direct action or protest camp. In a similar vein, Paolo Gerbaudo has referred to protest camps as 'magnetic gathering places' (2012: 95) in an effort to describe the allure of the physical space of the protest camp and the spectacle of its mediated presence across social, mainstream and alternative media.

A common feature of global justice mobilisations were 'convergence centres', often but not exclusively associated with urban protest mobilisations. Juris describes the convergence centre as a 'small, self-managed city, a "heterotopic space" of exchange and innovation' (2008: 129). Related 'social centres' (Montagna 2007; Hodkinson and Chatterton 2007; Leontidou 2007) are more permanent endeavours than 'convergence spaces'. As radical autonomous spaces, they are characterised by an autonomous politics and are often located in urban areas. With regards to student activism, Crossley (2008) has written about 'campus connections'.

Temporality is another important factor for understanding protest camps. The time frames of protest camps differ greatly, while central features of their organisational form remain linked to spatiality. Put more plainly, while some protest camps begin with no set end date, others are intended to run for a fixed period of time. In both cases, whether a camp is legally or illegally occupying land influences how long it continues. Likewise, when campers are occupying sites scheduled for demolition, such as trees, authorities often go to great lengths to remove the protesters. Routledge (2000: 33) draws on the work of Melucci (1989) to highlight how contemporary practices of resistance 'are characterised by diffuse, temporary and ad hoc organisational structures, and exhibit short term, intense mobilisations, reversible commitment [i.e. the possibility to instantaneously join and leave certain movements], and multiple leadership'. Here, the intense, yet temporal, nature of resistance fits well with an analysis of those short-lived protests often tied to global meetings such as the G8 or G20 summits, and could also be appropriate for some of the Indignados, Occupy and Climate Camps.

Whether protest camps last for an afternoon or a decade, they become places where people and ideas converge. As briefly discussed above, the concepts of the 'convergence space' and 'convergence centre' have received academic and activist attention as both physical and conceptual meeting points. Routledge (2000) has developed the idea of the 'convergence space' to refer to the conceptual arena where networks can align themselves and organise. Convergence spaces are defined by Routledge as:

Common ground between various social movements, grassroots initiatives, non-governmental organisations and other formations, wherein certain interests, goals, tactics and strategies converge. It is a space of facilitation, solidarity, communication, coordination, and information sharing. It is both virtual – enacted through the internet – and material, enacted through conferences and various kinds of direct action such as demonstrations and strikes (ibid. 35).

Convergence spaces take a material form when they manifest in a physical location where different groups and people come together. Protest camps may be seen as the materialisation of Routledge's 'convergence spaces'. To sum up, protest camps are defined and reflexively shaped by their overlapping location in material space, the spaces of the imagination and representational space. Therefore, any effort to study a protest camp requires a perspective on space that recognises these three overlapping and interwoven elements; the selection of a physical site for a protest camp is important for how the camp and its occupiers understand themselves (spaces of the imagination), and how they create, navigate and engage with spaces of mediated representation in their communication, self-representation, media framing and public perception.

Actor–network theory Another conceptual tool that informs our approach throughout this book stems from actor–network theory (ANT). ANT, particularly in its more contemporary versions and revisions, provides a method of thinking about how interdependencies between people, groups and objects emerge and function. It is particularly useful for thinking about how human and non-human actors are always enmeshed. Thierry Bardini offers this summary:

> [ANT] describes the progressive constitution of a network in which both human and non-human actors assume identities according to prevailing strategies of interaction. Actors' identities and qualities are defined during negotiations between representatives of human and non-human actants ... The most important of these negotiations is 'translation', a multifaceted interaction in which actors (1) construct common definitions and meanings, (2) define representatives, and (3) co-opt each other in the pursuit of individual and collective objectives (Bardini 1997: ft 3).

Employing this notion of 'translation', the process of joining together to maintain and operate a protest camp can be read as a series of engagements in which human actors (or people – campers, supporters, locals, government officials) and non-human materials (tents, tools, kitchen equipment, communication technologies, toilets) enter into particular relationships with each other. Each person participating might have a different orientation to camp life (experienced campaigner, first-time camper, weekend visitor, looking for shelter) and varying motivations for taking part, but through their operation of the tasks needed to achieve a common goal, participants negotiate (or fail to negotiate) a way to function together, manifesting a 'protest camp'.

While some critics of ANT condemn the model for failing to take account of how power relations shape interactions, those working with what is sometimes called 'ANT and After' (Law and Hassard 1999) or 'post-ANT' (Gad and Bruun Jensen 2009) argue instead that the tools ANT offers can help make explicit the ways in which power and difference are performed and played out in the many everyday associations and disassociations we make with one another, for example, how gender, race and class can shape meeting discussions or the division of cooking tasks (Alcadipani and Hassard 2010: 429).

Moreover, ANT approaches are concerned with questions not only about what is, but also about what could be (ibid.). How might the arrangement of tasks, division of roles and camp policies be altered in an attempt to create different effects and affects (emotions or feelings)? These approaches can also help direct our attention to the importance of physical objects and structures in how people interact, as well as to how things such as weather, climate and time of day form part of our political and social interactions. For example, how do outdoor meetings in the cold affect campers' discussions? What does the location and structure of the kitchen do to the flow of traffic and the conversations of camp visitors? In this book, we do not go into theoretical detail about different conceptualisations and uses of ANT, nor do we choose to use this now-outdated terminology. Instead, we engage with an ANT-informed approach, following Karen Barad, to rethink protest camps as entanglements of humans and non-humans and to treat objects and infrastructures as more than 'passive and inert' (Barad 2007: 245–6).

Affect In addition to using approaches drawn from ANT, our study is also shaped by theories of affect, emotion in social movements, and affective labour. Affect is defined in many different ways by thinkers from a variety of disciplines, including psychology, philosophy, cultural studies, media studies and human geography. While definitions vary from theorist to theorist, there are generally three ways in which 'affect' is viewed to explain social interaction and experience. In application, and even in theorising the concept of affect, these different approaches largely overlap and inform each other. We separate them out here in order to familiarise those new to these theories with this dense terminology (for a more extensive discussion of affect in protest camps, see Feigenbaum, McCurdy and Frenzel 2013).

First, affect can be seen as a way of thinking about sensations we do not (or do not yet) have the language to describe. This 'pre-discursive' or 'pre-personal' definition of affect sees affect as the pre-cognitive sensation that drives and moves the body; in other words, it is what makes us feel. For psychologist Silvan Tomkins, 'affect has the power to influence consciousness by amplifying our awareness of our biological state' (Shouse 2005). Second, affect is used to describe the ways in which sensations can move and circulate through physical and virtual spaces. Everyday examples of this include feeling the 'tension in a room', flame wars that erupt over listservs or emails, or online 'shitstorms' that hit corporations or people after they have made contentious comments. And finally, affect is found in encounters and interactions that move, stir or arouse something in us and produce a change. We see this notion of transformative affect expressed in many protesters' descriptions of their participation in actions and events.

Sara Ahmed's theorisation of emotion in political communities is particularly useful to a study of protest camps. Ahmed argues that collective formations emerge out of dialogical practices, 'the conversations, the doing, the work' (Ahmed 2004). Doing work and creating together at a protest camp can encompass everything from going through a meeting agenda to debating waged labour, to deciding whose turn it is to get tea. Through these interactions, especially as they occur repeatedly over time, campers form attachments to each other and to the protest camp. There are shared pleasures and practices, as well as persistent disagreements. These daily dialogues and debates shape campers' feelings towards each other, as well as towards ideas, activities and objects. Likewise, the technological objects utilised by protesters in the everyday life of creating and sustaining the protest camp are significant in terms of affect and feelings, and for understanding the importance of emotion in social movements. As we discussed in relation to ANT, objects mediate social interaction as they become invested with protesters' feelings and ideas.

Ecology Like many in the humanities and social sciences, in this book we borrow the language of ecology to make sense of how people live interdependently with other creatures, things and environmental conditions (Fuller 2005; Stengers 2005; Nardi and O'Day 1999; Treré 2012). Protests, and particularly place-based protests such as protest camps, lend themselves to this ecological thinking as human and non-human elements are in ongoing and constantly changing relationships with each other during the life of a protest camp. As Matthew Fuller explains, the term 'ecology' 'is one of the most expressive [terms] language currently has to indicate the massive and dynamic interrelation of processes and objects, beings and things, patterns and matter' (Fuller 2005: 2). Combined with thinking on technology and tactics, the language of ecology is well suited to our infrastructural reading of protest camps.

Also relevant to thinking about protest camps as 'protest ecologies' is Félix Guattari's work *The Three Ecologies* (*Les trois écologies*). Originally published in French in the late 1980s, and coming out of his engagement with social movements and training in psychoanalysis and Marxist theory, Guattari's short piece on 'ecologies' argued that we are entangled not only in an 'environmental ecology' but also in a 'mental' and 'social' ecology shaped and produced by 'integrated world capitalism' (IWC). IWC is a new phase of capitalism in which centres of power have moved 'away from the structures of production of goods and services, and towards structures of production of signs, of syntax' (Guattari 2005: 137). Guattari's understanding of ecology is particularly relevant to the study of protest camps because of the attention it draws to the importance of movement innovation, non-linear exchanges of knowledge and practices, and the complexity of enmeshed human and non-human networks. As Sy Taffel argues, Guattari's concept of ecology 'is far more than a concern for the environment, it is an epistemological system' (Taffel 2008).

Our thinking about ecologies is also informed by a recent turn in media scholarship to focus on the process of mediation and the related practices of the social in these environments (Couldry 2004; 2012; Silverstone 1999; 2007). Drawing on these works, protest camps are seen as unfolding within a media ecology that is both the product of and reflexively woven into the social, economic, technological and political fabric of society. In viewing media as an ecology, our goal is to explicitly acknowledge that social struggle takes place both on the ground in physical arenas (ranging from forest floors to public squares) and also – often simultaneously – in the representational arenas of mainstream media coverage and the wider mediated public sphere of alternative media, networked social media and other symbolic forms. Thus, an ecological perspective allows us to look beyond the tired binaries of old and new media, and mainstream and alternative media, and consider the broad media ecology that protest camps exist within and contribute to. Consequently, it frees us to examine the 'media practices' (Couldry 2004; 2012) of protest campers and the 'tactical' (Lovink 2011) uses and innovations of media at protest camps, and to consider both the representation and the symbolic significance of protest camps. The symbolic element of the protest campsite often attempts to draw attention to issues that are otherwise hard to make concrete, either because it is difficult to make them visible, for example the global system of consumer capitalism, or because the target audiences are otherwise disconnected from those issues. From this perspective, and drawing explicitly on Gamson and Wolfsfeld (1993), the symbolic role of the protest camp can serve to *mobilise* protest campers, *validate* their cause and/or *enlarge the scope* of the relevant issue. Protesters, conscious of the camp's symbolic significance and its public and representational resonance, may select sites that are believed to embody the issues they wish to highlight or where the protest camp may attain visibility.

Following on from these integrations and developments of ecological thinking, we argue that adopting an ecological viewpoint can transform not only the ways in which we think about the debates surrounding protest action, but also how people understand their own positions, and how they engage with other people and objects – both human and non-human – in the space of the camp as a site of ongoing protest and a community of resistance. Thinking about the protest camp as an 'ecology' helps us navigate the ways in which social movement ideas are exchanged and carried into the reproduction of protest camps' infrastructures and practices. As ideas of 'the best way to do things' compete, the desire for authority (or, as we will later call it, 'power over' as opposed to 'power to') can impede the 'experimental togetherness' of the protest camp. It is precisely this space of experimentation, of building together both to resist and to survive, that opens up what Stavrides describes as the 'collective inventiveness' of direct democracy (Stengers 2005; Stavrides 2012; Starhawk 1987).

Autonomy Picking up on the concept introduced in Hailey's categorisation of camps, it remains important to link autonomy to broader social movement studies and political science, for autonomy has become, to some extent, a central feature in the articulation of social movements. Böhm et al. (2010) identify the search for autonomy across social movements in three different terrains. They argue that social movements seek autonomy from capital, from the state, and from international, interstate organisations such as the World Bank and the International Monetary Fund. In this vein, authors who focus on autonomous Marxism, anarchism and feminism in particular have all formulated and expanded on notions of autonomy in different ways (Hardt and Negri 2000; 2004; 2009; Holloway 2002; Escobar 2004). As we will also show in this book, autonomy has moved to the centre of political theory explaining social movements because it has played an increasingly important part in such movements' practices.

We can see changes in organisational cultures and decision-making processes, as illustrated by the increasing use of protest camps, among other phenomena. This is confirmed in, for example, the observation that protest movements since the 1970s have increasingly rejected institutional frameworks to work within and have instead opted for the creation of new organisational forms, including network structures, affinity groups and single-issue campaigns (Crossley 2003). Movements are increasingly heterogeneous and comprise various struggles. The notion of the 'movement of movements', a term coined to describe the global justice movement, summarises this focus on diversity. In protest camps, we often see that modes of action follow the principle of a 'diversity of tactics' through an approach that favours autonomous political action by small affinity groups. Rather than agreeing an overall strategy for political action, the plurality of affinity groups, at times combined with a broad 'action consensus' (e.g. non-violence), leaves the decision over which action to take and how far to go with the individual groups. This also applies in the context of representation. Protest camps often defy the notion of representational politics. Protest camps, following examples from the World Social Forum and other global and local networking structures, tend not to formulate shared demands or aggregate them to coherent political programmes. This anti-representational drive is central to protest camps and also forms one of their key challenges, as we discuss in more detail in this book.

From the perspective of theory, we find it critical to raise a further issue here that is central to the contribution that the study of protest camps can provide to political theory and social movement studies. Of course, the question of autonomy is not new and does not derive solely from the political debates of the 1960s. Rather, autonomy, if understood as freedom, is a key question of democratic and republican politics and therefore points to a much grander and more universal political tradition. In pursuing political freedom, republican movements more often than not have found themselves confronted by the social question, the conditionality of freedom in light of poverty. The conflict was perhaps first spotted in the French revolution, and following on from there surfaced in the majority of modern republican movements and revolutionary attempts (see Arendt 2006). While we cannot expand on this controversial history here, we claim with the literature that there has been a stronger focus on the republican tradition under the banner of autonomy since the 1970s. Without question, tensions and critiques have arisen with regard to this re-focusing on autonomy, namely that the focus on autonomy has come at the expense of attention to the social question. Relevant in this context are observations claiming that new social movements have given up on class politics to pursue 'identity politics' (Offe 1987) or questions that concern the 'grammar of life' (Giddens 1991). An influential, and more recent, interpretation reads the demands of new social movements as being split into 'artistic critique' and 'social critique' (Boltanski and Chiapello 2005). An overt focus on 'artistic critique' – so the argument goes – has allowed social movement demands to be usurped by capital's desire for marketable difference. In this way, social movements have provided a lifeline for capital rather than working to overcome it. Boltanski and Chiapello's (ibid.) argument resonates with several debates within social movements, for example the questioning of 'lifestyle anarchism' as opposed to 'social anarchism' in Bookchin's writing. Clearly, these ideas are far more complex than presented here, but their gist is that many of the new social movements fail to address the 'social question'.

In the theoretical terrain, it is perhaps Hardt and Negri's (2009) interpretation of bio-politics that may best be evoked as attempting to bridge the apparent divide between republican (or autonomous) and social demands. In Hardt and Negri's reading of bio-politics, the political act is understood as one that concerns the question of living and the social being of society, as well as the production of autonomous subjectivities, for example through struggles over the role and recognition of reproductive labour (Federici 2004). Perhaps overcoming the separation between republican and social struggles, 'bio-politics' may offer a theoretical path to discuss working-class politics as being intimately linked to the politics of autonomy, rather than opposed to them. We aim to show in this book that, whether or not this is the case, protest camps, as places where republican politics and social reproduction often coincide and mutually depend on each other, offer a fascinating field in which to study how social movement activists do not simply address this theoretical issue but perhaps point towards answers in their political practice. In this sense, protest camps, as an outcome of a politics that focuses more exclusively on autonomy, may constitute a consequence of as well as a reaction to this trend.

Materials and methods Working from this concept soup, our book takes a multi-method approach. Our discussions are based on empirical data gathered across a range of protest camps, through a combination of documentary analysis, visual analysis and interviews. First, we look extensively at documentary materials on the range of protest camps covered, including media articles, camp newsletters, press releases, camp codes of conduct, publicity pamphlets, blogs, videos, photographs and reflective texts written by protest campers. Second, we draw from numerous interviews we have conducted with protest camp participants and organisers over the past eight years of our work on protest camps. These interviews offer extensive insights into the organisational dynamics, political environments and everyday life of protest camps. Third, we draw from our own experiences as participants at protest camps.

Our own position is relevant here in relation to our role as activist-researchers. Considering the camp inside and outside, we are both insiders and outsiders. We are insiders inasmuch as we have participated in some of the camps discussed in this book, but we are also outsiders because we have not been to all of the protest camps we write about. We acknowledge that in using, and further constructing, 'protest camps' as a universal signifier, we run the risk of glossing over differences and variances between camps, as well as the distinct ways in which protesters do or do not mark their practices as 'protest camping'. However, our argument is based on referencing a set of qualities shared between a variety of camps, despite their differences. In common language practices, we tend to refer to a table as a table, bracketing together all the different shapes tables can take. This similarly applies to anyone speaking about protest camps. In this book we pick up on conversations among protest campers about the fact that there is something that can be identified as a 'protest camp'.

This may appear to be basic semantics, but, certainly in the political terrain, semantics are deeply contentious and problematic. Activists are keenly aware of the potentially disastrous ways in which media representations of protest camps can undermine their political impact, lead to and justify violent policing, or simply gloss over their specific targets and ideas in gross generalisations and misinterpretations. Protest campers are dealing with the power of these representations, developing strategies and tactics to deal with the media, or, increasingly, replacing them with their own alternative media, as we will discuss in Chapter 2.

The problem of representation may be somewhat less dramatic, in the immediate sense at least, when social researchers represent protest camps. But we, too, need to be aware that there are important differences we may gloss over and simplifications we may produce and prolong when we speak of the protest camp as a universal signifier. We address this issue by stating the obvious: that the meaning and understanding of protest camps will not be definitively answered in this book. Rather, as we have indicated earlier, we hope to open a conversation on this practice, tactic, strategy and organisational form. It is through further work and in a broader research conversation that we may increase our understanding of what protest camps are. We also hope to be able to counter and to undermine deliberate misinterpretations as well as the open hypocrisy of some reflections in politics and the media that attempt to praise protest camps abroad as 'beacons of democracy' while dismissing them at home as 'irrelevant' and 'naive', or even 'fascist' or 'terrorist'. It is important for us to highlight elements of protest camping that seem to be independent of the context, ideology, movement and epoch in which they arise. Our proposal, for the purposes of this book, is therefore to pursue an analysis of the material cultures of protest camps, or what we call, in the course of this book, an infrastructural analysis.

Infrastructural analysis and book structure

To study protest camps, we have developed a theory and practice of 'infrastructural analysis'. The term 'infrastructure' captures how protest campers build interrelated, operational structures for daily living. These structures, along with the practices attached to them, function together, creating miniature societies able to disseminate information, distribute goods and provide services (such as non-violence training, medical care and legal support). This 'hands-on' and 'DIY' practice is central to how protest campers approach politics and is also, we think, the best way of researching protest camps.

As we will explain in more detail in the next chapter, this infrastructural approach first establishes a set of material criteria and general modes of operation shared between all camps. These were derived from preliminary empirical research and were identified as:

• media and communication infrastructures and practices (media strategies, distribution networks, production techniques);

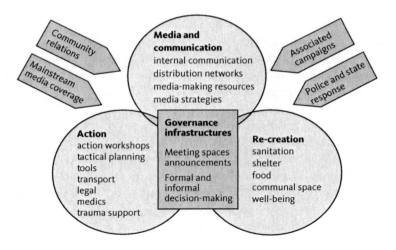

0.3 The infrastructures of protest camps

- action infrastructures and practices (direct action tactics, police negotiations, legal aid, medical support, transportation networks);
- governance infrastructures and practices (formal and informal decision-making processes); and
- re-creation infrastructures and practices (food supply, shelter, sanitation, maintenance of communal and private space).

As these four organisational dimensions interact, they enable and hinder each other, creating the distinct architecture of each protest camp (Frenzel, Feigenbaum and McCurdy forthcoming).

Looking comparatively at infrastructures across camps facilitates an analysis of how organisational designs, ideas and materials travel and spread in multiple directions. It allows us to compare and contrast divergent protest camps and to continue an ongoing conversation about them as emergent communities, and as places of political experimentation and innovation. In the chapters that follow we unfold a reading of protest camps that seeks to provide glimpses into other possible worlds, alternative forms – ephemeral and far from perfect – of living, sharing and building together. To this end, the book's argument unfolds as set out below.

Chapter 1 serves as a broad introduction to our thinking about protest camps and the infrastructures and practices that create, define and maintain daily life in them. Of interest are the organised services and facilities, from communal kitchens to legal support, developed to ensure the smooth running of the camp and which together create the 'homeplace' that is the protest camp. This chapter presents the core analytical framework for thinking about protest camps and introduces the reader to each of the infrastructures: media and communication, action, governance and re-creation.

The following chapters are dedicated to each of the infra-structures introduced in Chapter 1. Chapter 2 focuses on the media and communication infrastructure of protest camps. A protest camp's communication infrastructure allows campers to communicate with each other, with supporters, with mainstream media, state officials and the broader public. Media – in the broadest sense of the word – has always been an important terrain of struggle for social movements and therefore an important element of protest camps. Because of this, a wide-ranging repertoire of media practices has been developed to manage mainstream and activist media. To this end, the chapter splits its attention between analysing protest camp efforts to manage mainstream media (and the tensions caused by media interest at some protest camps) and the persistent endeavours of protest campers to create their own media representations of camp life. The latter range from setting up Indymedia centres at protest camps, to the use of documentary video and live-streaming technology.

Chapter 3 focuses on the action infrastructures of protest camps and is based on the premise that protest camps are places of action, places where engaging in direct action is normalised, and are protest actions in and of themselves. Of interest are the development and deployment of tactics that result from the animation of action infra-structures in protest camps. The chapter opens by reflecting on what makes protest camps unique as sites of ongoing protest action. Next, we consider how debates around the notion of 'diversity of tactics' have unfolded at protest camps and how protest campers reorient their tactics in response to collective reflections and interactions with the police. The chapter's second half introduces the idea of a 'protest action ecology', moving away from the binary oppositions that plague 'diversity of tactics' debates. Working through a series of examples, the chapter explores how a 'protest action ecology' perspective can provide room for understanding the complexities of both people and objects involved in protest camp infrastructures and allow for a more careful consideration of the spaces, objects and feelings that such tactics involve in protest camps.

Chapter 4 explores the development of governance infrastructures and examines how procedural and spatial practices shape and under-write the organisation of protest camps. Of interest are how processes and spaces of decision-making work together to make decision-making possible at protest camps, while, at the same time, they function as a laboratory for experimenting with prefigurative politics. To this end, the chapter traces the rise and spread of horizontal decision-making (HDM). However, the chapter argues that, even where they do not use HDM, protest camps often have the propensity to produce 'organic horizontality' among campers due to the spatial characteristics of the camp and the affective bonds the space creates between campers.

Chapter 5 looks at the protest camps' infrastructures of re-creation, which are designed to shelter, feed and protect campers. Included within re-creation are mobile kitchens, toilets, barricades, childcare and the like. However, rather than presenting an inventory of re-creation infrastructures, this chapter is concerned with the wider processes and practices at stake in creating and operating a protest camp. To this end, the chapter argues that re-creation infrastructures are more than functional facilities and services and instead point to the bio-political nature of protest camping. They may become political expressions of autonomy, often against the status quo, that seek to actively produce alternative worlds.

An historical review of selected protest camps

Before jumping into our protest camp infrastructural analysis, we first want to offer a sense of how different camps have looked at different times and in different places. We therefore provide this brief section on some of the layouts of specific protest campsites.

These selective and brief histories are taken from protest campers' first-hand accounts, as well as from handbooks and other print material. These examples provide an overview of some of the different forms protest camps can take, and how their distinct structures and systems arise not only out of social movement strategies, but also in

0.4 Welcome tents like this one at Occupy Bristol form a central feature of many protest camps

relation to laws, existing structural objects and environments, as we will discuss further in the following chapter. Sometimes what makes a camp unique is the unintentional result of other circumstances. Adaptation and improvisation mark the formation of protest camps as campers establish on-the-ground (sometimes quite literally grass-roots) contingency plans – often without any formal leadership. The camps highlighted here are used as primary case studies throughout the book, and we will return to them in more detail as we move to investigate practices relating to media and communication, action, governance and re-creation.

Resurrection City, Washington, DC From May to June 1968, civil rights and anti-poverty activists set up a highly organised 'tent city' that ran along the grassland between the Lincoln Memorial and Washington Monument in the American capital. An initiative of Martin Luther King Jr and the Southern Christian Leadership Conference (SCLC) as part of its Poor People's Campaign, Resurrection City sought to bring together America's poor on the doorstep of the US government. The campaign, which culminated in the creation of Resurrection City, attempted to craft a community of Native Americans, blacks, Hispanics and poor whites, taking action together against economic injustice, while the camp functioned as both a symbol of, and a base for, protest.

Under a sloganeering mandate to create a 'city-within-a-city', Resurrection City had its own city planners. Such an intentional protest camp project on this scale had never before been attempted, so the 15-acre encampment was modelled loosely on army camps and camps for migratory workers. The parkland was divided into a series of subsections or 'community units'. Architect and member of the Resurrection City structures committee John Wiebenson detailed in his planner's notebook:

The smallest scale was the single shelter unit that housed one family or, as a dormitory, five or six people. The next scale was nine shelter units (about fifty people) formed into a compound that backed onto a shower and toilet 'core.' Then, groups of four compounds (about 200 people) were formed with a leader's shack (also used for group storage and supplies) at its entranceway. Finally, a group of about 900 people would share a dining tent at their location on the main street (Wiebenson 1969: 407–8).

Dozens of volunteers helped set up and run a dental centre, health-care centre and kitchens serving three healthy meals a day, offering more than what many of the protest camp's residents had access to in their everyday home lives. In addition to services to meet basic needs, the camp set up infrastructures for well-being and places for knowledge and cultural exchange. In the City there was a Many Races Soul Center that served as the central cultural space of the encampment, a Poor People's University hosting classes and workshops, and the Coretta Scott King Day Care Center that provided activities for the camp's many children. There was also a bakery run by members of the Diggers, a Californian community group that ran free food and medical services in San Francisco, and propagated a vision of a property-free society. They took their name from the seventeenth-century Diggers of England, who freed 'common land' for the people. In a flyer that echoed the sentiments of both these Diggers groups, a brochure for Resurrection City read: 'The people had ... houses of simplicity, houses of creativity. But there was no jail and there were no landlords' (cited in Wright 2007: 348).

Auxiliary infrastructures – sites and/or services that are available outside the protest camp – have often played an important role at protest camps. Certainly, such services do not always work to the benefit of the camp, but they can complement and reinforce resources. Resurrection City employed auxiliary resources by hiring out a press office as part of the wider Poor People's Campaign, expanding off-site the media capacity of the City. In terms of housing, SCLC leaders drew on auxiliary resources to satisfy their housing requirements and stayed at a motel close to Resurrection City rather than at the City itself. This last example opens up a pathway for a critical exploration of the role and impact of auxiliary resources in the politics and practices of protest camps.

Greenham Common, United Kingdom Thirteen years after Resurrection City and across the Atlantic, in the midst of a global movement against war and nuclear armament that intensified with 1970s occupations at nuclear power plants in North America and Europe, Greenham Common became an epicentre of resistance. On 5 September 1981, a group of 35 protesters marched from Cardiff, Wales to the Greenham Common United States Air Force base in Newbury, England in protest at the 1979 NATO decision allowing US nuclear cruise missiles to be housed at military bases in Europe. Upon arrival at the base, the group demanded a televised debate with the Ministry of Defence. The women's request was not granted, so they refused to leave. As supporters and supplies came in, an encampment soon emerged.

Unlike Resurrection City, the Greenham encampment was not planned in advance. There were no permits, blueprints or months of organising supplies and volunteers. However, after a few months, thousands of women were coming to Greenham. In 1982 the camp became women-only and adopted the name Greenham Common Women's Peace Camp. Operational tasks such as cooking, cleaning and digging a 'shit pit' were taken on by volunteers on arrival. For shelter, Greenham protesters learned how to construct 'benders', something that was taught to them by travellers who came down to the camp during a 1982 peace caravan. These benders were made by bending hazel branches to create semi-circular structures over which insulating blankets and plastic tarpaulins could be placed. Benders offered a more affordable and practical way of creating shelters and dealing with repeated evictions (in an age before the pop-up tent).

In a set-up that looked very different from the neatly laid-out and pre-planned rows of A-frame tents at Resurrection City, the campsite at Greenham was divided into numerous camps set up outside access gates to the military base. Each one named after a colour of the rainbow, these encampments meandered around the 9-mile fence. Over time, the gates developed their own unique personalities. As the main gate, Yellow Gate was the most visited and most transient camp. Women there often hosted the press as well as international and male visitors. Located off a main road, Blue Gate attracted younger women and developed more of a punk anarchist environment than the other gates. Green Gate had a strictly women-only policy at all times and was nestled more deeply in the woods, further away from the soldiers and surrounded by the natural environment of the common. Women at Green Gate were often more likely to be engaged in eco-feminist and spiritualist practices such as Wicca and (neo-)paganism. Orange, Violet, Red and Woad Gates were set up rather more sporadically. Many women's groups who came regularly to visit Greenham would return to the same gate each time, developing an affection for their protest camp within a protest camp (Roseneil 1995: 75–82).

HoriZone, Stirling, Scotland In July 2005 the UK saw another major encampment, this time planned over a year and a half but lasting for little over a week. The 2005 HoriZone camp at Gleneagles grew out of the counter-summit model, developed at previous alter-globalisation gatherings and World Social Forums. HoriZone also drew from the experience of NoBorders camps, which brought together thousands of activists at migrants' rights action camps across Europe. Closer to home, HoriZone was informed both by Greenham and other peace camps of the 1980s, and by the camps of the anti-roads movement that spanned the UK in the 1990s.

With a planning process to match the intensity of that of Resurrection City, the HoriZone eco-village was organised before the G8 venue, the Gleneagles Hotel, was even confirmed. Among the protest networks that mobilised for the Gleneagles G8 Summit was Dissent!, which can be placed on a continuum of social movement activity dating back to the student movements of the late 1960s. Near Gleneagles, Dissent! established the HoriZone eco-village using land donated at the eleventh hour by Stirling Council. With a capacity for 5,000 people, HoriZone served as the primary living and social space for activists during the protests. HoriZone directly appropriated

0.5 Tents in the evening sun at HoriZone protest camp, Stirling, July 2005

the 'barrios' model used in Latin America, including in occupations in Argentina and in the Brazilian Landless Workers' Movement (Movimento dos Trabalhadores Sem Terra or MST) encampments (Sitrin and Azzellini 2012), as well as at the São Paulo World Social Forums. The model also draws on previous spatial organisations of camps into neighbourhoods, which date back to early protest camps including the 1932 Bonus Army camps, which in turn modelled themselves after military camps. The HoriZone campsite was divided into neighbourhoods that each had a meeting space and communal kitchen. There was also a wide range of working groups focusing on certain issues such as media relations (the CounterSpin Collective; see Chapter 2), a welcome tent, site security (the 'tranquillity team'), ad hoc troubleshooting (the 'bureaucracy bloc'), and medical and legal support. HoriZone was also home to the Activist Trauma Support group that came together to deal with the after-effects of police violence at the Evian counter-summit protests in 2003.

Creating an ecologically sustainable encampment took a great deal of effort. The camp had a double function, as described by organisers:

> The rural convergence centre was designed to be both a demonstration of the world we want and a base for action against the G8. The amount of energy spent in specifying exactly how the world we want would function was intense, and the original idea for a campsite was transformed into an idea for an eco-village to demonstrate sustainable alternatives to life under capitalism (Trocchi et al. 2005: 77).

Meat, milk and anything else that came from an animal was excluded from the food provided by the kitchens on site. Electricity came largely from little windmills, solar panels and bio-diesel generators. Scrap wood was the predominant building material on the site. Grey water, left over from washing dishes or brushing teeth, had to be dealt with in a sustainable way, as were human faeces. Compost toilets and grey-water treatment facilities clearly marked the campsite as an alternative to the world outside. That said, while the compost toilets on site at HoriZone were used, many campers displayed a preference for the standard portable toilets, which ultimately led to health and sanitation problems that lovingly became known as the 'shit crisis'.

In eco-village protest camps such as HoriZone, the ability to operate a camp outdoors is held up as an example of environmentally sustainable living and communal self-management. The process of planning, building and being at HoriZone went on to shape the 2006 Camp for Climate Action, which spread, under the abbreviated name 'Climate Camp', across four continents in four years (Frenzel 2011). The emphasis placed on the proliferation of alternatives in every aspect of life demonstrates that one of the central ways of 'making things public' at HoriZone was to physically create an alternative homeplace. Here, a village-within-a-village rather than a city-within-a-city, HoriZone shone a light (primarily via the mass media lens) on the issues of how we live together in ecologically sustainable ways. It showcased possibilities for sustainable diets, cleaner energy, and even what we can do with all our faeces.

Tahrir Square, Egypt While 2004 saw a large-scale protest camp with the Orange Revolution, which brought hundreds of thousands into the streets in Ukraine, it was not until 2011 that 'protest camp' became a common phrase across the world. In January 2011, Tahrir Square (Midan Tahrir) became a physical and symbolic hub of the Egyptian uprising. Protests in Egypt began in direct confrontation to repressive state policing. A 'Day of Rage' was called on 25 January 2011 against National Police Day, a national holiday created by then Egyptian President Hosni Mubarak in 2009 to celebrate the police force. The political climate in Egypt was marred by increasing poverty, a near 25 per cent youth unemployment rate, and widespread government corruption under the rule of President Mubarak. Protesters were also inspired by the successful revolution in neighbouring Tunisia.

Over the next 18 days, which culminated in the resignation of President Hosni Mubarak, Tahrir Square was transformed into a 45,500 square metre protest camp complete with street hospitals, waste and recycling stations, an ad hoc prison at Sadat metro station, decentralised day care, food stalls and guarded barricades (BBC 2011). As Tahrir Square protesters took over the public square in the heart of Cairo, their ability to construct an encampment on the cement, between large stone buildings, was greatly limited by the existing layout of the urban environment. As in other urban encampments that take place in squares, particularly when they are made of cement rather than parkland, camp infrastructures must largely be built around, on top of, and through a takeover of what is already in place. The circular shape of the square, with a dipped 'stage' area, lent itself as a place for larger gatherings and meetings. Tents were set up around this central gathering space, while existing shops and surrounding buildings were also put to use for the encampment. Urban planner and researcher Nabil Kamel described the siting of the encampment:

> Stages were set and a microphone and loudspeaker – a 'radio station' – provided outlets for speeches, entertainment, news and debates by public figures, opposition politicians, journalists, artists and the general public during 'open mic' hours. Sleeping quarters that started as mere blankets evolved into full-fledged campsites with tents, electricity rigged from street lights and supervised children's quarters. Memorials for fallen martyrs, artistic expressions, songs, dances, poetry and paintings were the spontaneous products of people from all classes and religious backgrounds (Kamel 2012: 38).

To protect the encampment, protesters erected barricades all around the square, and people would spend hours waiting in long queues being checked by ad hoc security groups. In a set-up similar to Resurrection City, what was happening on the ground in Egypt was not an openly accessible public space. To get in, you first had to pass lines of government security forces. Next, you had to pass the lines of revolutionary security. This separation was part of what made the physical square in Tahrir capable of being a space for democracy-building and collective resistance. Prior to entry, people were checked to see if they adhered to the common ground of protesters' claims (Mehrez 2012). These checks were designed to help keep out the police and those working for the government, although, like any security system, this was imperfect and undercover police officers were suspected of manning some of the barriers.

The camp in Tahrir Square served as a place for creating and disseminating media, for meeting and praying together, for sharing news and for maintaining a base for action. Medical care was central to the camp's function as part of the broader resistance. When those fighting police and soldiers on the streets to protect the encampment were injured, they were trolleyed back inside the square for medical care. Field pharmacies were also set up with various remedies to wash tear gas from the eyes and skin. In addition, and in support of the actions on the periphery, people inside the camp would break up pieces of the square to turn into stones for defence. These were often shuttled in wheelbarrows to the trunks of motorbikes, which carried them to those fighting on the front lines (personal correspondence).

Occupy LSX, London The protests in Tahrir Square inspired the Occupy movement. The initial Adbusters call-out for Occupy Wall Street urged Americans to make their own 'Tahrir moment'. Begun on 17 September 2011, within a month Occupy camps spread from New York City to 950 cities worldwide. Occupy reinforced the place of 'protest camps' in the common language and introduced this practice to a new generation. Occupy campers inherited experiences and camp-planning practices directly from the M15 movement in Spain, as well as from past movements including alter-globalisations and environmental movements (Zapatistas, the Argentinian uprising, counter-summits, NoBorders and Climate Camps). The largest camps in the US went up in New York, Oakland and Los Angeles, and the largest international camp took over a public square in the centre of London.

On 15 October 2011, about 2,000 Londoners took to the streets around Paternoster Square, home of the London Stock Exchange. Greeted by double rows of metal barricades, riot police, dogs and horses, it soon became clear that the camp was not going to be set up in the planned concrete courtyard outside the Exchange. After circling all of the entrances in the hope of a back way in, protesters found themselves in the square outside St Paul's Cathedral – the only space in the area big enough to handle such a large crowd. Without a central organising committee, people began to form small, ad hoc discussion groups to feed into a larger general assembly in order to try to figure out a plan B. Within two hours the crowd had decided, by consensus, that they would camp right there in the square outside the cathedral. Calls were made to start co-ordinating food, shelter and sanitation.

In terms of planning and organisation, Occupy LSX falls between the rigorously planned encampments of Resurrection City and Hori-Zone and the more contingent origins of encampments found in Greenham and Tahrir. As night fell and the cathedral heads asked the police to back off, more supplies slowly trickled in, adding to the sprinkling of pop-up tents set down earlier by occupiers. Over the next week, arrangements were made with the council for sanitation, and donations poured in for the kitchen, library and media centres. A tech

0.6 The library of Occupy LSX

hub and supply tent provided 24-hour support, while a prayer tent, wellness tent, 'tent city university', arts centre and later a women's space offered additional support and activity.

Also forming part of the camp's infrastructure was the local Starbucks, which served as a camp toilet, electronics charging station, public Wi-Fi hotspot, space for meetings and conference calls, and a personal escape where campers could get warm. Starbucks also served as a media hub for both mainstream and independent journalists and sold coffee to onlookers and as an occasional occupier indulgence. Appropriating existing urban infrastructures, Occupy LSX, like many urban encampments, took up both semi-public space and semi-private space (or the space of the privatised commons) for public use. Importantly, this highlights the interdependency of the camp and the existing infrastructures in which it operates, as we will explore in more detail in Chapter 5. Occupy LSX was condemned by some members of the Church of England and by the Corporation of London for causing a reduction in both tourist visits to the cathedral and the profits of the many chain restaurants and shops that lined the periphery of the occupied square (including, serendipitously, a Blacks camping store).

Occupy LSX, as part of the much wider Occupy movement,

reached millions. Occupy camps showed how protest camps can serve not only as a base for collective action and political convergence, but also as a space of home-building where the work of making the camp together forms an integral part of the process of protest. In such acts of reclaiming and occupying city space, it is often the self-sufficient aspects of the encampment's governance and decision-making processes that are highlighted as both a showcase of, and a demonstration of public demand for, more direct forms of democracy. This sentiment was emblemised in the M15 slogan 'Real Democracy Now' and the popular Occupy mantra: 'This is a process not a protest.'

Community section.

1 | INFRASTRUCTURES AND PRACTICES OF PROTEST CAMPING

Shoulder straps dig in at either side of my neck, my tent swaying as I walk, smacking the skin of my legs. I go over my backpack's contents one more time in my head: jumper, water, toilet roll – toothbrush? Setting off I looked just like any other camper or festival-goer, only my destination was a protest. We arrived on site at dusk, the day before the camp's official opening. The night before the campsite was successfully squatted as dozens of climate activists took to the land, securing the entrance with tripods. Tents and tarps went up. Supplies were wheel-barrowed in along make-shift roads paved with hay, plywood and cardboard. I turned up as the central marquee was being assembled. A huge white canvas construction still dotted with the paint of protests past. Campers were tugging on long, thick lengths of rope as others drove stakes into the ground to lift this fabric shelter that would become our communal home for the next week. Part carnival, part boot camp. I looked on awestruck and a bit afraid. What was this alternative world I had just walked into? (Climate Camp, Heathrow, 2007)

Introduction

What makes protest camps distinguishable from other modes of protest is largely their attempt to create sustainable (if ephemeral) structures for ongoing protest and daily living. Whether in the forests of Tasmania or the crowded streets of Thailand, to function at the most basic level as sites of ongoing protest and daily living, camps need to figure out how people will sleep, what they will eat, and where they will go to the bathroom. This aspect of protest camping is similar to recreational camps, as well as base camps and other campsites (Hailey 2009). Beyond basic bodily needs, as sites of ongoing protest, protest camps develop ways for protesters to communicate with one another and methods for organising their campaigns, direct actions and day-to-day operations. There is also often some form of legal support and medical care available to protesters. Additionally, many

↱ Still see as 'supporting'.

protest camps contain spaces for well-being, including places for prayer, meditation, entertainment, socialising, education and cultural exchange. To create these spaces, protest campers bring together and develop particular infrastructures and practices. As campers build communal kitchens, libraries, education spaces and solar-powered showers, they become entangled in experiments in alternative ways of living together. Their communication, governance, protest actions and practices of re-creating everyday life are shaped through their communal relationships. This is perhaps what most makes protest camps distinct from other overt forms of protest, such as marches and demonstrations. They are at once protest spaces and homeplaces.

Protest camps and crafting a homeplace

Building on the work of bell hooks (1990), Jeff Juris (2008) refers to alter-globalisation convergence centres (some of which involved protest camps) as 'homeplaces'. For hooks, the homeplace is not something structurally static or already there, but rather something that is made. Describing spaces for refuge and nurturing built by black women to resist capitalist patriarchy, hooks argues that the 'task of making homeplace' involved constructing a safe space for growth, development and to 'nurture our spirits'. For hooks, it is a task that is shared, a task of 'making home a community of resistance' (hooks 1990: 184). This idea echoes much Marxist feminist work on the reproductive labour of homemaking and bio-politics (Cowan 1983; Federici 2004), while also invoking the structural home itself as something active, affective and vibrant. Zoe Sofia calls structures such as the home 'container technologies', arguing that rather than passive and static objects that merely hold and store, they instead actively shape what they contain. The home becomes invested with the labour that goes into its making and remaking, and this affects what is inside (Sofia 2000).

Juris adapts hooks' idea of the homeplace as a community of (and for) resistance, describing the convergence centre as a 'small, self-managed city, a "heterotopic space" of exchange and innovation' (Juris 2008: 129). The creation and operation of the protest camp as a 'self-managed city', an eco-village or a revolutionary home-place involves both labour and leisure. The combination of work and sustenance, as they form part of the home-making process, is well captured in a number of protest campers' recollections of their experiences at camps. For example, Jill Freedman's documentary photography book recounts these sentiments in relation to the vision of life at Resurrection City:

> No clocks, just time. Nobody better, only equal. Respect for where you're at, not where you're from. Work for everyone who wants it. Kids your own age to play with. Making music. Building a home. Calling your neighbour brother. Mornin' sister. Soul City. Getting it together, making it work, because it's yours. Feeling it. For the first time. Feeling free. Couldja dig it? (Freedman 1970: 119).

Merrick's recollection of his experience camping in treetops at the Newbury bypass anti-roads protest sites in 1994 carries a similar affection for the protest camp:

> It becomes so much. Your camp is not just a piece of natural heritage that you are defending, it's your home. You know every bit intimately, you've watched it change, you know how it runs day to day … It's where you live. And it's your work, you labour hard to make things happen here, that's what you spend most days doing. You become familiar, attached (Merrick 1996: 90).

These feelings of what it means to take part in a protest camp echo bell hooks' (1990) description of making a homeplace as a site of resistance and nurturing. They draw attention to ways in which care is bound up in protest campers' acts of making together, positioning the individual in relation to others and to the environment, and they highlight the ways in which we become entangled in the distinct space–time of camp life. As a place of work and leisure, the protest camp is a space of production and reproduction, where value and values are produced by campers as they go about the day-to-day work of making home while making protest.

Across protest camps, we see practices, objects, structures and operations come together to create this homeplace, a space that seeks to be both a place for ongoing protest and a site of nurturing, a community of resistance. To organise a more in-depth discussion of the ways in which protest campers build these homeplaces and spaces for ongoing protest together, we engage the term 'infrastructure'. By common definition, infrastructures refer to the organised services and facilities necessary for supporting a society or community. We use the term with this basic meaning in mind to capture how protesters build interrelated, operational structures for daily living. Whether ad hoc or planned out in advance, these infrastructures work together to create miniature societies able to disseminate information, distribute goods and provide services. Thinking about these structures and operations as infrastructures helps us make sense of the ways in which protest campers develop and employ practices that negotiate (and fail to negotiate) ways of living and protesting together around and through the objects, structures and environments available to them.

The facilities offered at the protest camp sometimes also serve to highlight the lack of free, public infrastructures available to people for gathering, eating, discussing, relaxing or playing, something we discuss in more detail in Chapter 5. A large part of the impact made by protest camps on the public comes from their visible disruptions of the normative routines of daily life, which see us move primarily through privatised places and spaces of consumption. Protest camps interrupt the ways in which people move through 'public' spaces, how they see a park or forest, a parking lot, public square or government lawn. As convergence spaces, protest camps bring strangers together. This disruption of the status quo is particularly true of protest camps formed of, and focused on, populations already deemed illegitimate and out of place (or of no place), such as refugees, those who are homeless and impoverished, and those divested of their land. In these camps, the homeplace, as a space of bodily vulnerability and scant resources, is often intentionally exposed to the public, mirroring the unjust conditions of the nation state back to itself and its citizens. This is seen, for example, in the American Indian Movement's communiqué from its encampment Occupation of Alcatraz Island in San Francisco in November 1969:

> We feel that this so-called Alcatraz Island is more than suitable for an Indian Reservation, as determined by the white man's own standards.
>
> By this we mean that this place resembles most Indian reservations, in that:
>
> - It is isolated from modern facilities, and without adequate means of transportation.
> - It has no fresh running water.
> - It has inadequate sanitation facilities.
> - There are no oil or mineral rights.

- There is no industry so unemployment is great.
- There are no health care facilities.
- The soil is rocky and non-productive; and the land does not support game.
- There are no educational facilities.
- The population has always exceeded the land base.
- The population has always been held as prisoners and kept dependent upon others ...

A similar approach of making visible those issues, bodies and communities that politicians often attempt to sweep aside can be found in those protest camps that form around a lack of recognition and resources. Examples include the Landless Workers' Movement (Movimento dos Trabalhadores Sem Terra or MST) encampments on government lawns, the Australian Tent Embassy in Canberra. On 27 January 1972, the day after Australia Day – the country's national holiday which commemorates the landing of British colonisers on Australian soil – a group of indigenous activists went to Old Parliament House in Canberra, the nation's capital, to set up an Aboriginal Embassy. The action was a direct response to the then government's handling of Aboriginal land rights. Pitching a beach umbrella into the lawn (because they couldn't afford a tent and were instead donated an umbrella), the men announced outside Parliament House that they were a sovereign people. While such an act of protest would normally be cleared quickly by Australian police, the laws of the lawn allowed camping as long as there were fewer than 12 tents. Aboriginal activist Gary Foley, who was involved in the Tent Embassy, recalls how the visibility and exposure of the camp largely led to its success:

> The inability for the Government to remove this embarrassing protest from in front of their Parliament House captured the imagination of not just Indigenous Australia. Within days the site had established an office tent and installed a letterbox in front. Tourist bus operators became aware of the new attraction in town and began bringing their busloads of tourists to the 'Aboriginal Embassy' before escorting them across the road to Parliament House. The Koori activists would solicit donations and distribute educational literature about their cause. Local residents of Canberra would bring food and blankets and invite Embassy staff into their homes for showers and dinner. Students at the

nearby Australian National University opened their union building for support activities and the mass media began to display great interest. The Aboriginal Embassy very quickly became the most successful protest venture yet launched by the Aboriginal political movement (Foley 2001: 17).

As Nick Couldry has argued in relation to Greenham Common, the protest camp moves the normative frame of debate from inside the walls of parliament to the place of the encampment as a site of contestation (Couldry 1999; see also Chapter 2). In the case of protest camps pitched on the lawns of government buildings, political debate is physically moved from the legitimated inside to the heretical outside (Cresswell 1996). Protest camps create alterations in the landscape, building alternative infrastructures for communication, decision-making, dissent and daily care. In doing so, protest camps both expose the failures of the nation to attend to its inhabitants, and simultaneously generate a homeplace carved into the very same land that denies them a place to be at home with others.

Infrastructures

To generate discussions about protest camps that focus on the practices and infrastructures that make protest camps unique as a political form, it is useful to first imagine what an inventory of a protest camp's objects, technologies and key spaces might look like. From our research and first-hand experience at protest camps, we have found that one could produce similar lists of objects, spaces, structures and operations that apply to a range of different protest encampments, albeit in very different forms and formations. The kinds of items, roles and spaces one might find in a protest camp include, but are not limited to: kitchens; toilets/showers; shelters; donations/supplies; rubbish bins/recycling stations; grey water and waste disposal systems; communal tents; religious/prayer tents; tranquillity spaces; education spaces; libraries; crèche/childcare facilities; a welcome area; security fences; electricity/power generation; police liaison; medical tents; legal tents; storage/tat tents; tools; stationery supplies; art supplies; transportation, from bikes to vans; computers; internet access; mobile phone charging; art, music and performance spaces; media tents; queer/people of colour (POC)/women's spaces; and announcement boards and schedules.

To make sense of this long list, and indeed a slew of other items, we identified four key sets of objects and operations, or what we refer to as 'infrastructures' (Frenzel, Feigenbaum and McCurdy forthcoming). These are:

- *media and communication*: mainstream media tents, liaisons and policies, distribution lists and phone trees, along with camp media ranging from radio stations and newspapers to social media;
- *protest action*: tools, police liaison, and legal, medical and activist trauma support;
- *governance*: meeting spaces, megaphones, announcement boards and decision-making policy guidelines; and
- *re-creation*: the infrastructures and practices needed to reproduce everyday life in the camp (food supply, shelter, sanitation, maintenance of communal and private space).

We derived these four sets of infrastructures from our previous empirical studies on Greenham Common (Feigenbaum 2008; 2010; 2013), the 2005 G8 counter-summit's HoriZone eco-village (McCurdy 2008; 2009; 2010; 2011a; 2011b; Frenzel 2009), Climate Camps (Frenzel 2009; 2011; 2013; Feigenbaum 2007), and the G8 camps in Germany in 2007 (Frenzel 2009), as well as original and archival research conducted for this book. From our research, these four sets of infrastructures and practices appear generalisable to all protest camps. These four sets are not discrete, nor are they the only way to think about how people, things, spaces and environments come into operation together at a protest camp. Instead, they are presented here as a lens through which to study camps.

Recognising these limitations, we use these four categories in order to be able to identify important similarities and differences between and across protest camps, in an effort to better understand how activist knowledge, tactics and material resources develop and travel, as well as how broader social movement practices can become both reified and innovated during and beyond the life of a protest camp. Our interest is in how practices and processes are negotiated both with and through structures and objects, as protest campers work together to sustain a homeplace and space for ongoing protest. We use these divisions between sets of infrastructures and practices in our attempt to examine how social movement tactics and practices are developed and adapted in the space of the protest camp, and how conflicts are generated through daily interactions and the challenges of building together. In what follows, we briefly introduce the four key sets of infrastructures, each of which has a chapter of this book dedicated to it.

Media and communication By bringing protest to the site of contestation, the locations of protest camps often pose challenges for journalists seeking to 'expose' the camps through media frames. Photographer Ann Snitow wrote that getting good footage of Greenham, in industry terms, was difficult for television crews:

> Meetings without podiums, spontaneous acts that can erupt anywhere without notice, a world without hierarchies of space or time – this is the Greenham that has every intention of maddening the media which always demand a controlled orchestration of event (Snitow 1985: 45–6).

Nick Couldry makes a similar argument in his media analysis of Greenham's television coverage, writing that Greenham disrupted the 'specific spatial order implicit in media production' that the 'right place to debate on issues such as nuclear weapons is a place at the "centre" (Whitehall, Westminster, television studios), rather than the site of the weapons themselves' (1999: 339).

While all campaigns and movements require ways to spread messages, protest camps are distinct in that the action centred at the camp is one, localised part of what is often a much broader protest ecology. Dispersed actions, working group meetings, support groups, food supplies and speakers must all be co-ordinated. Some of this happens at the campsite, while other organisation occurs off-site. In efforts to communicate between these diverse groups and activities, protest campers establish infrastructures to enable them to communicate with each other, with supporters, with the media and with the broader public. UK anti-roads activists used phone trees, where people were responsible for spreading information by calling each other in a designated order. In their descriptions of this practice, we can see how the camp, as a base, must develop methods to communicate with its larger network of supporters and campers who are not on site:

> [phone trees] are used in two broad ways: as an emergency alert (e.g. for the start of work or an eviction) to get people to respond as quickly as possible; or as a general, regular means of spreading

information through a group without one person having to ring everyone! (Road Alert 1997).

In recent years, phone trees have widely been replaced by social media platforms (Twitter and Facebook groups), private SMS and listservs. As communication technologies have developed over time, becoming smaller, faster and more mobile, so too have protesters' uses of these technologies at protest camps, particularly in organising actions. By the mid-2000s, multiple modes of digital communication – alongside non-digital forms – were being used to organise and mobilise protesters. Describing some of the ways in which protesters in Ukraine utilised media technologies when hundreds of thousands of people took over city streets in Kiev in 2004 to protest about the national elections, journalist Matthew Collin writes:

> The protesters used text-messaging services to distribute bulletins and orders to hundreds of mobile phones; telecommunications companies even had to set up temporary phone masts in central Kiev because of the overwhelming demand (Collin 2007: 140).

These digital forms have proliferated with the use of social media, as evidenced in the misguided celebration of Tahrir Square's revolution as the 'Twitter revolution' in the Western media as well as the rise of livestreaming from the Occupy camps and actions.

However, despite the increased ability to communicate that digital media brings, even in the mobile media age, protest campers often rely on a wide range of old and new technologies. A problem faced in the encampment inside the capitol building in Wisconsin was the noise generated by the number of people and the acoustics of the building. Occupiers tried out various solutions to make accommodations and enhance their communication infrastructure. As one protester explained: 'We would show [the general] assembly on TV with speakers, but people couldn't hear so we'd write it up on our official low-tech Twitter' (see Democracy Now! 2011). The 'low-tech Twitter' she refers to here was a vertical scroll of blank white paper that was used to display short update messages written in various coloured marker pens.

As protest camps are often sites of mainstream media interest, camps and campers often develop systems, strategies and tactics for dealing with media interest. Moreover, these strategies are often the source of debate and contention within protest camps. Media –

1.1 A noticeboard at Heiligendamm anti-G8 camp in Germany, 2007 – these boards function as camp communication infrastructures

analogue and digital – made by campers themselves is also included under the umbrella of communication infrastructures. Many camps, often as part of the wider movements in which they participate, have published their own papers – utilising both on-site media-makers (reporters, editors, newspaper folders) and off-site facilities (printers, photocopiers) to form part of their camp-based, grassroots media infrastructures. For example, in 1968, Resurrection City had the *True Unity News*; in the 1980s Greenham Common produced a range of newsletters including the early *Greenham Women's Peace Camp News* and then the *Green & Common* newsletter series. The Oaxaca protest encampment in Mexico in 2006 had its own newspaper, as well as radio stations and a squatted television channel, and recently many Occupy camps physically and digitally distributed their own papers, including *The Occupied Wall Street Journal* in New York and *The Occupied Times* in London, to list just a few examples.

While it can be hard for people today to understand how protesters communicated in previous times, communication practices and infra-structures are always shaped by available media technologies, as well as by past movement cultures that influence and inspire contemporary activism (Reed 2005). In addition, technologies and media tactics do not function in isolation, but rather operate together, sometimes complementing each other (a co-ordinated action sent out by a press release team), at other times generating competition and conflict (two newspapers vying to represent camp life and movement positions). The interactions between different practices, people and technologies form part of the distinct communication and media ecology of each protest camp, as we will discuss in more detail in the next chapter.

Protest action The protest camp is a place of and for protest action; this is expressed in a variety of ways. First, protest camps are places where protest actions are planned to take place on site or nearby. They are places where people are trained and where care for protesters' 'bodies in action' is provided. In this sense, protest camps function rather like a 'base camp' where meetings are held, supplies are stored, and people are nourished and sheltered. At sites such as Tahrir Square and Oaxaca, the camp serves as a base that is protected by those on the defensive lines, pushing back police, government or military attacks. In 2006, after a repressive crackdown on striking teachers who were demonstrating in *plantones* (ongoing sit-ins), thousands came out on to the streets of Oaxaca, connecting the issue of poor school conditions highlighted by the teachers with their own understanding and experience of poverty, discrimination against indigenous populations and repressive government rule. To defend against police violence and to reclaim both their right to resist and the right to their own city, protesters began to protect the *plantones* through a co-ordinated system of guarded barricades set up around the city. Reflecting on this practice of barricading, Silvia, a sociology student who was part of the protests in Oaxaca, says:

> The barricade was part of the political strategy. It was a way of demonstrating the government's lack of capacity for governance through civil disobedience … It was a way to put pressure on the state and federal government, but also a means for our own protection. All over the city, barricades were built to protect the sit-ins, our *plantones*, and to prevent the police and paramilitary troops from driving around the city shooting at people under the blanket of total impunity (Denham and C.A.S.A. Collective 2008).

1.2 The Oaxaca encampments in 2006 filled the city's streets

These barricades were built from building scraps – wood, wire, piping – as well as appropriated fencing and often overturned cars and trucks. There were also barricades whose constituent components depicted the struggle: entanglements of chairs and desks. The barricades were occupied mostly by young men who served as guards and watched out for the police. Many others contributed to the workings of the barricades, bringing food, song and conversation. In this sense, the barricade is not merely a structure or place, but a set of interactions, a grouping or assemblage of technologies, bodies and practices. It has what Jane Bennett has termed a 'vibrant materiality', a vitality found not solely in the bodies of the barricaders, but generated by all of the people, materials, exchanges and interactions that make up the life of the barricade (Bennett 2010; see also http://momentofinsurrection. wordpress.com/2012/07/29/elements-of-a-barricade/).

Second, protest camps are places in which people become 'active' or 'activate' their politics. As sites for planning, skill-sharing and training, protest camps often provide sessions and workshops on direct action, civil disobedience, how to deal with the police and the legal issues involved with protesting. Together, these aspects of the camp help make them a community of resistance that nurtures, as well as justifies and normalises, participation in direct action. As John Jordan writes, engaging in direct action is a potentially transformative experience on a number of levels, and can both materialise and communicate resistance:

> Direct action takes the alienated, lonely body of technocratic culture and transforms it into a connected, communicative body embedded in society. Taking part in direct action is a radical poetic gesture by which we can achieve meaningful change, both personal and social. Direct action is the central strategy of creative resistance, a strategy that, unlike the rationality and objectivity of most politics, revokes the emphasis on words and reason and demands the acknowledgement of intuition and imagination (Jordan in McKay 1998: 134–5).

Finally, protest camps can also be protest actions in themselves. In such cases, the presence of the protest camp is itself antagonistic, a physical and direct intervention at the site of contestation. This type of protest camp commonly comprises protesters occupying trees set for clearing, as with the Newbury bypass anti-roads camp in the United Kingdom, the Minnehaha Free State anti-roads camp in Minnesota, Julia Butterfly Hill's two-year anti-logging tree-sit 55 metres off the ground in a giant redwood in California, and with many more.

Other camps of this nature see activists construct (or occupy) barriers and dwellings in the pathway of proposed construction. Examples include the Claremont Road protests in London in 1994, where activists squatted rows of terrace houses set for demolition, and the 2012 campaign in Fullerton, New South Wales in Australia, where residents of all ages decided it was time to take direct action and 'reclaim the cove', establishing a blockade encampment at the entrance to the pilot coal-seam gas project site. Protesters might also camp out at sites of government power, occupying spaces in ways that prevent or detract from work to be done, as in the occupation of the Capitol Building in Wisconsin in 2011. As we will argue in Chapter 3, together these action-related aspects of protest camping not only constitute the 'action infrastructures' but also form 'ecosystems' of protest action. They are sites of entanglement, vibrancy and innovation, where tensions around tactics are played out, and strategies never seen before are unleashed.

Governance In order for things to get done at a protest camp – whether those things are making dinner, sharing out donations, or deciding who will guard the gate that night – decisions need to be made. We use the term 'governance infrastructures' to refer to the processes (voting, consensus), spaces (meeting tents, assemblies) and technologies (markers, megaphones) that may be employed to make decision-making possible at a protest camp.

While some protest camps, such as Resurrection City, Seabrook, HoriZone and Climate Camp, employed guidelines thought out in advance for meeting structures and decision-making, other camps, for example the Wyhl anti-nuclear camp in Germany and Greenham Common, had more ad hoc modes of meeting and getting things done. But wherever on the spectrum of formalised governance structures a protest camp can be placed, in each case a set of practices

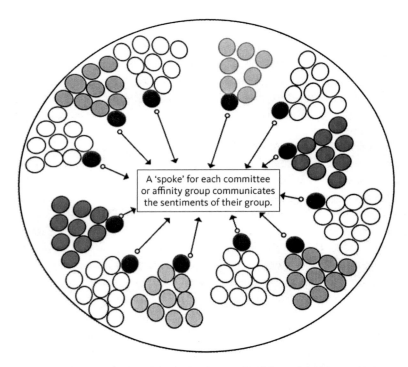

A 'spoke' for each committee or affinity group communicates the sentiments of their group.

1.3 The spokescouncil model – in this decentralised form of decision-making, neighbourhoods communicate with each other through 'spokes' to make camp-wide decisions

emerges that allows for decisions to be made and camp matters to be attended to. As we will discuss in more detail in Chapter 4, many protest camps often intentionally employ modes of horizontal and consensus decision-making that stand in radical contrast to forms of representative democracy or autocratic rule that define a nation's formal political system. Even in those camps that do not intentionally use these methods, there is a form of 'organic horizontalism' that emerges as campers come together to tend to the needs and nurturing of their communities.

What makes protest camps' governance structures different from those of 'legal channels of protest' involves both the procedural and the spatial reorganisation of who makes decisions, when and where. Describing their experiences as part of a demonstration against nuclear power at the Seabrook plant in 1976, a protester reflected:

> The round of interminable 'spokes' and decision-making body meetings about ongoing strategy had begun and a 'community of resistance' sense of potency prevailed, something which the legal channels of protest had failed to create (Crown 1979: 23).

This 'spokescouncil' model of decision-making was used in anti-nuclear occupations of the 1970s and 1980s, by the Zapatistas, at the counter-summits of the alter-globalisation movement, by NoBorders and Climate Camps, and was adopted by Occupy. It is often described by English speakers using the image of a bicycle wheel made up of many spokes. The visual metaphor of a wheel, with spokes coming together from an outer circle to an inner circle, provides a representation of how a spokescouncil works organisationally and spatially. In a spokescouncil model, a number of small groups discuss an issue at the same time, then each group sends one person to a group discussion or meeting nearer the centre of the 'wheel' to put forward their views. This person then reports back to their smaller group at the outside of the circle.

These practices of direct democracy and horizontality generate a different feel or atmosphere to that of other kinds of political space. Writing about her time at the Minnehaha Free State camp, which was protesting against the destruction of sacred native land for a road-building project, one participant wrote:

> The first day that I came out to the Free State, I sat in one of

the daily circles: ideas were shared, updates were given, tactics discussed and I was so impressed by the organised, articulate, effective, respectful and meaningful communication that was taking place in front of me (quoted in Egan 2006).

Like many camps, Minnehaha Free State used circular seating for its meetings. The circle allows every member to engage in face-to-face contact and, as there are no raised seats or separate seating areas for meeting leaders, the non-hierarchical framework of the discussion is apparent in its spatial form. This contrasts sharply with the layout of the parliamentary halls and auditoriums of politicians and political parties. These structural and procedural practices of creating and operating alternative and autonomous forms of governance together, commonly found in protest camps, are explored in detail in Chapter 4.

Re-creation In addition to functioning as a convergence space and homeplace in the sense described by Jeff Juris, protest camps also become the site of interactions and exchanges that usually happen in the privacy of the home – whether these are bathing, going to the bathroom, washing laundry, or making a cup of tea. Creating and sustaining an outdoor community means braving the elements, and figuring out how to undertake daily tasks such as eating, cleaning and caretaking on cobblestone streets, in muddy grasslands or, at times, up spiky trees. For Tim Cresswell (1996) this marks how the protest camp becomes 'a place out of place', where the rituals of daily life – from cooking and bathing to parenting and displaying affection – are offered as an 'alternative aesthetics' to those of the normative, surrounding geography (ibid.: 124).

The idea that someone would live outdoors to protest – exposed to the world and weather, and often among strangers – invokes responses of bewilderment, intrigue, compassion and disgust (Feigenbaum 2008). The volume of media coverage focused on questions such as where protesters go to the bathroom is evidence of the ways in which such basic needs evoke a point of connection, returning us to our shared 'species bodies', while at the same time revealing and reproducing anxieties around class and cleanliness – notions about what, where and who is dirty and does not belong (Douglas 1996).

Offering structures for day-to-day living, the facilities provided at the protest camp again highlight the lack of free and public infra-

1.4 Compost toilets are part of the holistic, permaculture-inspired, ecological outlook of protest camps

structures available in cities for taking care of daily bodily needs. Barbara Ehrenreich drew attention to this in her widely circulated commentary on Occupy:

> What the Occupy Wall Streeters are beginning to discover, and homeless people have known all along, is that most ordinary, biologically necessary activities are illegal when performed in American streets – not just peeing, but sitting, lying down, and sleeping (Ehrenreich 2011).

The shelter, kitchens, toilets and sanitation that form part of the rituals of daily life are fundamental infrastructures of any protest camp. Infrastructures and practices of re-creation refer to the wider ideas and principles that guide protest campers' systems and the building of the structures needed to reproduce the protest camp as a homeplace and site for ongoing protest.

Some protest camps go to great lengths to build ecologically sustainable camp villages. In Rossport in Ireland, activists gathered to help support local residents' ongoing campaign Shell to Sea; this is a protest against the damage brought about by oil giant Shell's refinery and planned pipeline on their well-being and the environment. At Rossport, the protest camp's kitchen and sanitation systems formed part of participants' commitments to sustainable living. Speaking of his experience when he arrived at the Rossport Solidarity Camp, one protest camper wrote:

> I remember turning up on site the first time and thinking to myself, have I dropped a clanger here? Middle of nowhere; no chippy, no kebab shop – oh my god, what have I done! But the lack of takeaways was more than compensated for by the people I was about to meet ... From the organising of the picket run, to the shopping, cooking and general running of the camp, even the waste was composted. Not a nice job. It was a community within a community, although not without its own small differences of opinions on minor issues (Rossport Solidarity Camp n.d.: 23).

At camps such as Rossport, strong ecological sensibilities, grey water systems, composting and even gathering and growing food are common practice and often part of broader permaculture politics. According to permaculture, the 'problem is a solution' (Starhawk 2005b). Starhawk, who has published extensively in this field, exemplified this in reflections on the HoriZone eco-village:

> Conceiving of ways in which problems might become solutions, waste can be transformed to resources, physical structures support directly democratic social structures and people might be encouraged to wash their hands (Starhawk 2005a).

Whether intentionally or not, the re-creation infrastructures protesters build together are frequently regarded as being outside the political sphere; they are seen as add-ons to the real business of meetings and direct action. Sometimes coded as 'women's work', the physical and affective or emotional labour – as well as the materials and spaces – that go into caring for our bodies are often overlooked and undervalued. More than a mere backdrop or accessory to action, the people, objects and operations required to keep camps running are essential to the political life of the camp. Acts of re-creation are, in their own right, political acts that have much to tell us not only about the nature of protest camps, but also about social movement and cultural politics more generally. In her reflections on Occupy

Wall Street, Manissa Maharawal discusses how it was common for cultural events, random announcements, working group meetings and general assemblies to be taking place at one time in the small space of Zuccotti Park. Thinking through this dynamism, which produces both tension and conviviality, she writes:

> Maybe this is how movements need to maintain themselves, through recognition that political change is also fundamentally about everyday life and that everyday life needs to encompass all of this: there needs to be a space for a talent show across from an anti-patriarchy meeting, there needs to be a food table and medics, a library, and everyone needs to stop for a second and look around for someone's [lost] phone (N+1 2011: 36).

We will explore these larger issues and questions surrounding protest campers' struggles to build autonomy and community in Chapter 5.

Exposing the law

An encampment's infrastructures are always embedded in, and interdependent with, the existing operations and laws of the city or town in which it is located. The laws, or even the by-laws, of the land are often used to police and prohibit what may seem to be minor elements of a protest camp. For the police, these laws provide a means and excuse to exercise control.

A look at the legal history in the United States of camping in tents as a form of protest sheds light on the tensions around protest camps as sites of exposed living and re-creation. While US courts have repeatedly upheld the status of tents as a form of protected symbolic communication, it is generally when the tents move from being 'merely symbolic' to being actually usable structures for sleeping, eating and other forms of re-creation that 'reasonable time and place restrictions' are trotted out to remove or limit them as part of a protest. In one case, 'fake sleeping' was deemed acceptable while 'real sleeping' was not (Filip 2011). In this sense, displaying the infrastructure and putting it into operation is a challenge to the idea that protest should remain symbolic. When the protest camp's tents are seen to be too much like actual living spaces – when they begin to threaten the established, settled, normative state – they are no longer allowed.

In the UK, this view was made explicit in recent years following

Imperial College is the freehold owner of this land and has not given permission to any person or organisation to have access to and/or to occupy these fields.

Any person who gains access to and/or occupies these fields is doing so unlawfully and should vacate the field.

Imperial College reserves all its rights, including any claim(s) for damages and costs, against all and any occupiers of these fields.

Monday 13 August 2007

1.5 Laws and legal battles can form part of the struggle to create camps

the ruling to evict Occupy LSX. Sarah Ludford, the Liberal Democrat MEP (Member of the European Parliament) for London, commented on the verdict:

> Protests should not morph into tent cities. The right to protest is too precious to be undermined by long-term encampments which disrupt normal life to an unacceptable extent, beyond the inevitable and legitimate inconvenience of a one-off demo (Davies 2012).

In other words, it is the distinct space and time of the camp and its efforts to re-create life out of place that serve as a questioning of the status quo, of the settled order.

In the wake of many protest camps, governments have also enacted legislation that explicitly prohibits or severely limits protest camping. Following Resurrection City, a law was passed prohibiting camping on national parkland, a law that would be used decades later to clamp down on the Occupy movement. Following the eviction of a peace camp on Parliament Hill in Ottawa, Canadian Public Works Minister Roch La Salle created and passed a nuisance regulation directly targeting the camp, prohibiting camping on Parliament Hill, and giving police the power to evict campers immediately (see Kinloch 1985).

A similar situation occurred with the Parliament Square Peace Campaign, started by Brian Haw on 2 June 2001 in front of the Palace of Westminster in London. After almost a decade of legal battles and appeals to local and national government, the Police Reform and Social Responsibility Bill was given its first reading on 30 November 2010 in Westminster, steps away from Haw's protest camp. The Act banned 'any tent or any other structure that is designed, or adapted … for the purpose of facilitating sleeping or staying in' and received Royal Assent on 15 September 2011 (see http://services.parliament.uk/bills/2010-11/policereformandsocialresponsibility.html).

In the end, the law was never used to evict Haw as he died of lung cancer at age 62 on 18 June 2011, 11 years after setting up his protest camp and three months before the very bill designed to remove him came into force. Yet while the police never evicted Brian Haw from his Parliament Square Peace Campaign, they did raid his camp. As is often the case, Haw's camp, which consisted largely of graphic banners, signs and a collection of tents pitched by supporters, was subject to over-policing. The camp's first raid took place on 23 May 2006, when almost 80 police officers descended upon it in a heavy-handed night-time operation. When first reported, it was initially thought that the police action cost around £7,200, but it was later revealed to have cost £111,000 (see http://news.bbc.co.uk/2/hi/uk_news/england/london/5017142.stm and http://news.bbc.co.uk/2/hi/uk_news/england/london/6897656.stm).

'Travelling' infrastructures

Just as protest camps must be situated within the legal contexts that give rise to their distinct practices and infrastructures, so too must they be situated in relation to the broader ideas and practices they inherit from social movements and (sub)cultures. The resources and plans that go into constructing a protest camp are often passed on by previous or simultaneous movements. Whether it is a shared marquee or instructions for building a tree house out of wooden pallets, architectural materials and knowledge are often exchanged between protest campers. We have used the term 'promiscuous' to identify how the organisational designs of these infrastructures travel and spread in multiple directions (Artivistic 2011; Feigenbaum 2011). Those looking

1.6 Infrastructures travel, with tripods being used at different UK Climate Camps, including here at Kingsnorth in 2008

for linearity in processes of social change, like those concerned only with large-scale structures, often misunderstand or misrecognise the micro-structures that facilitate and propagate protest camps as they appear and disappear across cities, countrysides and continents. Just as the negative cultural meaning of promiscuity has been politically contested in relation to bodies, we here reclaim the word 'promiscuous' to capture the often cunning and seemingly chaotic mobility of the organisational dynamics that give life to protest camps.

Conceptualising and studying protest camps through the lens of travelling or promiscuous infrastructures can help us recognise existing connections between camps, campers and social movements. While movements have always shared knowledge, in an age of digitally networked communication and high-speed travel, this knowledge now spreads and circulates quickly. As social movement participants and protest campers alike pass on, share, learn from and adapt past experiences, they modify their communication, action, governance and re-creation practices. While the majority of our examples and our own experiences come out of social movements in Europe and North America, focusing on how practices and structures travel between movements in space and time draws attention to the way in which global flows of ideas and actions are multidimensional and multidirectional (Pickerill et al. 2011). The list below sets out some examples of these kinds of transnational exchanges between protest camps:

- Media and communication: A logistical handbook from a 30,000-person nuclear power plant occupation in Germany in 1975 was used as the basis for information pamphlets circulated in the US two years later by the Clamshell Alliance (Crown 1979).
- Protest action: The 19-month Occupation of Alcatraz in 1969–71 by the American Indian Movement inspired eviction resistance by protest campers at Minnehaha Free State in Minneapolis in 1998 (Egan 2006).
- Governance: Spokescouncil models for organising meetings in factories and neighbourhoods in the Argentinian uprising of 2001 were adopted in Spain in 2011 during the M15 movement (Sitrin and Azzellini 2012).
- Re-creation: A group calling itself the TAT Collective stored and delivered tents, marquees and kitchen supplies to protest camps around the UK throughout the 2000s, with recipients including Climate Camps and NoBorders camps.

The highly publicised and widely popularised 'human microphone' created in Zuccotti Park provides an excellent recent example of how infrastructures and practices travel transnationally. Banned by the police from using amplified sound devices, campers at Zuccotti developed a system whereby a speaker's words would be repeated by a larger group of people, allowing the sound to travel further through large crowds and through the space of the encampment.

In what some have called a display of symbolic solidarity (Pickerill et al. 2011), and what can equally be seen as an embodied performance of Occupy identity, protest campers across the globe replicated the 'human mic'. By being replicated across the globe, this form of communication both created a highly affective transnational resonance and drew critique. At sites such as Occupy LSX, the following question was raised: 'If a camp does not face a ban on amplified sound, does the affective force of the "human mic" outweigh the functionality of a PA system or megaphone?' This kind of consideration, which occurs both explicitly (on a meeting agenda) and informally (in camp chats), can be applied to a wide range of activities and operations that structure camp life. At the founding of the Occupy Ottawa camp, for

1.7 Note of solidarity at Occupy LSX

example, facilitators deliberately avoided an amplified sound system for the gathering in order to use the 'human mic'. While it proved difficult, at times, to transmit information and debate issues in this way, it allowed Occupiers to enact and embody a practice linked to what it meant to be an 'Occupier', regardless of its practical utility and contextual necessity. Other examples of adaptive and imaginative approaches to governance – with varying degrees of success – are discussed in Chapter 4.

In the case of the human microphone, and in the examples listed previously, a combination of people, technologies and ideas was exchanged and travelled across time and space. These kinds of network exchanges shape the ways in which new protest camps materialise around the world, whether in the trees of California or the parks of Tel Aviv. Using our four sets of infrastructures and related practices as threads to read across and through protest camps helps us account for how ideas, objects and organising structures travel across time and space, becoming adopted and adapted as they circulate – simultaneously moving through social movement networks and creating new ones (Feigenbaum 2011).

Most recently we saw this phenomenon on a global scale as protests in Tahrir Square went on to inspire Spanish, American, Israeli and Greek protesters to challenge their governments, erecting encampments in the spring and summer of 2011. However, while a 'Tahrir Square, City of Westminster' street sign went up in Occupy LSX and placards declaring 'From Tahrir to Puerto del Sol: Democracy for All' were carried in Madrid, there are significant differences in the social, economic and political realities between each movement, including in the level of repression faced by activists. Official figures recognise the deaths of 847 individuals and injuries to 6,000 more during the 18 days in January 2011 preceding the 11 February resignation of Egyptian President Hosni Mubarak (Knell 2012). While the Egyptian uprisings in January and February of 2011 were non-violent in spirit, reading Tahrir as an example of non-violent direct action does not tell the full story. It overlooks the role that antagonism played in protesters' struggles against the corrupt state, and it often detracts from the intensity of violence inflicted on protesters by both the police and hired 'security'. Protesters' chants of 'salmiya, salmiya' (peaceful, peaceful) did not reflect the atmosphere in Cairo, but rather sought to draw attention to the use of physical and coercive violence by the state against its people.

As the model of the public square encampment from Tahrir travelled across the globe, protesters in Cairo were conscious of these elisions and of the realities masked by Western portrayals of their struggle. In a solidarity letter sent via social media and picked up by online news sites including the *Guardian*'s 'Comment is Free', occupiers from Egypt told the US-led Occupy movement:

> We faced such direct and indirect violence, and continue to face it. Those who said that the Egyptian revolution was peaceful did not see the horrors that police visited upon us, nor did they see the resistance and even force that revolutionaries used against the police to defend their tentative occupations and spaces: by the government's own admission, 99 police stations were put to the torch, thousands of police cars were destroyed and all of the ruling party's offices around Egypt were burned down …
>
> Had we laid down and allowed ourselves to be arrested, tortured and martyred to 'make a point', we would be no less bloodied, beaten and dead. Be prepared to defend these things you have

occupied, that you are building, because, after everything else has been taken from us, these reclaimed spaces are so very precious (http://anticapitalprojects.wordpress.com/2011/10/24/solidarity-letter-from-cairo/).

This call asked Occupy activists to recognise both the realities of the violence of the struggles in Egypt and the fact that the state will not simply hand over change to Occupiers on demand. At the same time, captured in this letter is the larger vision of participatory democracy and of reclaiming space that all of these protest camps share. As a protester camping in the Capitol Building in Wisconsin in 2011 told a reporter during a guided tour of the occupation:

I think that most people agree that the people of Egypt really inspire people here. There's this whole issue with equating the two situations, which I think is a false equation, but there's no doubt that people here have been inspired by that to really see that a group of people without official leadership can get together and really do something (Democracy Now! 2011).

As this young protester points out, drawing connections between occupations and encampments is not the same as saying that their situations are identical. Tents and tarmac do not make movements equal, or equally in it together. Rather, the idea is to highlight patterns. On the one side, there are patterns of state corruption, state repression and the uprisings that they ignite, an increasing number of which are taking the form of the protest camp, at least in part. On the other side, there are patterns of practices and infrastructures, ways in which planning, tactics and resources travel and become entangled in specific cultures and contexts. The question is how to draw out these patterns, how to make the connections, while attributing political significance to their differences in ways that foster collective learning between movements. Governments, media pundits and police forces tend to portray each act of civil disobedience, every march, every direct action and every protest camp as being unconnected, both to each other and to broader political struggles; it is clear who benefits when the links are not made.

Messages of solidarity and support, like the ones from and for Tahrir Square, make manifest or visible the transnational links between movements, and the ways in which their structural forms, tactics and practices are reproduced and adapted across borders, cultures and causes. As they travel transnationally, between camps and beyond, these messages tell their own stories of how people's struggles for resistance learn from each other. These lessons can cross borders, making and shaping the protest camps yet to come. Likewise, they can tell us stories of what gets lost in translation.

Conclusion

Throughout the following chapters, we seek to understand protest camps by looking not only at people's ideas and interactions but also at what the structures, objects, environment and laws of an encampment 'make humans do' (Latour 2005). By framing questions around the ways in which protesters must negotiate not only with each other but with the objects and structures that are brought together in the making of an encampment, we are able to explore tactical developments and tactical failures. This approach draws attention to what is possible, focusing on the experiential and experimental terrain of the protest camp.

In a practical sense, looking at how circumstances and events that are sometimes beyond our control come to shape political negotiations can help expand our tactical thinking and collective problem-solving skills. It can make us shift and rethink attributions of fault and blame to better allow for contingency, for the unexpected to become a political actor, mutating our protests into new forms. Likewise, being attuned to the ways in which ideas circulate with and through the objects, structures and environments that make up acts of protest can help create new spaces for reflection and transformation of practices, as we make room for different ways of seeing each other and ourselves.

Processes of social change cannot be mapped out in clear chronologies or through a series of linear exchanges. For example, one of the impacts protest camps have on the public is the visible disruption of the normative routines of daily life and how they disturb people's movement through 'public' spaces. This crucial aspect of protest camps is hard to capture with such approaches.

Looking instead, as we do, at the infrastructures and at the practices and processes associated with protest camps, we are able to analyse and look seriously at the encampment itself. We can study how people, ideas, objects and organising structures are always entangled. We can draw out the similarities and differences in how protest campers have gone about 'building together'. This can help further illuminate the ways in which people and objects interact, how specific protest camps come to life, and what we can learn from an examination of them. By showing how protest camps configure their infrastructures and practices, shaping experiences of participation, collaboration, collectivity and mutuality, we hope to contribute to the wider understanding of alternative forms of social and political participation.

As we will argue in more detail, shifts in political organising are both played out and developed in the space of the protest camp. As others have argued, the protest camp, in all its distinct forms, is a temporary autonomous zone (Bey 1991), an autonomous geography (Pickerill and Chatterton 2006), a space of production that creates a 'new commons', always messy and evolving (Pusey 2010). In the midst of this messiness, this experimental and partial autonomy, protest camps provide a space to fundamentally renew and reshape how a community is imagined, organised and run. Treating infrastructures as threads, we use them to tie together diverse sets of protest camps and their campers' practices, as we have begun to do here. This approach allows us to weave together the many research-oriented and personal reflections offered on protest camps over the years. Many of the ideas and examples introduced in this opening discussion of camp infrastructures are explored in greater detail in the chapters that follow, beginning with media and communications.

2 | MEDIA AND COMMUNICATION INFRASTRUCTURES

I had brought my video camera to the anti-G8 protests in Gleneagles, but I never filmed inside the camp. There were several reasons. Of course, filming or taking pictures inside the camp was also officially banned. A distinct policy was in place, that no cameras would be used. A total blackout, decided in advance, that applied to anyone: media, campers, whoever. How could we tell who was 'undercover' and who wasn't?

It also simply didn't feel right. There were people brushing their teeth or cooking in the kitchen tent. Others were sitting together over maps, plotting ways to circumvent major roads on the way to the conference hotel. Filming them would have been an intrusion into their privacy. It sometimes felt, as well, that the camp was a sanctum that shouldn't be polluted by representation.

One day, as a film team did enter the camp, they were immediately surrounded by angry protesters and asked to leave. The policy was defended; the camp was not to be represented. Afterwards there were hardly any pictures or videos from the camp and this was a shame. For the most part the camp had been amazing but we didn't have many pictures to show it. (HoriZone, Scotland, 2005)

Introduction

This chapter examines how protest campers attempt to work together to manage mainstream media and to create their own media representations of camp life and broader campaign or movement politics. To do this, we draw from previous analyses of the communication strategies of social movements, but we also look at how the spatially and temporally unique setting of the encampment adds further dimensions to how we understand the activist media strategies taking place at protest camps.

The presence of media – anticipated or actual, overt or undercover, activist or mainstream, digital or analogue – transforms the space of the protest camp. With media attention, protest camps often become sites of media reportage and public interest, and the protesters are brought under the gaze of media-makers. As convergence spaces (Routledge 2003), protest camps are often home to competing and conflicting ideas of what – if any – strategies should be deployed to communicate with the public via mainstream and activist media, from complete hostility to sheer excitement, from utter fear to professional decorum.

Aware of the importance of media as an arena for struggle, protest campers must navigate the range of views, experiences and existing strategies to develop their own systems and practices for managing mainstream, activist and social media. Yet, as this chapter demonstrates, managing protest camp media does not merely require protest campers to develop, refine and deploy a repertoire of media practices; simultaneously, they must navigate the camp and the wider social movement politics to do so. To this end, we discuss protest camp-based media practices, including media policies, media stations and the making of promotional materials, press releases, newsletters and documentary video. We view protest camps' media as part of a broader historical trajectory of activists' media practices, from pre-internet and pre-digital cultures to the live streaming of videos of camp activities and protests. We argue that the communication practices and infra-structures we see today are shaped to a great extent by past movement cultures as they come into contact with new devices and platforms.

In making our argument, we pay attention to the ways in which protesters' strategies are entwined with each other, as well as with their material environments. From concerns about internet and mobile phone connections to undercover reporters infiltrating action planning meetings, the human and non-human elements that make up protest camp life affect the media and communication practices of the protesters. While some media strategies deployed by protesters are planned and based on long histories of social movement campaigning (e.g. spokespersons, media liaisons, camp-based newsletters), others emerge spontaneously or are improvisational as protesters make do with available resources. In some cases, protesters monitor the media and file complaints against slanderous coverage. Engaging a range of strategies, media teams at protest camps figure out how to find, protect and generate the resources needed to both make their own media and respond to mainstream media reports. At Occupy Wall

Street, the campers needed electricity for their communications and therefore devised a system for bringing generators into the park. In Tahrir Square, protesters rewired street lamps to get electricity to run computers and charge mobile phones. In Oaxaca, women took over existing infrastructure, occupying a broadcast television station to film and air their own programming.

We begin by briefly introducing and discussing Rucht's (2004) 'Quadruple A' framework for understanding social movements' media strategies and discuss how it may be used for our purposes. Next, we consider how protest camps have engaged with the four strategies Rucht outlines in their efforts to manage both backstage and front-stage aspects of the protest camp, and to create their own representational forms for communicating campaign goals and wider movement issues, and, in some cases, for showcasing life at the camp.

Given the breadth and diversity of media and communication practices used in protest camps, it is important to develop a typology that can help focus attention on how such strategies play out in the various camps studied. We can achieve this by adapting Rucht's historical overview of the media strategies of social movements. Beginning with the student movements of the 1960s and running up to the Global Justice Movement, Rucht devised a model for charting a social movement's 'reaction' to mainstream media interest based on four different – but not mutually exclusive – strategies: alternatives, attack, abstention and adaptation. Rucht defines these terms as the 'Quadruple A' framework (ibid.: 37):

> Alternatives: 'the attempt by social movements to create their own independent media ... in order to compensate for a lack of interest, or bias on the part of established media'.
>
> Attack: 'consists of an explicit critique of, and even sometimes even violent action against, the mass media'.
>
> Abstention: 'born out of resignation based on negative experiences with established media ... it implies the withdrawal from attempts to influence the mass media and retreat to inward-directed group communication'.
>
> Adaptation: 'means the acceptance/exploitation of the mass media's rules and criteria to influence coverage positively'.

Using these four categories, Rucht argues that 'the question is, under which circumstances social movements tend to which, or which combination, of the four non-mutually exclusive options?' (ibid.: 38). Like Rucht, we too are interested in the evolution of media strategies. However, we are particularly interested in how strategies and practices come into contact with and are influenced by both each other and the wider social/political context within the space of the camp. As a result, we need to recognise that camp media practices – the issuing of a press release, the maintenance of a Facebook page or the creation of a camp newsletter – do not unfold in a vacuum. Instead, camp politics are often interwoven with, and come to a head around, issues of media representation; the politics of representation are often a core issue debated at protest camps. The repertoires of media practices and the accompanying strategies used within a single protest camp may overlap with, anchor, complement, militate against or contradict each other. Moreover, while groups tend to emerge within protest camps to 'manage' different aspects of media (from overseeing a media tent to deploying a social media strategy), it would be a mistake to assume that a protest camp always has a consistent media strategy; even if a strategy exists, there may still be tensions within the camp.

To better account for the place-based dynamics of the protest camp, we direct our gaze primarily towards two of Rucht's categories – 'adaptation' and 'alternatives' – and within each of these broader groupings we fold in the strategies of 'abstention' and 'attack'. Consequently, we begin by considering how protest camps 'adapt' to the needs of mainstream media and we follow this with an examination of how protest campers have chosen to present themselves using available media technologies. Both strategies are equally important for understanding a protest camp's media practices and infrastructures. Our approach complements the literature of social movement and media scholarship, which has tended to focus either on managing mainstream media (what Rucht calls 'adaptation') or on social movement media ('alternatives').

Although we have separated out these practices for discussion purposes, we see activist media strategies as taking place within a wider media ecology. The media ecology view takes account of the ways in which the infrastructures, objects and environments of mainstream and alternative media-making are intertwined – albeit very unevenly as far as access to and distribution of resources are concerned. Those seeking to understand our rapidly changing systems of media and information communication have employed such ecological perspectives. Nardi and O'Day (1999) describe 'information ecology' as 'a system of people, practices, values, and technologies in a particular local environment'. Treré (2012) argues that their conceptualisation allows us to move away from thinking of technologies as tools used by individuals to achieve aims (e.g. 'Twitter revolutions') to a view that is 'able to grasp the interrelations among tools, people and their practices', paying attention to both group processes and specific localities (ibid.: 5). While Nardi and O'Day are interested in libraries and education, Treré's application of their concept to study the information ecologies of autonomous social centres highlights the importance of reflecting on the complex ways in which old and new technologies are brought into contact with each other, while drawing attention to the continuous negotiations people make as they both generate and work through tensions and conflicts (ibid.). Combining this ecological approach to media technologies with an analysis of the physical and infrastructural spaces of media-making and audience reception, Altha Cravey describes the city of Oaxaca during its ongoing encampments:

> In Oaxaca's central marketplace in summer 2006, call-in commentary on Sit-In Radio (Radio Plantón) wafted through the air and, from time to time people stopped what they were doing to listen intently to a compelling narrative. Women-run Saucepan Radio (Radio Cacerola) blared from taxis as they navigated to the edges of the permanently barricaded central city ... Visual imagery also exploded ... newspaper photos and stories hung from zigzagged twine throughout the insurgent *zocalo* (Cravey 2010: 10–11).

Here, Cravey captures the dynamic processes, infrastructures, objects and even soundscapes of a rich media ecology in which protest camps are interwoven.

Adaptations

In this first section, we explore adaptive media strategies as they arise out of protest campers' efforts and innovations in managing mainstream media interest and interactions. While Rucht's framework sees adaptation as a one-way process, we do not think that this is the case. Protest campers certainly make accommodations for the media and adjust their practices according to media norms. However, they also adapt their practices to reflect social movement traditions, particularly in regard to critiques of representation and corporate- and government-controlled media power. We therefore see protesters' use of these strategies as a *dual adaption* in which they adjust their practices to fit with both mainstream *and* internal movement norms. Moreover, at times the mainstream media also adapts to protest camp- ers' policies and mandates. While any complete or total abstention is not really possible in an age of 24-hour news cycles and social media, the issue of abstention remains relevant. In fact, it is arguably even more important during this period of media saturation, as it becomes increasingly difficult for protesters to find ways to be both visible and invisible to the media. We explore these issues in the next section, which examines protest campers' strategies of adaptation when the protest campsite becomes a media stage.

Strategies of adaptation: protest camps on the media stage Place- based and spatially bound, protest camps function simultaneously as a 'staged' and symbolic protest for the media and the public, and as 'activist spaces' where protesters plan, organise and live. Therefore, in protest camps there are often inherent tensions between its 'front' or 'media stage' attributes and its 'backstage' components. It was sociologist Erving Goffman (1959: 92–122) in his famous study of face-to-face interaction who popularised the differentiation between front stage and backstage. Referring to the way in which individuals control and present themselves, Goffman defined the front stage as the area where the show is put on, the part that is visible to the public and that is consciously made visible (ibid.: 93). Backstage, on the other hand, was defined as the area that is kept hidden and protected from view, where secrets are kept and where performances can be rehearsed (ibid.: 97–109). Extending Goffman's work, Benford and Hunt (1992: 43) introduced the front stage/backstage dichotomy to social move- ment literature as a means of conceptualising the challenges faced by social movement actors in maintaining 'backstage control' over their activities. To this end, the authors differentiated between front stage (presentation to the public and media) and backstage (activist organising). Thus, a demonstration is held on the front stage, but its organisation and the political debates over who speaks when and who marches where are kept hidden in the backstage. The tensions between front stage and backstage are arguably more pronounced at a protest camp than in other kinds of protest. From the perspective of managing media interest at the protest camp, there is a significant dilemma as the camp is often 'inside' the media event of the protest yet at the same time is a homeplace for protesters (McCurdy 2008). As Couldry (1999: 344) argues in his discussion of Greenham Common:

> home ... lies beyond the media frame. At this level of background expectation, events at Greenham were profoundly disruptive. The peace camp was at the same time a 'domestic', 'local' space where women lived and a public, mediated space of national significance.

In this way, protest camps may disrupt given media frames of protest. While gaining media representation is often a key component of having a protest camp, the media's interest in and presence at the camp inevitably changes a camp's dynamic. This often prompts campers to enact specific policies for managing both mainstream and movement media. Protesters develop strategies and tactics for interacting with journalists and for handling the dynamics between those elements of protest camp life that do and do not want media attention. Activists at protests camps tend to possess a reflexive awareness of the presence and logic of media and often attempt to adapt the media and communication infrastructures of their camps accordingly.

To manage the camp's status as a media stage, protesters develop specific strategies of adaptation. In what follows we investigate strategies of building boundaries; instituting 'open hours', where mainstream media are allowed a chaperoned protest camp visit; creating media mandates; and establishing 'media tents' for media liaison teams and individuals interested in speaking to the media. We begin by briefly looking at Resurrection City's attempts to construct boundaries and the tensions faced by City residents and campaign organisers when trying to establish a consistent media strategy. We then look at how a collection of UK-based protest camps, from the 2005 HoriZone to the 2010 Edinburgh Climate Camps, developed and carried forward a range of media management practices. Specifically, we chart the creation, evolution and consequences of the use of an 'open-hour' media strategy. In discussing the 'open hour' below, it is not our intention to present it as a generalised practice deployed in all protest camps. Instead, it is offered as an example of how protest camps develop and share media practices within a specific social, political, economic and media environment. We then focus our attention on media mandates and media tents.

Establishing media boundaries at Resurrection City Pitched in view of the Lincoln Memorial on the National Mall, Washington, DC, and at its peak with about 3,000 residents, Resurrection City was literally too big to miss. Indeed, that was its point; as Amy Nathan Wright notes, the City was built to 'both display and protest', to make visible the poverty and destitution many Americans experienced in their everyday lives (Wright 2008: 46). By bringing the poor to the government's doorstep in Washington, DC, the symbolic and physical site of national power, the protest made visible and visceral to politicians, media and the public that which was often otherwise invisible. In fact, as a planned event with the major campaign goal of garnering national media attention, Resurrection City was the culmination of a media and awareness campaign initiated by Dr Martin Luther King Jr. After his assassination, the campaign was carried forward by leaders of the Southern Christian Leadership Conference (SCLC) and the organisers of the Poor People's Campaign (PPC).

To mark the City's arrival, campaign organisers held a press con-ference on 13 May 1968 for a symbolic 'ground breaking' ceremony. Much to the displeasure of waiting journalists, the event began hours later than its announced start time. Fager's (1969) account of Resur-rection City's opening ceremony notes that:

> the situation quickly became a standoff, with angry reporters
> crouching or sitting on the grass but keeping their places while
> marshals and marchers kept up constant but less insistent cries for
> them to move (ibid.: 35).

Eventually, Reverend Ralph Abernathy arrived on site to mark the City's construction, journalists got their news story for the day, and the event signalled the start of the protest camp – while also fore-shadowing the tensions between some of Resurrection City's protest campers and mainstream media journalists that were to continue.

As noted above, friction between journalists and residents of Resur-rection City began with the camp's construction. Although the camp was intended as a spectacle for media, journalists had difficulties while on site. In theory, the City was open to the media, a position confirmed by the PPC, which wanted the press to be able to access the camp as they pleased. Some members of the PPC even offered the media tours of Resurrection City, a tactic that has been used at many protest camps, as we will see. However, such tours were usually escorted; if prominent tour guides, often from the SCLC, left journalists on their own, marshals would forcefully banish the journalists from the City and move them to positions outside the improvised City boundaries, which were constructed using snow fences (ibid.: 38).

Thus physical – even if somewhat flimsy – barriers were created to divide camp space from park space, media space from City space, and these barriers were actively reinforced by marshals. This led journalists, who were surprised by the hostility they encountered, to congregate outside the City's entrance; here, PPC officials would sometimes gather to reassure them. From Fager's perspective, the constant on-site intimidation and harassment of journalists probably had a negative impact on protest camp coverage (ibid.: 37). This view was shared by Tom Offenburger, Director of the Department of Information for the SCLC and head of press relations for the PPC (and therefore also of Resurrection City's media relations). However, from Offenburger's perspective, tensions between City residents and journalists may have been somewhat stronger because it was the Washington press corps that tended to report on Resurrection City and not the seasoned reporters who had covered the civil rights movement and were therefore familiar with the movement's cultural nuances (Offenburger 1968: 40). While this in no way excuses the harassment encountered by the press, Offenburger's view could account for some of the frustrations expressed by journalists about the delay and lack of process experienced at the protest camp. Moreover, Offenburger saw press corps journalists as having a special relationship with government and being used to covering the process of government. Because of this, Resurrection City – the environment, politics and process – would undoubtedly have seemed quite unfamiliar to many journalists. In fact, this observation can be extended to the wider protest camp phenomenon, where camps are exceptional sites on many levels, as we will discuss further in Chapter 5.

Of course, the purpose of many media groups at protest camps is to try to facilitate this process. In fact, there was a press team at Resurrection City and Offenburger was at its head. It began as a skeleton crew of six people from SCLC Atlanta and was expanded with the City's founding to include a team of press volunteers. As part of the wider PPC campaign, and as a media base for Resurrection City, an off-site press office equipped with a Xerox machine and funded by the SCLC Finance Committee was secured in advance of the camp's founding (ibid.: 43). At times, the team was in charge of much more than just press relations; its responsibilities included scheduling television and radio interviews, printing, and programming camp entertainment and exhibits (ibid.: 41). It should be noted that the full-time volunteers included professionals who worked without pay, while a small core of paid public and press relations professionals were hired to work full time using a small grant from the National Council of Churches (ibid.: 42). In recruiting press and public relations people, there was a conscious effort to have people from different groups, such as the First Nations and the Mexican American community (ibid.: 59).

In short, a large amount of resources – relative to the size of the organisation and the number of people involved – were invested in the media side of the PPC and Resurrection City. Reflecting on the media strategy of Resurrection City, Offenburger pointed to two significant failures: journalist harassment and the lack of a consistent media policy. With regard to the second issue, Offenburger was critical of the:

> inability to keep a consistent policy about the access of the press to Resurrection City that is in terms of hours of the day or night and about the access of the press to the people … whether or not they can interview on the campsite (ibid.: 48).

Interestingly, as opposed to ideological or political differences between campers about the role of the media (a definite cause of tension for protest camps discussed in the next section), Offenburger attributes the lack of a policy to:

> [T]he very lack of an overall management of the entire city as a city. This was never done. In a sense, it was never desired. I desired it as a press officer because I know that the press will respect and really won't complain if you say they can be in the campsite, for example, for one hour a day and you tell them what that hour is and adhere to it, stick to it straight about what the press could do on the campsite. Could they take pictures any time if they were allowed on there, or could they freely roam around the camp or be escorted by marshals. Time and again we tried to set up policies and it never got done. I think it is a failing of SCLC that we didn't do that and it case [sic] a lot of problems between us and the press (ibid.: 48).

Offenburger's critique is based on a perceived failure of the PPC's initiating organisation, the SCLC (of which he was a director), to successfully implement a top-down media policy. Offenburger's view is that such a policy for the protest camp was desirable because the press required structure, and he believed in the need to 'adapt' camp practices to facilitate media coverage. Given the governance structure of Resurrection City and the fact that it was run by a civil rights non-governmental organisation (NGO), such a media policy would have been possible – but it did not happen. However, in other camps, such as HoriZone and the Climate Camps, their application of autonomous politics has directly influenced and limited the type of media policy possible. Nevertheless, hostility towards journalists at protest camps is still widespread.

'Opening' HoriZone to the media The 2005 HoriZone protest camp in Stirling in Scotland was initiated by the autonomous and anti-capitalist Dissent! network. The dual function of HoriZone as both a media space and an activist space presented a challenge in how to manage the front-stage and backstage aspects of the site. Whereas the presentation of HoriZone as a media space, such as in the press release, was premised on media access and media visibility, its function as an activist space was premised on preventing media access and managing invisibility. HoriZone campers were aware of the media event status of the G8 Summit they had mobilised against. They were also aware of their visible role as 'protesters' and that of the protest camp within the media event. As a result, many Dissent! activists anticipated the media coverage and developed specific practices for dealing with media enquiries and for managing the protest camp as a site of media interest.

Stemming from Dissent!'s interpretation of horizontal and autonomist politics (see Chapter 4), press statements from HoriZone were strictly limited to formal written statements, often produced via consensus and sanctioned at network and camp meetings. It was press release by committee. This committee-led process of interacting with the media, while being an effort to enact the movement's politics, was slow, cumbersome and did not sit well with the time pressures and demands of news media. To compensate for this, some Dissent! activists formed an autonomous media group – the CounterSpin Collective (CSC) – to manage media interest, as will be discussed shortly. In advance of HoriZone's opening, Dissent! set out a policy barring mainstream media from entering HoriZone while the camp was up and running (McCurdy 2009). However, on 29 June 2005, two days before the camp officially opened, news media were invited to take a one-hour, escorted tour of the campsite. The one-off 'open hour' event was agreed upon at a HoriZone camp logistics meeting in an effort to offer a timed and restricted media window '... out of respect for those who did not want to be subjected to any coverage, and in order to control mainstream media access to the site on our own terms' (CounterSpin Collective 2005: 324).

The fact that journalists were prohibited from entering HoriZone did not prevent them from showing up at the camp's entrance or from sneaking inside. One of the jobs the CSC took on was to inform journalists of the camp's media policy. As the CSC recounts, journalists were not happy with the restrictions that greeted them at the camp:

> Some journalists were upset by this and would argue one or two positions. They would either demand their right of access to a public space, or they would try and cajole us by asking us how they could provide a fair coverage under such restrictions (ibid.: 327).

As will be discussed shortly, the CSC did more than just inform journalists of the camp's rigid media policy; it proactively facilitated interactions between activists and journalists. Of interest here is the tactic of having an 'open hour' against the backdrop of a 'no media on site' policy, and what it suggests about the tension between the camp as both a media space and an activist space. It is important to know that within the camp, and within Dissent!'s wider political culture, the issue of media interaction was a contentious one. Referred to, almost in code, as the 'media debate', whether or not to interact with news media and to what extent was often seen as a bitterly divisive topic within Dissent! (McCurdy 2010). As such, HoriZone was, at times, an antagonistic environment for CSC activists, who were met with outright hostility by some fellow campers:

> We experienced repeated hostility and encountered inaccurate gossip about what we were doing. In one instance at the Hori-zone, activists speaking to journalists were screamed at and threatened with physical violence and then had bottles thrown at them from inside the site (CounterSpin Collective 2005: 328).

2.1 No access to mainstream media beyond this point – entrance to the HoriZone protest camp, Stirling, July 2005

It was as a direct result of these tensions that the media was banned from entering HoriZone and the 'open hour' was only held prior to the camp's opening.

While some media coverage of HoriZone was gained from the 'open hour', it was largely contained within Scottish borders, as the media event the protest camp was built around was not yet on the international media's radar. The nature of the international news cycle meant that significant interest in the camp and its occupants was not generated until six days after the 'open hour', on 5 July 2005, just one day prior to the start of the G8 Summit. By the time interest had flourished in the camp, its patrons and their planned actions, journalists were met with the aforementioned 'no media' policy that banned journalists from entering the camp.

Dual adaptation in Climate Camp's 'open hour' policy The 'no media' policy and the 'open hour' tour were products of the political and cultural environment of the Dissent! network and the HoriZone camp. The tactic was an attempt to adapt to the demands of media yet still operate within the political confines of the camp. The end result was a tactic that, while having some impact, was far more restrictive than many CSC members would have liked (McCurdy 2009). Nonetheless, the tactic was carried forward from HoriZone to subsequent Climate

Camps by some members of the CSC. The proposed hosting of an 'open hour' ended up being an issue of contention during the second Camp for Climate Action held on the edge of London's Heathrow Airport. As part of a co-ordinated media effort, the 2007 Climate Camp organisers entertained the following proposal:

> Media wanting access to the camp will be invited to come on site between 11 am and 12 noon. All visits will be over and journalists off site by 1 pm at the latest. Journalists will be given a tour of the site, accompanied at all times by two (or more) members of the media team, who will carry a flag to make the journalists/ photographers identifiable. Journalists will be required to stick with the tour and will not be allowed to go into marquees or meetings and workshops unless invited at the agreement of all participants (SionPhoto 2007).

This proposal was adopted by Climate Camp but eventually amended so that, instead of a one-off camp tour, there were daily one-hour tours on each day of the camp's duration, from Tuesday 14 to Friday 17 August 2007 (Indymedia 2007).

The camp's media policy became the object of harsh criticism from journalists. In a widely distributed letter to Climate Camp written by John Toner, freelance organiser of the National Union of Journalists (NUJ), Toner remarked:

> While I can understand your apprehension that coverage of the camp by mainstream media could be negative, the conditions you have stipulated are guaranteed to attract criticism from all professional journalists, whether supportive of or hostile to your views (ibid.).

The Climate Camp media policy was also openly criticised by journalists such as the *Guardian*'s environment editor, John Vidal, who in a scathing editorial commented:

> A small but anonymous faction of the old protest movement at the climate camp had decided from the start that the 'corporate' press is actually the enemy, and therefore has to be excluded. There was to be no appeal and the policy was rigorously enforced via a media police team. As a sop, the press was allowed a guided tour of certain parts of the camp for one hour a day. I refused to go

on the absurd camp tour ... If there is one thing more aggravating than a British policeman stopping you on suspicion that you are a terrorist when he knows for a fact that you are not, it's a jobsworth protester trying to have you thrown out of a site that he himself has squatted (Vidal 2007).

Many journalists thought that the 'open hour' inhibited free speech and impeded their right to report on activities as they so desired. Aware of these criticisms and the tensions they caused, the Climate Camp media team commented as follows:

> This policy is a compromise that attempts to provide reasonable media access whilst respecting camp participants' right to privacy. Past protest events similar to the camp have had a no-access policy, and last year's [2006] media hour, which worked well for all concerned, was, we thought, a major step forward ... The media team will do our best to make sure that journalists get what they need, within the framework set out above. Please do be aware though that we are facing multiple opposing constraints, and please bear with us as we attempt to negotiate these pressures (Indymedia 2007; Camp for Climate Action 2007).

The above passage makes reference to 'multiple opposing constraints' faced by the Climate Camp media team in attempting to create a camp media policy. One constraint was obviously the pressure placed by journalists to open up the camp. However, pressure also came from within Climate Camp. As with HoriZone, there were political divisions within Climate Camp concerning the degree of media access, and some activists pushed quite hard to limit media access to the camp. This was, effectively, a continuation of the 'media debate' (McCurdy 2010) and touches yet again on the tension between activists envisioning the protest camp as a symbolic place to 'showcase' politics in practice and activists viewing it as a place to live, plan and work without media interference. Of course, it can try to be both, but that often requires compromise, which is what ultimately produced the 'open hour'.

The 'open hour' strategy developed at Climate Camp was an attempt to 'adapt' (Rucht 2004) to journalists' needs yet also devise a solution that respected the protest camp's internal political divisions over mainstream media interaction. However, in the end, the strategy had a hard time making anyone happy. Journalists felt slighted by the restrictions placed on them; some activists felt any interaction with media at the camp was too much, while many wanted to see media interaction increased. Saunders (2012), writing about the 2008 Camp for Climate Action, argues that the camp was a space where a heterogeneity of viewpoints, from radical to reformist, converged. This diversity in perspectives, Saunders argues, created the tensions between campers that ultimately led to the Climate Camp network's demise. The media policy adopted by Climate Camp must be seen as both the embodiment and the consequence of these larger heterogeneous debates surrounding camp politics.

Media activists continued to refine the 'open hour' media policy during the Camp for Climate Action cycle. In 2010, the last year of the Camp for Climate Action, the camp developed a dual media strategy that differentiated between 'photographers and TV crews' and 'radio and television journalists'. The former group was invited to attend a modified and extended 'open hour' that permitted them on site daily between 1 p.m. and 6 p.m. However, photographers and television crews wishing to enter the camp were given an 'assigned camper' or minder; according to the camp's media access policy, this was to ensure that 'campers and journalists are kept happy, and can ensure that consent is obtained from people being filmed and photographed' (Camp for Climate Action 2010). Meanwhile, in imitation of military strategy, radio and television journalists were able to embed themselves with Climate Campers. The invitation to participate read as follows:

Print and radio journalists – bring your tents!
This year, print and radio journalists have the option of staying for as long as they choose in order to get a fuller insight into camp life and the many activities. We request that print and radio journalists register upon arrival, and sign up to a short code of conduct. The camp media team will provide a 'buddy' who will provide a point of contact and can also try to facilitate your access to the type of campers or activities you may be hoping to profile. We request that media badges are worn at all times, and that you inform people that you engage with that you are a media professional covering the camp (ibid.).

The Climate Camp received some media coverage as a result of its efforts to embed journalists with activists. One example was a news item run on the BBC London evening news that told the story of Climate Camper Elly Robson, a twenty-year-old, middle-class university student who passed up a holiday with her parents in Thailand to attend Climate Camp; the narrative largely focused on the 'secrecy' of activists and the policing of the camp. However, despite the further increase in media access, 'off-limit' areas at the Climate Camp remained. These off-limit areas were made explicit to journalists in the advance media briefing:

> Certain neighbourhoods and work spaces may decide to 'opt out' of the media access policy, and no journalists of any kind should go to these spaces in any kind of capacity. This is not because these areas have 'anything to hide' but because the camp process respects the right of those neighbourhoods and working groups who don't feel comfortable engaging with the media. Our ability to provide wider access to the camp depends on us being able to respect the decision of these groups to opt out like this. Journalists will be informed by the media team on arrival which neighbourhoods and spaces have opted out. The neighbourhoods that opt out may change during the week (ibid.).

The justification for the 'no-go' area again captures a tension common in many protest camps between the camps as sites of media interest and as places of activist living. The compromise that allowed media to tour the camp was a strategy of dual adaptation – adapting to conflicting activist demands and to the needs of media. Yet it was also a strategy of 'abstention' (Rucht 2004), as some neighbourhoods explicitly avoided media interaction. In fact, much like HoriZone before it, the camp did have critics who retrospectively labelled the 'open hour' policy as 'kowtowing to mainstream media' (a g.r.o.a.t 2010: 14). Such critiques were extended to the camp's media strategy more generally; the charge was that it was run by reformists, not radicals, and therefore represented only a middle-class perspective, ultimately framing the camp as being more liberal than some would wish (ibid.: 13).

This perspective, of course, is just one way of viewing the camp's media policy. Those on the camp's media team, on the other hand, did not see themselves as bending or 'kowtowing' to the media. Instead, many believed that something should be done to try to influence the camp's image in the media, since the presence of mainstream media at the camp was inevitable (Lewis 2009). The tension and difference in campers' perspectives on media interaction was often bound up in broader ideological views of the media, and such debates are what ultimately shape the media access and strategies of the camp.

In considering discussions about mainstream journalists being able to access Climate Camp, it is worth briefly highlighting a more fundamental debate between journalists and activists over what constitutes a 'public' space. Both HoriZone and Climate Camp positioned themselves as 'public spaces': areas that members of the public were openly encouraged to attend and explore. However, journalists, with the exception of a time-restricted window, were excluded from this activist reading of 'public space'. Here, then, the camps are implementing an exclusionary reading of 'public' that restricts journalists' access. Put differently, the protest camp is a 'media-free' public space. While this move certainly militates against a traditional understanding of 'public', it can be understood by unpacking the media dynamics of a protest camp.

The media policy at Climate Camp was part of an intentional strategy to create and sustain a boundary between 'activist space' and 'media space'. This move may be seen as a defensive one, protecting the backstage of the camp from adversarial, intrusive and sensational media coverage. Yet, equally, such a policy works against the premise of using the protest camp as a place to 'show' alternative living, as a media space. Of course, Climate Camp was not the only protest camp to ban media access. In 2005, HoriZone implemented a policy banning journalists from entering the camp. While this did not stop undercover journalists from sneaking in, it meant that overt journalists – those carrying television equipment or expensive cameras, and often wearing press passes – were prohibited entry. As a consequence, the camp's fortified and guarded entrance quickly became a media focal point. At HoriZone, as with Climate Camp, crudely constructed barricades, staffed by volunteer campers acting as de facto security, policed and enforced the activist/media divide.

Greenham's women-only mandate Another strategy that protest camps can adopt is a mandate that specifies the journalists or publications with which protesters will interact. One strategy used by activists at Greenham Common was the implementation of a 'women-only' media mandate whereby the women of Greenham would interact only with female journalists (Feigenbaum 2008). This policy was intended to confront the sexist treatment and misogynist representations of Greenham women in the media.

When the women-only mandate was in effect, reporters and crew members had to be women in order to gain access to the protest campers. In a report on the first December mass action, 'Embrace the Base', Alma reported in the internationalist feminist newspaper *Outwrite*:

> A row [took] place when the women at the main gate refused to talk to the smartly dressed creeps who did not hesitate to put women down: 'shut up you stupid woman – if we had not given you such publicity (when?) you would not have had ... this turn out' (piss off you silly git) ... the women did not shut up and continued shouting for women reporters (not many around). When women photographers turned up at the gate, the women were pleased to oblige (Alma 1983).

Just as the insistence on women-only spaces at the protest camp encouraged women to develop technical skills and work collaboratively with each other, implementing this policy had many of the same effects for television crews. As women were significantly underrepresented in these fields, the policy both called attention to women's exclusion and provided opportunities for the few women performing these technical jobs.

However, women-only mandates and investing trust in women journalists were not always successful strategies. The assumption that women journalists' loyalties would rest with Greenham women rather than with the institutions they worked for was at times misguided. The British tabloid press would often exploit Greenham women's commitment to working with other women by sending in undercover reporters or soliciting women to go to Greenham to produce 'insider stories'. In November 1983, a 'Sun Special Inside Report' appeared on Greenham Common, lambasting Greenham women's separatist politics and sexual expression. With a headline in capital letters, 'I MEET THE GREENHAM MANHATERS', the *Sun* special contained a large-font pull-quote reading: 'Four in every five are lesbians – all are united in their hatred of men' (Ritchie 1983).

The homophobia of some women journalists, as well as that of the media institutions in which they operated, also prevented them from forging alliances with Greenham women. On some occasions, the disloyalty of women journalists to Greenham women cost protesters their jobs and family support as these exposé-style reports named women as lesbians and drug-takers (Roseneil 2000: 290). At the same time, producers and editors intentionally employed women to create intragender divisions that delegitimised the Greenham Common protests. The disappointment some campers felt following the publication of journalists' exposés illustrates women's more general anxiety around the relationship between gender and (feminist) politics. Many women at Greenham discovered first-hand that 'sisterhood' did not organically emerge from women's gender identity – a reality that the Women's Liberation movement at the time was confronting more broadly.

Media tents as spaces for media management The media tent has also been a feature of many protest camps. As media and media strategies have evolved, and depending on the social or political context of the protest camp itself, the location and composition of the tent and its contents have varied. In the case of some camps, distinct tents have been erected for both mainstream and alternative media. We will touch upon the alternative components shortly, but first we examine the media tent from the HoriZone protest camp.

At HoriZone, the CSC, working within Dissent!, established a 'media gazebo' to serve as a base to co-ordinate their media efforts (Gipfelsoli 2005). The media gazebo was a small, white marquee with a couple of small chairs and a dining-sized table with a constantly refreshed selection of newspapers – mostly tabloids – covering the G8 protest activities. Outside the gazebo was a hand-painted sign that read: 'Journalists report here.' Located 15 yards from HoriZone's gated entrance, the media gazebo was a satellite space, intentionally distanced and differentiated from the protest camp itself. The media tent's purpose was twofold. First, it provided a base – a tactic in and of itself – from which the CSC could employ its repertoire of media practices. Briefly, this included fielding interview requests by journalists, sourcing activist interviewees, giving media interviews, and distributing press releases and a 'media contact list', which supplied a select list of 'good' journalists with privileged information and access to activists (for more information, see CounterSpin Collective 2005; McCurdy 2009; 2010; 2012).

2.2 A media tent is part of many protest camps

Second, the gazebo was used as an outpost to try to control the news media – a vantage point from which journalists could be tracked on a two-way radio system and approached before nearing the entrance gate in order to maintain the boundary between front stage and backstage, between media space and activist space. The gazebo acted as a 'honey trap', a site to attract journalists in an effort to contain and control news. The gazebo, staffed with volunteers willing to engage with the media, deflected journalists from the camp's entrance, which helped enforce site boundaries.

In both instances, the position of the gazebo and the role of the CSC outriders were about control: trying to control, in a defensive manner, the mainstream media. These practices also sought to maintain the division between front stage and backstage, between media space (outside the camp) and activist space (inside the camp), by acting as symbolic security guards trying to prevent journalists from sneaking into HoriZone, though not always successfully.

Challenges to adaptation strategies As noted before, protest camps are often themselves forms of direct action and, as such, they need to take and sustain immediate action. This can involve an ongoing blockade, securing barricades and police defence. A challenge posed by media interest in the camp is that the campsite is transformed into a media stage or a set for media production. Accompanying this metamorphosis are the expectations of journalists who, often with a sense of professional entitlement, demand camp access. However, the glare of the media in such circumstances has the potential to flatten camp politics, often sensationalising violence while marginalising the camp's objectives, as discussed in the previous chapter. Under the intense scrutiny of mainstream media, the camp risks becoming a performance in its totality. As a result, campers who do not want to be recorded planning or participating in actions, or who just want the privacy to rest, shower and eat without being recorded, cannot escape the media lens or the journalist's pen.

Protest camps therefore face dilemmas in establishing their adaptation strategies. By interacting with reporters and letting journalists behind the scenes view the camp's daily operations, you lose a space to retreat. Yet if you ban mainstream media, you still cannot prevent undercover journalists from sneaking into the camp, and, as the experience of Climate Camp and Greenham suggest, such bans or restrictive mandates may even encourage exposés. Additionally, as the example of Resurrection City shows, if protest campers fail to adapt to the professional time-keeping of media schedules, journalists will grow frustrated and coverage may disappear or become more negative. The decorum of behaviour demanded by journalists can be incredibly irritating for protest campers, as the feeling of being constantly on show can become tiresome or upsetting. But when protesters respond with impatience or with the taunts or disdain that many feel the media 'deserves' – particularly the tabloid press – they potentially face even higher levels of negative coverage. These numerous challenges in adapting to the mainstream media result in protesters – in and outside protest camps – making and creating their own media. In the remainder of this chapter we explore protesters' 'alternatives' strategies to mainstream media and journalism.

Alternatives

Adaptation to mainstream media is only one of the media strategies engaged at protest camps. Protest camps function as ecosystems, allowing alternative, independent media to arise from the space of the encampment. Media produced at protest camps and by protest campers ranges from fliers and banners to newspapers, documentary films, live blogs and streamed video. Protest camps often become experimental spaces, laboratories for media production, as innovation occurs in both the methods for communicating information and the tools used to record and transmit media. In fact, some would argue that alternative, radical or social movement media are far more important than adaptations to mainstream media (Atton 2003; Downing et al. 2001; Langlois and Dubois 2005; Downing 2010).

Much has been written about alternative media and the role it plays in relation to social movements. In particular, attention has been paid to the rise of Indymedia, an international network of independent media centres that facilitated the digital publication of text, images, audio and video. Born out of the 1999 protests against the World Trade Organization (WTO) in Seattle, Washington, Indymedia centres were a common feature at global justice movement mobilisations (Frenzel et al. 2011; Atton 2003; Downing 2002; 2003a; 2003b; Downing et al. 2001; Wolfson forthcoming). Indymedia was driven by an ethos that empowered activists not just to watch media but to 'be the media' and represented a significant stage in the evolution of social movement media production and distribution, although radical media certainly existed before Indymedia. Today, with the spread of social media, the idea of 'Indymedia' is more powerful than ever, while the organisation has lost much of its role in activism. Existing scholarship on activist media tends to focus, understandably, on information and communications technology (ICT) without necessarily taking into account how physical environments, weather, shelter and the availability of electricity affect media strategies.

The embedded nature of media-making at the site of a protest camp means that reporters and documenters cannot be passive observers (Ostertag 2006: 3). Some protest campers, already working as freelance journalists and photographers, cover stories of the protest camp for one or more existing media outlets. Often, these journalists are already involved in the social movement or have close ties to others taking part in the camp. In addition, there are always a number of what Ostertag terms 'accidental journalists' – people who do not necessarily have any formal training or institutional support who come to a camp to take on the task of documenting protest activities (ibid.: 10). The broad range of participant–observers covering events at protest camps

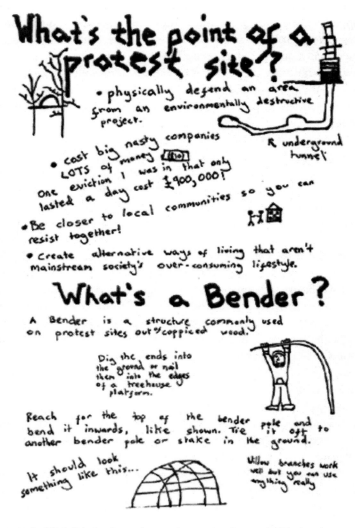

What's the point of a protest site?

- physically defend an area from an environmentally destructive project.

R underground tunnel

- cost big nasty companies LOTS of money. One eviction I was in that only lasted a day cost £900,000!

- Be closer to local communities so you can resist together!

- Create alternative ways of living that aren't mainstream society's over-consuming lifestyle.

What's a Bender?

A Bender is a structure commonly used on protest sites out of coppiced wood.

Dig the ends into the ground or nail them into the edges of a treehouse platform.

Reach for the top of the bender pole and bend it inwards, like shown. Tie it off to another bender pole or stake in the ground.

It should look something like this...

Willow branches work well but you can use anything really.

2.3 Mainshill Solidarity Camp zine teaches readers how to build a bender

leads to exchanges across diverse activist communities and social networks. Many participants who are active at any given camp will have also participated in various political groups. Some belong to a specific political party, unions, communist and socialist groups, various international solidarity groups, or anti-fascist and feminist groups.

When these people converge to create a camp-specific publication or run a camp-based media centre, they are often working from these previous political experiences and modes of organising. Consequently, connections and conflicts, as well as new strategies and tactics, frequently come into play during the building and running of protest camp media and communication infrastructures (Feigenbaum 2008).

Protest camp media practices are part of broader historical trajectories of social movement media-making. Looking across time reveals how communication tactics and techniques arise out of the nexus of available resources, emergent technologies and existing activist media strategies. A great deal of research over the past decade has explored the changes new media technologies have had on activist cultures (de Jong et al. 2005; van de Donk et al. 2004). In recent years, digital technologies have become increasingly used as activist tools, while handheld digital recorders, cameras and now smart phones are used both by grassroots media journalists and for protesters' personal documentation. These digital documentary practices have developed from earlier (and often much heavier) forms of mobile recording devices. The advent of the VCR and videocassette allowed images of protest camps to travel faster and farther, marking an increase in the visual documentation of police brutality and in the transnational circulation of footage of small-scale direct actions. The CD saw an increase in collections of clips and short documentaries of actions and made the distribution of video documentaries cheaper and more mobile. Today, YouTube and similar video-hosting platforms serve as sites for activist knowledge exchange and archiving. As many older recordings of protest camps and their actions become archived on these sites, mediated knowledge exchange has taken on an increasingly 'rhizomatic' quality, with inspiration and imaginative ideas coming from different time periods and locations, although this can also create problems as events and actions become de-contextualised (Cowan unpublished).

Phones are also a frequently employed technology for communication at protest camps. They allow protesters to alert each other to their location, police presence, arrests, surveillance and other obstacles. Phone trees evolved into 'ticker tape' SMS updates on mobile phones in the early 2000s, and platforms such as Twitter are now used to keep people informed about various events and actions as they unfold at and around the protest camp. In this section we look at particular forms of alternative media and communications arising from and used at protest camps, drawing attention to how available resources and technological developments shape the alternative media strategies of camps over time. Whether videos, newsletters, postcards, internet memes or songbooks, social movement media both create movement cultures at the time of their production and carry movement ideas and infrastructures into the future. A story told orally, a manifesto, a recorded interview, a picture of a mass demonstration – they can all circulate across time and space. And through this circulation, ideas and artefacts are transformed and incorporated as different people encounter and interpret these cultural texts in different ways (Feigenbaum 2013).

Print-based media

Radical printing has always been a mainstay of activism as it allows activists to express themselves and offer perspectives that challenge mainstream discourse. They can also provide avenues and outlets for communities to share information and construct common, collective identities. When Resurrection City was formed, there was an existing newspaper called *Soul Force*. Founded in February 1968, it was the official paper of the SCLC, the primary organisation behind the City. However, while the SCLC published and distributed a few issues during the Washington, DC protest camp, each with a run of 100,000 copies, it was not a paper for and by the residents of Resurrection City (Offenburger 1968: 20). Among the organisers, there was a desire to fill this void and so *True Unity News* was created as the protest camp's newspaper, although its founding took some time: it did not start until June 1968, about three weeks after the protest camp had been established.

While the SCLC helped produce the newspaper and printed it at the off-site Resurrection City press office, it was largely run by and featured content from the camp's inhabitants. The newspaper highlighted camp events and featured news reports, letters to the editor and the experiences of camp participants, as well as their poetry and art (Wright 2008: 451; Mantler 2010: 46). As Tom Offenburger, press relations co-ordinator for Resurrection City, described it: 'It was a grass-roots kind of thing for the people of Resurrection City.' This vision was also captured in the newspaper's objective, which was to 'write what has to be said to help advance the goals of the

TRUE UNITY NEWS

OF RESURRECTION CITY

Who Runs The Unity News

ᴸrvine Akbar

Eric Kindberg

PURPOSE

CULTURAL PRIDE--LAND--SELF DETERMINATION

SELF HELP AND ECONOMIC CONTROL

To Accomplish the Goals:

"No matter what religion or philosophy you may have,
let's unite."   --Akbar

News of what goes on in the city

1. local news

2. international news

NEWS MEETING

SATURDAY 4:00 P.M.

RESURRECTION CITY

CITY HALL

2.4 *True Unity News* was published in the Resurrection City camp

people; Self Help – Economic Control – Cultural Pride – Land – Self Determination' (as cited in Wright 2008: 451).

Given the limited technological resources at protest camps, the easiest media form to put together before laptop computers, internet connections and social media was the handwritten newsletter, which could easily be reproduced outside the camp. At Greenham Common, newsletter materials were created and collected mainly at the camp. Sometimes a support group would be responsible for producing multiple copies; at other times a woman with a car would go into Newbury to make a set of photocopies. On a few occasions, particularly for larger events in the earlier years of the camp, the Campaign for Nuclear Disarmament would take responsibility for producing materials. A limited number of copies, ranging from a few hundred to a few thousand, would be produced and then sent back to the camp and distributed to campers, support networks and those on any Greenham mailing lists that were available at the time (Feigenbaum 2013).

Individuals and groups receiving materials would sometimes be asked to make additional copies for further circulation. Larger publications, such as the February 1983 newsletter covering the time from November 1982 to mid-February 1983, were also sold in independent bookshops and women's centres for a price of around 30 to 50 pence. The undated broadsheet *Greenham Women's Peace Camp Newsletter*, which came out in about October 1983, is marked with 'Donations appreciated' on its leader. Unlike the sleeker activist newspapers we see today, at Greenham there was very little consistency in format or layout; very few of the Greenham newsletters used standard layout techniques, nor were they produced on set dates. In the early period of the camp's life (1981–83), newsletters were far less frequent and 'news' could cover a span of several months. For instance, on one occasion in 1984, campers published both 'June News' and 'More June News', while in 1985 they published 'August and Most of September News'. This illustrates the unique sense of time protest camps develop, which is often out of synch with the mainstream world of work, demands and deadlines (Griffiths 2004) and is an aspect of camp life that can cause frustrations for both journalists and participants. Camper Liz Galst recalled the newsletters' production process: 'One of us would go, "Oh yeah, it's time to do the newsletter."' They

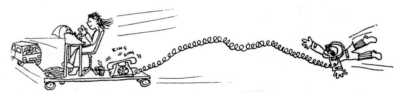

2.5 Greenham Common's communication infrastructures included on-site media-making and off-site offices

would then walk around the base, gathering bits of writing or drawing women had done, as well as news and updates from each gate (Galst in Feigenbaum 2008).

These newsletters allowed movement participants to explore and experiment with political ideas. They gave women a venue to share poetry, writing, journal entries, sketches, political comics and other artwork. As such, they encouraged forms of expression often absent from both mainstream and pre-existing social movement publications. While the newsletters were not read or contributed to by all the women, they often offered a sort of crystallisation point where the major issues and conflicts of the time were addressed from a diversity of viewpoints. In this way, protest camp newsletters are well suited to capture the 'everydayness', spontaneity and fluidity of life at the camp (Feigenbaum 2013). Thus, as unique historical records, these kinds of protest camp artefacts provide an insight into the intricacies and ideas that accompany transformation and changes both within an encampment's politics and in social movements of the time more generally. Such intimate, detailed accounts are often absent from both movement commentary and dominant historical archives (Feigenbaum 2010).

Thirty years later in the Occupy movement, we saw the tradition of protest camp newspapers carried forward. This strategy seemed surprising to some, as rises in digital production have made print often seem too expensive and time-consuming to produce. *New York Times* journalist David Carr reflected on *The Occupied Wall Street Journal*, which emerged from some participants of the Occupy Wall Street encampment:

> Forgive an old newspaper hack a moment of sentimentality, but it is somehow reassuring that a newspaper still has traction in an environment preoccupied by social media. It makes sense when you think about it: newspapers convey a sense of place, of actually being there, that digital media can't. When is the last time somebody handed you a Web site? (Carr 2011).

Here, Carr drew attention to how the spatiality and temporality of the encampment shaped the forms of media that the activists at Occupy Wall Street engaged and created.

The newspaper eventually evolved beyond the physical encampment and became a movement publication that was very much in the same spirit of the *True Unity News*. *The Occupied Wall Street Journal* also

2.6 The debut issue of *The Occupied Wall Street Journal*, October 2011

published the thoughts of campers, although the content leaned more towards the polished and emboldening prose of public intellectuals such as Chris Hedges and Naomi Klein. A special issue curated by Occuprint was dedicated to the art of the Occupy movement. Additional camp newspapers were also created, such as *The Occupied Chicago Times* and *The Occupied London Times*. While activist in content, the titles of all these newspapers sought to actively subvert or 'culture jam' the names and brands of mainstream media. In many ways, the publication of the newspapers at the Occupy camps was a form of protest action in and of itself, and a challenge to the ability of massive news corporations to construct and represent reality. Therefore, the 'Occupied' versions of these newspapers did not merely inform activists but directly challenged the representational hegemony of mainstream news organisations. The Occupy newspapers also echoed the publication ethos of the colourfully designed *Madrid15M* from Spain, which had been shaped by the years of social movement media that had come before it: 'We believe the same way you need to reclaim public space to meet and come together as human beings, taking the squares, rebelling and creating, you should take the press' (http://madrid15m.org).

Activist video at the protest camp In addition to often having rich print cultures, protest camps' media ecosystems frequently involve activist video-making. The documentary film *Carry Greenham Home* was probably the first full-length documentary of a protest camp as a site of ongoing protest and daily living or re-creation. Beginning in December 1982, two young film students, Amanda Richardson and Beeban Kidron, went to the camp as part of a filmmaking assignment for their university course. Beeban recalled that at their first filming session, during the December 1982 'Embrace the Base' demonstration, they were surrounded by all-male crews. The police were letting the male crews through the police lines, but not them. As they squeezed past to get footage, women protesters cheered and they 'were accepted as part of the protests' (City Limits 1984). Drawn into the energy and passion of the protest, Beeban says that at one point she was crying behind the lens, while Amanda was holding up the boom and singing. As the women continued to return to the camp for more footage, Beeban reflected that 'the film became part of the politics' at Greenham. Rather than becoming accidental journalists (Ostertag 2006), Beeban and Amanda became, in a sense, accidental protesters. At times, Beeban and Amanda would pretend to be filming so 'the police didn't get so heavy'. Beeban referred to a particular moment in the film where a woman is singing 'Which Side Are You On?' to some police officers, commenting: 'There's no way the camera wasn't behind that dance, that questioning of the police. We were the witness.'

Amanda and Beeban did not make the footage into a film until the summer of 1983, when the Greenham peace camp was being vilified in the press. Beeban said: 'Then it seemed necessary.' Once it was available on videocassette, *Carry Greenham Home* circulated both nationally and internationally. Greenham support groups in cities across the United Kingdom would play the video in meeting halls, church basements and school classrooms, often with a Greenham protester or two on hand for discussion. As video-recording became an everyday technology in the UK, available either on loan or in people's homes and workplaces, duplication was relatively cheap and easy. At the same time, a documentary protest video was still a fairly new phenomenon and a novel way to spread the word. Even a few years previously, the cost of production and duplication would have been far greater. This meant that the video could travel around quickly and harness people's new-found excitement with home movie technologies.

Of course, these technological aspects are not the only reason why the film was such an accomplishment for the filmmakers and the Greenham network. A passionate review of *Carry Greenham Home* in *Outwrite* newspaper outlined the reasons for the film's celebration and success as a resource for mobilisation:

> The fundamental difference between this film and anything produced on Greenham before … is that it is made by Greenham Women … The outcome of this is the most true to life representation of the Peace Camp that you are ever likely to see. Those who have been there will remember the atmosphere and relive the feelings that the film evokes, particularly the joy and strength of women participating together.

This 'real-life' effect is the result of the diverse actions and interactions the film documents. Beeban and Amanda's film captures both the spectacular actions and mundane moments of Greenham's activist life. *Carry Greenham Home* shows images of the 30,000 woman-strong 'Embrace the Base' mass demonstration and blockade; images of women dancing on the missile silos; views of the Rainbow Dragon Festival, where women sewed together a four-and-a-half-mile-long dragon tail and weaved in and out of the base with it; the Teddy Bears' Picnic, where women dressed in teddy bear and Easter bunny costumes to break into the base and have a picnic there; and the bike lock action in which women locked shut the main gate to the base using the strongest bike locks available. In this scene we see soldiers produce larger and larger bolt cutters in an attempt to break the locks, until they accidentally knock down the gate (with the locks still intact) using five-foot bolt cutters that required a number of men to operate them. The film also includes glimpses of tense conversations and spontaneous small pleasures of life at the camp, from breakfast on a cold winter morning, to singing by the roadside, to fighting over funds at a money meeting.

In an article on the film, the reviewer, Carol, points out that 'not all the emotions evoked are pleasant'. Shots of evictions and the rough policing of blockades capture fearful and violent moments of protest. Carol suggests that this gives the film depth, showing the camp 'warts and all' rather than offering a simple message. Often, documentary video of protests focuses solely on moments of intense action, confrontation with authorities, property destruction and instances of collective joy. While these kinds of images certainly contain and evoke strong emotions, they remain detached from the day-to-day context of organising, eating and protesting. The Greenham documentary intersperses images of these different occasions, thereby creating a sense not only that viewers could 'carry home' the sentiments of the Greenham protest but also that they could make Greenham home (albeit a temporary one for most people).

While Greenham marks one of the first widespread uses of video-cassettes in the spread of protest camp documentaries, the film *People's Guelaguetza: Oaxacan People Take to the Streets*, which documented the uprisings in Oaxaca in 2006, captures how the use of DVDs made activist footage more accessible. Describing the role that DVDs played in the local media environment of Oaxaca, Altha Cravey writes:

> [T]ourists and other shoppers passed over clothing vendors in favour of a ten peso ($1) DVD that was selling faster than the famed Oaxacan rugs and pottery. Crowds gathered to watch the DVD's violent moving images wherever vendors were selling it (Cravey 2010: 11).

Footage for these films was taken by protesters with mobile phone video cameras and uploaded and edited quickly for turnover as DVDs. According to Cravey, one of the film's producers, the documentary 'aired in classrooms, film festivals, scholarly meetings, and public libraries' (ibid.: 12). Named after a large-scale festival reclaimed by Oaxacans during their occupation of the city centre, *People's Guelaguetza* features a wide range of movement participants. It engaged 'simple oral communication strategies', including interviews and poetry readings, to share 'local stories with international audiences' (ibid.: 11). The film countered mainstream media reports that did not cover the state-sponsored violence of the police against the Oaxacan people by presenting these violent images alongside people's hopes and aspirations (ibid.: 11).

This activist documentary filmmaker's reflection demonstrates the ways in which emergent digital technologies (beyond social media) created new developments in social movement media and communication strategies. These strategies combine 'old' (oral storytelling) and 'new' (uploaded mobile phone video footage) media elements. Playing documentary footage DVDs on public television screens in high-traffic areas of the city centre in Oaxaca prompted those who passed by to stop and witness acts of violence outside the mainstream media frame. As many police attacks took place in the middle of the night, these violent scenes were left off the media stage. DVDs and outdoor television sets made the repression of the police and government visible.

Desert.Indymedia and the vulnerability of reporting Since the arrival of the internet and the increase in mobile media, protest camp eco-systems have grown to include digital stations for media-making. In fact, protest camps are fertile ground for nurturing media strategies and innovations that allow the rapid diffusion and circulation of information into and out of the camp. At many protest camps since the WTO in Seattle, Indymedia tents have offered spaces for people to upload and file text, photographs and video. Laptop computers and generator-powered or solar-powered internet access enabled these autonomous media stations to be set up within the encampment. At their best, these Indymedia stations created space for participatory news publishing and skill-sharing. People could communicate the day's events straight on to the internet, offering a diversity of perspectives and outlooks. In the period before social media platforms became more widely available (although not as widely available as the mainstream's 'Twitter revolutions' would have us imagine), Indymedia tents were particularly valuable.

One particularly interesting example of Indymedia could be found at the 2002 NoBorders camp in Woomera. The existing terrain of the Woomera encampment meant that Indymedia participants had to innovate infrastructures and practices for reporting from a desert. The hot, dry weather and lack of existing infrastructure led to the site being hosted from a hotel room using a local internet service provider (Pickerill 2003). In addition to the demanding environment of the encampment, the emotional intensity of participating in actions with migrants imprisoned in an isolated detention centre raised questions about how to communicate 'news' from within the vulnerable and violent contact zones of protest. John, from 3CR Community Radio, interviewed Desert.Indymedia reporter Alex soon after the fence action at Woomera (see Chapter 3). Their exchange begins:

JOHN (3CR): Now, there's been conflicting stories in the media with regard to what has happened out at Woomera. Maybe you'd like to tell us first what exactly occurred yesterday and last night.

ALEX: Sure. Firstly, I'd just like to say that I'm extremely tired. I haven't slept much over the last few days and am pretty emotional as well. If I do have to take some time or break down, deal with me, okay?

JOHN (3CR): Not a worry.

In an exchange that one is unlikely to find (not edited out) in mainstream media coverage, Alex begins the report by familiarising the interviewer and listeners with the emotional intensity of the situation and with her bodily well-being. This invocation of mindfulness in a media report is of note here because, rather than 'biasing' the report by masking her feelings, Alex uses this articulation of her affective state in order to be able to give testimony clearly and factually. After describing the events, she explicitly draws attention to the journalistic ethics of the situation:

JOHN (3CR): A lot of the mainstream media, *The Age* and *The Australian* included, have actually reported that there's still about five people, I think, that are 'at large', shall we say …

ALEX: Well, as I said before, I don't really want to speculate in the interests of safety. I mean, for a lot of people who are involved in Indymedia we had a really intense situation where we had incredible possibilities for stories last night. We had access to amazing interviews, footage, stories, but it was a situation of: is it worth doing media about this if it is going to compromise the chances of these people to a genuine possibility of … freedom? So I suppose, I haven't heard that … but I'm elated to hear that there seems to be five people still unaccounted for. I don't think I'd like to speculate on that any further at this time.

Drawing attention to Indymedia's position within a wider ecosystem of social movement media and communication, Alex ends by asking listeners to extend the media chain, contacting media outlets, NGOs and Amnesty International, in an echo of the Greenham ethos to 'carry protest home'.

Occupy media tent, Zuccotti Park With the evolution of social media, the ecosystem in which protest campers produce and share information from the site of the camp has changed rapidly. As evidenced by the recent Occupy movement, protest camps can function as media hubs, combining 'old' media approach of print production with video-making and a range of social media practices including the use of Facebook, Twitter and livestream. But along with these advancements in what technologies can do come the practicalities of how to keep all of this media running. In a similar fashion to the Indymedia tents of the early 2000s, since the rise of smart phones and social media, camp media centres have had to figure out how to have constant electricity and mobile, sufficiently fast internet connections to keep pace with the speed of digital news cycles.

Moreover, as protest camps are outdoors and subject to the elements, either technology must be adaptable or the practices need to adapt to the technology. In Alaska, at Occupy Anchorage, for example, at times the weather was too cold to use computers, getting down to −23 degrees Celsius, which meant that the livestreaming had to be stopped. The campers adapted to the elements by bringing in propane heaters to keep the computer at a comfortable temperature. Camping outdoors, there is, of course, rain and water, which never mix well with electronics. To protect the New York City media tent from the elements, a system was developed whereby, if it looked like rain, media team members would line commercial-sized skips with tarpaulins. They would then begin by switching off equipment such as computers, wrapping them like presents in tarpaulin and donated rain ponchos, and placing them carefully in the skip. Next, non-vital equipment would be turned off, given the same treatment and placed in the skip, which functioned as a safe container. The use of the appropriated skip was an innovation; before this, equipment had been wrapped in spare rain ponchos and placed on a table – itself covered with a tarpaulin – creating 'mounds' of technology.

The aim of the Occupy media tent at Occupy Wall Street was to provide an outlet for camp-produced media, ranging from photography to livestreamed content. The Occupy media tent was initially demarcated by a very large umbrella fixed in a bucket of sand, but it also attempted to make use of the cement tables in Zuccotti Park, incorporating these into its existing infrastructure. Reminiscent of the early Australian Tent Embassy's beach umbrella, at Occupy Wall Street this architectural solution was a response to the structural limitation of 'no freestanding objects' imposed on the encampment. The police turned off electricity at the park, and so, as the media tent needed power, protesters brought in a petrol generator. Occupiers would take taxis to petrol stations, fill jerrycans with petrol and taxi back. The petrol would be transported manually from the taxi back to the park using a trolley, the fuel canisters draped with a cloth in order to smuggle them in.

Crowdsourcing dissent: Tahrir Square media tent Included among the myriad decentralised resources in Tahrir Square was a media tent run by a collective of between 10 and 15 experienced and technologically savvy political and human rights activists. These media activists, the majority of whom were long-standing friends, established the tent at the onset of the 25 January occupation of Tahrir Square. Recognising the prevalence of digital devices capable of taking pictures and recording video in the square, they sought to provide a physical hub to manually crowdsource digital material (images and video) from Tahrir Square itself. In doing so, activists wanted to offer evidence to national and international audiences that countered government narratives downplaying the extent of the protests. They also saw this as a means of providing evidence of the Egyptian government's lethal and excessive use of force against protesters (interview with Ramy Raoof, 12 September 2012).

According to Ramy Raoof, a key member of the media tent collective and prominent human rights and ICT activist, equipment for the media tent was collected by pooling the personal resources of team members. They brought together an assortment of technologies including routers to create computer networks, laptops, external hard drives, USB hubs, memory cards and memory card readers, as well as cables to connect the various devices. Depending on need, data brought to the tent would be transferred in any number of ways, including via secure digital (SD) card readers, USB, infrared, wireless and Bluetooth. Thus, in order to make images taken from Tahrir Square available to a global audience, media activists needed webs of hardware as well as 3G and internet services, which, as we outline below, were not readily available in the square itself.

Of course, all this work at the media tent required electricity, which was obtained by using the electrical wires from street lamps in the square. As mentioned earlier, these were also used as a means of charging mobile phones. 'Stealing' electricity from lamp posts is a common practice, with how-to techniques circulating among squatter and favela communities. This again points to how tactical knowledge

2.7 The Tahrir Square media tent

and skills converge in and around the space of the protest camp as it seeks the resources needed to re-create daily life and ongoing protest. In addition to drawing electricity from street lamps, some individuals would take batteries or mobile phones with them away from the square and bring them back fully charged. This is similar to the use of office photocopiers or printing services; charging phones away from the site highlights the importance of auxiliary and support spaces that go beyond the 'boundaries' of the camp.

The Tahrir media tent was run in a decentralised fashion. A paper sign was hung on the tent and read, translated from the Arabic, 'Point to gather pictures and videos' (Raoof 2011). Members in the collective asked those in Tahrir Square to give them any pictures or video of the events taking place in the square. Data gathered at the media tent would then be transferred to an external hard drive. As internet access in the square was restricted, and entirely cut off for a period, media team members would regularly take external drives away from Tahrir Square to an off-site location with internet access, often at six-hour intervals (interview with Ramy Raoof, 12 September 2012). Data was then uploaded to the internet using free image-hosting platforms such as Flickr. All digital content uploaded by the team was shared under a creative commons licence that allowed anyone, including mainstream media, to use the content freely as long as appropriate attributions were made. The use of a creative commons licence by the media team was a deliberate strategy to ensure the maximum use and visibility of the material they had gathered.

Although the media tent was a hub for collecting and sharing crowdsourced content, it also ended up fielding requests from news media organisations during the January–February occupation. Often Raoof and other collective members were contacted for details of what was happening in the square. Given that many of the media team volunteers were trained human rights researchers, they applied and adapted their skills to gather, vet and report information for enquiring mainstream journalists, such as the number of deaths and the number and type of injuries.

In terms of journalists accessing the protest camp of Tahrir Square, security was incredibly tight and the Egyptian government was keen to prevent images from the protest camp getting out. Consequently, it was not uncommon for the police and army to try to seize memory cards or force individuals to delete content from their devices. Forcing activists to delete content is a common police tactic used at many protests and protest camps. At Tahrir, activists and journalists alike had to adapt their media practices in and around the square to protect their data. For example, journalists and some protest campers would carry around multiple memory cards for their phones, often hiding cards of value and passing dummy or blank cards to the authorities. To document the protest and the protest camp, many activists also carried around multiple memory cards so that they could continue recording while passing on a memory card to be uploaded off-site.

Given the limited internet access at Tahrir Square, off-site locations played an important auxiliary role, as mentioned above. However, a curfew set by the government and enforced by the army regulated when people could come and go at the protest camp, and thus when they could reach auxiliary sites and services. The Tahrir Square camp could be accessed before curfew – which varied from 3 p.m. to 6 p.m. – but the army running the perimeter would tell activists that they could go into the square but could not come out (interview, 27 July 2012). This meant that many people would stay in the square in the evenings and, when the curfew was lifted, they would go home, upload photographs and video, make phone calls, gather supplies, shower and the like. The imposition of this curfew shaped the media environment of the camp; media activists both adapted to these regulations and re-created an infrastructural network of laptops, memory cards, readers, USB sticks and external hard drives. Powered by re-routed lamp-post electricity and the collective energy of skilled media activists, Tahrir's media tent worked within the confines of limited mobility to create and share stories of what was happening in and around the square.

Livestreaming Occupy While there were a number of activists who offered livestreaming from Tahrir Square, the use of livestreamed video really took off in the Occupy movement. Practices of livestreaming during the occupations of 2011–12 open up a number of questions about the future of social movement journalism. The use of livestream at protest camps is particularly noteworthy as it is a manifestation of the evolution from static Indymedia coverage, with the DIY ethic it offered the protest camps of the global justice movement, into the real-time coverage we saw emerge with Occupy. This evolution was not a spontaneous invention but rather a rolling innovation; many Indymedia reporters were active proponents of livestreamed audio in the early 2000s. As with livestreamed audio, the use of video livestreaming can inspire and connect protest camps, enabling people who cannot attend to witness camps from afar. Like other media technologies, it allows engagement between different camps, extending feelings of solidarity nationally and transnationally (Juris 2012: 267). As images circulate to an increasing extent, we see the widespread use of symbols of transnational solidarity, an advanced visual communication of connection across movements, struggles and nations (Pickerill et al. 2011). A protester from Occupy Anchorage in Alaska described her use of livestreaming as a 'connection to the world', a networked link between camps. The uses of livestreaming in Occupy camps included:

- making call-outs, including requests for donations, and answering questions about what was required by campers;
- providing live coverage of meetings and general assemblies, as well as covering camp actions and evictions;
- offering a 'summary' or end-of-day recap to viewers of the goings-on at the camp;
- documenting and monitoring police actions and transgressions; and
- providing a connection with viewers and other camps and the ability to interact through networked communication.

For the viewers of the Occupy livestream, it provided:

- a real-time opportunity to bear witness, show solidarity and engage with Occupy camps and other camps separated in space;
- first-hand accounts and content to supplement, if not challenge, mainstream narratives; and
- the ability to participate in meetings for those who could not be there; for example, at Occupy Chicago and Occupy Montreal, among others, individuals could watch the livestreaming of general assemblies and have their voices heard by putting their remarks in the livestream chat interface.

When live footage of major events is brought to us via television news, mainstream media reporters have access to helicopters, well-equipped news vans, salaries and often assistants on hand. In contrast, livestream movement journalists can be equipped with as little as a mobile phone strapped to their body, an app such as Bambuser (which was banned in both Bahrain and Egypt), and a 3G connection. Out on the streets, in the midst of protest action, livestreamers are vulnerable to police repression for being at the site of the protest, just like other kinds of movement journalists (and at times mainstream journalists). They can also be specifically targeted as they are often there to record police violence and the abuse of power. Reflecting on his year of livestreaming from Occupy spaces, Michael Pellagatti wrote in *The Huffington Post*:

> This year has not been easy for me. Despite finding a vocation that I am passionate about, and being an active participant in the revolution of journalism, it has come at a cost to my health, as I deal with constant back pain, tendinitis and shoulder pain. Such has also come at a cost in terms of my relationship with my family, who have been burdened with my absence. Livestreaming the news, at this point, is still a revolutionary concept, which is accompanied by the risk of danger. We do not get paid (aside from donations), we do not have benefits, or a pension, or insurance. What we have is a mighty sense of social justice and the desire to keep putting our well-being at risk to deliver the news as it should be ... Close up and in real time!
>
> The future of journalism has arrived, and it can be found in the hand of a livestreamer (Pellagatti 2012).

Pellagatti's article points out the structural and resource constraints in which livestreamers work. In the early days of Occupy New York, livestreaming operated thanks to donations: money was crowd-sourced and used to purchase some equipment, while further equipment was donated. The media group in New York also sent out equipment and related material to other cities, occupations and countries. One of the ways in which donations were sourced was through the use of livestreaming, as appeals were made for money and materials to be sent to a post office box located a block away from the Zuccotti Park protest camp.

In addition to the question of resources, Pellagatti draws attention to two other aspects of protest campers' alternative strategies that we seek to highlight throughout this book. First, the technologies and objects we use do not simply 'empower' us. Just as we shape them to our needs, they can shape us, as we reorient our bodies to their materiality. The back pain, tendinitis and shoulder pain Pellagatti mentions emerged from his use of the technologies of his trade. Filming in an environment filled with the affective intensity of the violent and vulnerable contact zones of protest action took a toll on

Pellagatti's health and well-being (an issue we will discuss further in Chapter 3). Second, Pellagatti's discussion of both his bodily well-being and the health of his relationship with his family illustrates how the issues relating to re-creation extend beyond the camp and into our other home lives. Similarly, it poses questions of participation and care work. Who is able to come to the camp and who stays at home significantly shapes the environment of a movement encampment, as we will discuss further in Chapter 5. Also of note is the fact that, while one of the major motivations for livestreaming from protest camp meetings and actions is to extend the boundaries of participation, the amount of time and availability required to be a livestreamer greatly limits who can take part in this kind of activist media-making.

Conclusion

Protest camps differ across geographical space and time and in the resources they can call on. Some camps are decades and miles apart, yet the strategies they implement for communicating, both with mainstream media and internally, share striking similarities. The reason for these similarities lies in the challenge faced by all protest camps: they have to cater for both the mainstream media and the protest campers themselves, and they need to respond to and proactively deal with their own representation. The challenge, as we have argued, arises because protest camps combine qualities of front stage and backstage; they are protest sites as well as homeplaces. The camp is a place where journalists and photographers can go to get a story, where the architecture and objects of the encampment provide a sensational backdrop that lends itself to a spectacularised media image. But it is also – and simultaneously – a backstage space where political strategies are devised and discussions held, and where conflicts and arguments occur and are resolved. Moreover, the camp itself is a home space. As we argued in the previous chapter, protest campers sometimes render public and visible what is normally confined to the private sphere. In terms of media representation, protesters make what is normally a backstage area into a front stage, but, at the same time, they expect and often demand privacy in a protest camp setting. This is why protest campers from Resurrection City to Occupy have attempted to impose barriers and limits on reporters.

However, this challenge also breeds opportunity and creativity, and protest campers have developed a range of adaptation strategies in their media management to address it. Importantly – as we have shown – adaptation has included the idea that mass media has to adapt to the logic of protest camps; this is what we have described as 'dual adaptation'.

Moreover, protest camps have dynamic media ecologies; activists have innovative media strategies, experiment with new technologies, create independent media, crowdsource data and proactively debate issues of representation and media management. We use the notion of media ecology here in reference to Treré's understanding of 'information ecology', but rather than focusing only on technology and environment, for us the term 'media ecology' points to the spatial and temporal character of a protest camp as a living ecological system. It is from within the entanglements of this ecosystem that protest campers develop a broad range of media strategies and tactics. Here, material resources and conditions, perhaps especially in their limitations, play a central role in shaping innovative activist media and communication strategies. The media strategies of protest camps are moulded by resources and conditions, including the latest technology, as well as the lack of electricity, mobile coverage and shelter from bad weather. Decisions about and implementation of technology are therefore influenced by the elements, objects and terrains that make up the physical site of the encampment, and activist media practices have to adapt accordingly. As we argued earlier, we propose reading the protest camp from this materially dynamic – or ecological – perspective. As protest campers try to navigate and adapt in media ecologies, they are both negotiating and adapting their practices within protest camp infrastructures. Through training and skill-sharing, through discussions about the limits of mainstream media representation, protest campers aim to generate fertile ground for the shaping and development of activist media strategies. In the next chapter we extend the concept of ecology – that is, approaching protest camp action as an ecological system – to a discussion of the way in which protest campers, as well as objects, affect the environments and infrastructures that make up the camp, and shape political action and activism.

3 | PROTEST ACTION INFRASTRUCTURES

At the camp there had been trainings in the 'five-finger tactic' on a regular basis since I had arrived. As the big day of action came closer, I was very keen to take the training myself. We were to attempt to take and block three roads leading to the conference centre of the G8 in the Baltic Sea resort of Heiligendamm, no easy task. When I joined the training session, it went all really quick. Half the group became police, the other half were protesters. 'How do the police control space?' asked the trainer and answered: 'They stand in a row.' But between two policemen there is always space. Then he showed us what he meant. As he approached the fake police line he headed for the space between the two police. The two police moved to stop him, opening large spaces to their respective other side. 'Here,' the trainer said, 'now you have space'; and all the other protesters stormed through.

'Don't look at the police,' he said, 'look at the space between them.'

In the morning of the action day, the opening of the 2007 G8, about 6,000 protesters had gathered in the Reddelich camp. Another 4,000 gathered in Rostock and 2,000 came out of the third encampment during the G8. The choreography of the blockade had been rehearsed, and nearly all of the protesters staying in the camps had been trained. In the camp there had been discussions and parties, sometimes boredom, always food and shelter. But now the time in the camp, the training, discussions, etc., started to make sense. Leaving the camp, I felt like I had joined a massive peaceful peasant army, about to challenge the ruling class. We were all part of colour-coded groups. As we marched off together towards the G8 access roads, we soon met a police blockade. However, rather than running into it, the five fingers stretched and each of the colour-coded teams left the main road in different directions, taking about 1,000 protesters with them each. The police attempted to follow the different groups but whenever there was a new police line, the protesters simply split into the fingers, stretching out and overstretching the police capabilities. In three hours, all 5,000 Reddelich protesters had reached the road and sealed it off. We heard from the Rostock march that they equally, dodging water cannons and truncheons, had managed to outwit the police. Only one road remained open and it took the police thousands of men, eight to ten water cannons and a whole cavalry of helicopters with special police to keep it open. They managed, just about. (Heiligendamm, G8 protest camp, 2007)

Introduction

As we discussed in Chapter 1, the protest camp is a place of and for action in multiple ways. First, protest camps are places of action. Second, protest camps provide spaces that normalise engagement in direct action, and as such become places in which people 'activate' their politics. And third, protest camps are protest actions in and of themselves; sometimes they are a physical and direct intervention at the site of contestation (as with a blockade camp), and often they are a direct, communicative intervention steeped in symbolism, exposing injustice. As described in Chapter 1, on infrastructures and practices, when we speak of protest action infrastructures, we are referring to the spaces and objects that go into planning, preparing and carrying out actions. This can include maps, pamphlets, training workshops, bolt cutters, locks, tools and textiles, as well as 'support' structures and practices such as legal, medical and trauma support. As a community of resistance and a site of ongoing protest action, the protest camp embodies multiple forms of protest action simultaneously.

In this chapter we focus on the development and deployment of tactics that create and are shaped by action infrastructures in protest camps. We begin by reflecting on what makes protest camps unique as sites of ongoing protest action and places where tactics are discussed, developed and deployed. We then highlight the role protest camps and similar kinds of convergence spaces have played as sites of conflict and debate around tactics, and particularly the notion of 'diversity of tactics' as it has emerged and developed in recent years. Offering a brief re-reading of these tactical debates from the perspective of the protest camp, we draw attention to the ways in which protesters reorient their tactics in response to collective reflections and interactions with police. We look at how these reorientations take place in and through the violent and vulnerable contact zones of protest action.

3.1 Protest camping as direct action – No Dash for Gas scale a power station's chimney in 2012

In the second half of the chapter we introduce the idea of a 'protest action ecology' as a move away from the binary oppositions that plague 'diversity of tactics' debates, often reductively framing and limiting reflections on and understandings of protest actions (for example, symbolic/direct, violent/non-violent, soft/hard, pink/black, fluffy/spiky, hippie/punk, liberal/anarchist). Working through a series of examples, we explore how a protest action ecology approach provides room for the complexities of both people and objects, allowing for a more careful consideration of the spaces, objects and feelings that tactics are always entangled in and entanglements of.

At the same time, we use the idea of a protest action ecology to make two main arguments. Firstly, we argue that protest camps are often 'laboratories of insurrectionary imagination', spaces in which experimental, collaborative and richly creative actions are dreamed up and deployed (see the Laboratory of Insurrectionary Imagination at www.labofii.net). From hundreds of women dressed as witches cutting down fences at Greenham Common for a Halloween action to blockades of Clandestine Insurgent Rebel Clowns armed with feather dusters and disruptive humour, protest camps are sites where new tactics are tested and existing ones are adapted and developed. The temporality of a protest camp (some lasting for at least a few days, others for years) and the close proximity in which protesters live and work with each other can provide time and space to expand and explore tactical repertoires (Tarrow 1998), passed on from existing social movements and from previous protest camps' infrastructure and operational designs and practices.

Secondly, infused with art, protest camps often include designated areas for creative productions and performances of music, art and theatre. When creativity is used not only as an escape or accoutrement but as central to strategies of action, colourful and effective forms of resistance take shape. In protest camps, protesters mesh together existing tactics with new ideas and available resources, generating ways of navigating particular security circumstances and police repression. Merrick captured the ways in which protesters, technologies and creative thinking come together in the protest camp in his memoir of the Newbury bypass anti-roads camps: 'With a few simple tools, but imagination, wit, resourcefulness, drive and a little absurdity, we're hindering all these trained people and expensive plans' (Merrick 1996: 39).

Protest camps as places of protest action

As place-based protests that may last for days, months or even years, protest camps are unique in their development and deployment of protest action tactics. While, as we have discussed, protest camps arise out of broader movements and contexts, carrying existing debates with them, there are particular features of the campsite that shape experiences of action. The affective intensity of encampments as ongoing sites of protest action means that protesters not only have increased contact with each other but also must deal with police, the media and state authorities, often on a daily basis. As a result, protest campers frequently live in a state of increased vulnerability, at a site of exceptional state-sanctioned harassment and violence. This violence is, at times, carried out through – and as – a spectacle of state force.

Protesters living in an encampment can face intense covert and overt surveillance as well as harassment. Lines of police often stand guard at camp entry points, with 'reinforcements' in the form of armoured vehicles, attack dogs, tanks and so on, either on site or nearby. Helicopters can patrol day and night, creating 24-hour surveillance zones while disrupting sleep and rest. Stop and searches can occur at any time or in any place. In other cases, police rules about where one can walk, sit, sleep or urinate can change frequently over the course of a day with little or no explanation. In some camps, protesters must also contend with local and sometimes hired vigilantes, in addition to state-sanctioned police violence. This was seen in the highly publicised 'Day of the Camel' in Tahrir Square, when hired thugs wielding swords, sticks and guns rode through on camels and horses in order to run down, hit and shoot protesters. On a smaller scale, such violence was recently seen in the October 2012 arson attacks on the anti-logging Camp Florentine in Tasmania, and, throughout the 1980s, it formed part of daily living at many women's peace camps. More generally, the level of violence at protest camps varies greatly, but similarities can be seen in the ways in which violent contact zones transform or reorient protesters' relationships to their objects and environments, and therefore to their protest tactics.

These multiple forms of violence and surveillance – enacted through bodies and objects – shape the protest camp as a space of vulnerability. The protest camp is, of course, far from being the only space where such levels of violence are part of daily living. Rather, the heightened police presence and risk of violence and harassment that are intensified in the protest camp reflect the daily state-sanctioned conditions of those living in ghettoised enclosures, estates, housing projects, prisons and detention centres, or those working as street workers, domestic servants and others in 'states of exception' (Agamben 1998), and reveal the everyday violence of the state (Feigenbaum 2010). Importantly, it is often at the site of protest – and particularly at public, place-based protests such as the protest camp – that those bodies not generally exposed to police violence or street-based harassment confront it for the first time (Scholl 2012).

The point then is not – or not so much – that protest camps are exceptional because there are heightened levels of violence and vulnerability at them; rather, the question is how tactical decisions, discussions and innovations emerge in and through the protest camp as a vulnerable contact zone. At the protest camp, protesters encounter the violence of the state, as well as its many reproductions found both in vigilante attacks and at times, in campers' interactions with each other. As protesters encounter their own and others' vulnerable bodies in an insecure environment, the contact zone of the protest camp can intensify those violent behaviours (of speech, of taking up space, of sexuality) that are already part of our internalised practices. Re-reading debates about tactics from this ecologically and emotionally attuned vantage point can help us better understand the role of affect and emotion in political decision-making. It can reorient our focus towards tactical innovation and problem-solving, rather than trap us in failure (Ahmed 2004). It can highlight the interdependency of well-being infrastructures and practices that sustain protest action, in and beyond the protest camp.

The question of violence

While debates about tactics go back much further than 1968, for the purposes of this chapter we begin again with Resurrection City. Following the riots that erupted in major cities across the United States, the organisers of Resurrection City felt it was especially important to conduct the campaign as a testament to the efficacy and empowering potential of non-violent civil disobedience. Writing of the association between the Poor People's Campaign (PPC) and recent race riots, in his last major article before his death, Martin Luther King told his readers:

> We believe that if this campaign succeeds, non-violence will again be the dominant instrument for social change – and jobs and income will be placed in the hands of the tormented poor. If it fails,

non-violence will be discredited … the talk of guerrilla warfare is going to become much more real … the urban outbreaks are a 'fire bell in the night' clamorously warning that the seams of our entire social order are weakening under strains of neglect (cited in Fager 1969).

The analysis King offers here positions Resurrection City and the demands of the PPC as a way of addressing problems of racial injustice and economic inequality that had erupted in urban riots. This article came just a month after he deemed riots 'the language of the unheard' in a speech given on 14 March 1968. We find it remarkable that over 40 years later, in 2011, this quote again graced news headlines and spread across social media, this time in reference to Greece and to the August riots that spread across the UK.

King was assassinated before the A-frame tents of Resurrection City were constructed on the Washington Mall. His speech reflected the ambivalence many campers at Resurrection City felt about the possibilities of non-violent civil disobedience in the context of on-going police violence, and the social and economic injustices that seemed without end. The rise of the Black Power movement and its commitment to building and defending community power was on many protesters' minds (ibid.). As Resurrection City's permit reached its expiration and protester numbers dwindled, many of those who remained in the camp felt demoralised. The muddy conditions and incessant police presence had taken their toll, and participants questioned whether or not their tactics could produce change. On the night of the eviction of Resurrection City, police shot tear gas canisters into the encampment over and over again, for an hour. Campers of all ages were, for the most part, asleep in their tents during the attack. Recalling the events of the night, Jill Freedman describes how people were gagging, crying and vomiting. They came together in the centre of the camp, trying to escape the gas:

All at odds-and-ends, pajamas and nightgowns and depressed pleats and blankets and curlers and an old lady who's lost her teeth and towels and handkerchiefs. Coming together, looking around, talking low, waiting for the meeting to begin. The chairs gradually fill, and still people are coming, absorbing all the space within the tent, then spilling out over the sides. Finally a man gets up and speaks of cruelty. The cruelty of sneaking up on people in the middle of the night and gassing them in their beds. Brutalizing, and being brutalized. What being poor in this country is all about ... (Freedman 1970: 126).

Freedman goes on to recount some of the comments made in the meeting, as people tried to reflect on what it would all mean the next day:

'I came on this because the only solution I could see was non-violence through Martin Luther King. But now King is dead, my kids are sick, and I'm getting tired.'

'This ain't my first time and this ain't my last. But Lord, I'm runnin' outa cheeks.'

'Me I'm getting me a gun. Nonviolently.' ('Me too, brother.') ('Amen!')

'What kinda fool talk is that? Is that what Dr King died for?' [...]

'How you gonna protect us when they shoot you down like a dog? Badmouthin' Charlie 'bout your riots and guns. But them bodies is always black.'

'Well, man, when I go, a whole lotta pigs goin' with me. Believe it.'

(Clap, Clap) Ungawa. (Clap-Clap) Black Powa (ibid.: 126).

This conversation captures the intensity of protest camps as sites of state violence, particularly during the spectacular displays of force that go into camp evictions. The intimacy and immediacy of the discussion highlights the particular space–time of the protest camp that brings protesters into close contact with each other (here huddled together in the entertainment tent), as well as with the people, objects and environments of state force (policemen, batons, tear gas, sirens). Protesters together make the link between this act of violence and the general conditions facing the poor, and particularly the black poor in America. This act of linking, amidst a storm of tear gas deep in the night, reorients protesters to the meanings and purposes of non-violence.

Looking at the last 40 years of developments in social movement activism, we can see similar tensions crystallise in the space of other protest encampments. Parallel debates and discussions take place across these convergence spaces produced for and by activists' exchanges.

Tactical turning points and moments of heightened awareness and transformation are commonly fuelled by such intense moments of police violence. When the state not only fails to hear its people's demands but actively represses them, we see bodies and objects reorient towards new tactics.

Such debates over whether to pursue violent or non-violent means of social change have become a central feature of social movements, at least since the time of Resurrection City. After Resurrection City, we find it significant that this debate is so closely linked to the development of protest camps. Protest camps emerged as forms of action, as occupations, in the context of West German anti-nuclear protests. These occupations were pursued as non-violent acts of civil disobedience where protesters gathered en masse for days at a time and put their bodies in the way of construction, blocking and occupying the sites of future power plants. We discuss the role these occupations played in the formation of protest camps' governance in the next chapter, but what is significant here is that the peaceful occupations became such a successful strategy that the police needed to employ violent tactics to prevent them from happening. After highly successful anti-nuclear occupations in Wyhl in 1976, there were protests against a nuclear power plant to be built in Brokdorf near Hamburg in northern Germany. Protesters pursued the same tactics of non-violent civil disobedience, but the occupation was evicted with military-style police strategies on the premise that, as one West German politician put it, 'if Wyhl is repeated this country is no longer governable' (Vollmer 2007: 271). The following months saw a massive escalation of the conflict. Policing and protest tactics intensified to unprecedented levels, often resembling battle scenes. The protesters remained peaceful for most of the time; however, under the sustained onslaught of the paramilitary police force, there was an increasing cohort of protesters ready and willing to fight back.

The Brokdorf escalation stopped after a successful legal challenge that revoked the granted planning application. While the protests calmed down, German politicians attempted to split the anti-nuclear opposition by alleging a difference between 'legitimate protesters' and 'violent lawbreakers'. The split was affirmed by some activists and perhaps helped to prevent another attempt at occupying the site, when a new court ruling allowed the building to continue in 1980. Brokdorf nuclear power plant was built and is still in operation.

In the radicalised part of the movement, there was an increasing resolution to fight police brutality; this led to the development of the Autonomen movement and to the 'black bloc' tactic, which was associated with the group's rise.

Diversity of tactics

Der 'Schwarze Block', the black bloc, travelled from West Germany to the US in the 1990s, mainly as a uniform dress code and a way to march in demonstrations as a block of protesters, essentially mirroring the uniform character of marching police units. The first recorded occurrence of a black bloc in the US was at a Pentagon protest in 1989. The 1991 Gulf War protest march and the 1996 Democratic National Convention both saw black blocs, along with other smaller demonstrations (Van Deusen and Massot 2010). Borrowed tactics of face-covering from the Zapatistas, an inspirational source for many autonomous alter-globalisation protesters, were mixed with German and European practices of self-defence and makeshift body armour. Then, in 1999, protests against the World Trade Organization (WTO) meetings in Seattle brought these tactics to the fore.

Seattle saw the black bloc engaged in corporate property destruction, at times prompting other street protesters to stand between the black bloc and its targets, and even, on occasion, to turn black bloc demonstrators over to the police. This marked a breakdown in communication around tactics and called on movement participants to better account for the different kinds of mobilisation (Hurl 2004). Discussions over what coalitions should be including and condemning featured prominently in meetings, online forums and movement publications following Seattle. During the organising for the Summit of the Americas to be held in Quebec City in 2001, the term 'diversity of tactics' was put forward (quite possibly its first use as an English translation of a discussion in French) to describe a position that embraced multiple kinds of tactics. This allowed for groups and individuals to self-determine what tactics they would engage in, and to agree not to endanger each other or hand each other over to the police.

Following Quebec, the term 'diversity of tactics' and the debate that accompanied it became a salient feature of the alter-globalisation movement, both guiding and characterising many of the counter-summit demonstrations in Prague, Genova, Cancun, Evian, Gleneagles and Heiligendamm, and some NoBorders camps, and carrying over into Climate Camps. Endless debates have occurred, focused mainly on forms of black bloc tactics, their ethics, deployment and utility. In these counter-summits and alter-globalisation protests, and as these tactics spread internationally, they often mixed with other, contextual police defence strategies, forms of creative resistance and traditional left-wing tactics of labour protests.

Most recently, debates around diversity of tactics have been common in the Occupy movement. Like counter-summits and the German anti-nuclear occupations, Occupy served as a 'convergence space' (Routledge 2003), as people from many different experiences and backgrounds came together in parks and squares around the world. In many encampments, early policy-making and discussions of principles at general assemblies (as well as in everyday and working group conversations) were shaped, in part, by protesters with experience of participating in the alter-globalisation movement, familiar with the language of 'diversity of tactics'. In many of these conversations there were also people with different movement experiences who adhered to a stance of principled non-violence; and there were others discussing tactics in these terms for the very first time. These divergences in experiences of, and orientations towards, different tactics at some Occupy camps led to endless debates, and issues related to tactics were often carried over or tabled for later meetings.

After the majority of Occupy encampments had been evicted, the debate about diversity of tactics took centre stage following the publication of a piece by well-respected journalist and social movement participant Chris Hedges. In an article published on 6 February 2012, Hedges declared the black bloc 'The Cancer in Occupy', stating that its tactics were dangerous, led to increased police violence, were antagonistic to the left and played into the hands of the state (Hedges 2012). Hedges was referring mainly to actions of property vandalism and defensive attacks on the police that had taken place as part of wider actions at and around the Occupy encampment in Oakland (whose larger movement strategies included strikes, port blockades and marches). In his piece, Hedges argued: 'The Black Bloc's thought-terminating cliché of "diversity of tactics" in the end opens the way for hundreds or thousands of peaceful marchers to be discredited by a handful of hooligans.'

Within days, Hedges' article was re-posted, blogged, Tweeted and

Facebooked around the internet. Responses and commentaries rolled in, some supporting Hedges' position, others seeking to tease out some of his damning claims. For instance, while Hedges asserted that the black bloc stood in opposition to the Zapatistas, others argued that the Zapatistas have served as an inspiration for many people who join black blocs, particularly with regards to the tactic of 'masking up'. Another widely republished and circulated critique of Hedges' position by activist scholar David Graeber highlighted the danger in calling part of the Occupy movement a 'cancer' as it justified violence against those seen to be taking part in black bloc tactics (ibid.).

What we can see in these discourses around Occupy tactics is a reframing of the tactics debate; instead of being a binary opposition between violence and non-violence, it became what A. K. Thompson (2012) has described as a boxing match line-up of 'nonviolence vs. diversity of tactics'.[1] This elision between 'violence' and 'diversity of tactics' equates 'diversity of tactics' with 'supporting violence', rehashing the logic used to demonise autonome tactics in early 1980s Germany. In an account that feels eerily current, Geronimo, the author of *Fire and Flames*, recalls:

> Large parts of the Peace Movement clearly distanced themselves from the Autonome. A 'violence debate' followed that isolated the Autonome even further. Comrades from Hamburg observed that 'the term "autonomous groups" is systematically used by the state to reduce our politics to nothing but the issue of violence' (Geronimo 2012: 116).

A large part of the reason for this is the continued ambiguity about whether certain acts, such as self-defence and property damage (e.g. graffiti, fence-cutting, breaking windows), constitute an act of violence. While there is a long-standing social movement tradition of principled non-violence, the particular, contextual acts that do

---

1 This elision can also be seen prior to Occupy; see, for example, www.greenpeace.org/canada/en/Blog/nonviolence-vs-diversity-of-tactics-the-case-/blog/12075/ and www.trainingforchange.org/diversity_of_tactics. Part of the Alliance of Community Trainers (ACT) wrote an open letter to Occupy arguing against 'diversity of tactics' and for strategic non-violence for a number of reasons, primarily focused around accountability. ACT argued that 'diversity of tactics' is often shorthand for 'anything goes' and can replace organised discussions about tactics and longer-term strategies. (See http://starhawksblog.org/?p=675.)

and do not fall under this category are often debatable even within these circles. Instead of revisiting such debates surrounding what Uri Gordon calls the 'messy definitions' of violence (Gordon 2008), here we want to challenge the ways in which the violence/non-violence binary has come to over-determine reflections on and understanding of the dynamic unfolding of protest tactics in and outside the protest camp. If we only read and recall actions as 'smashy smashy' or 'fluffy stuff', which is how English-speaking activists often refer to this debate, are we missing what goes on in between and beyond this binary? While a return to the binary of the violence debate seems a permanent feature of social movement activism, we want to show that the black bloc and 'diversity of tactics' are approaches that emerge in certain specific circumstances, often at sites of convergence and activist exchange – such as protest camps. Moreover, in the next section we further the concept of an 'ecology of action'. Here, we expand on the idea that protest camps are places where the academic and activist binary of violent and non-violent are insufficient. Instead, we argue for the need to understand protest camps as spaces where a broad spectrum of debates, tactics and practices are negotiated and exchanged. They are spaces where the tactics and strategies of 'resistance can be imagineered' in that they take both physical and representational forms (Routledge 1997: 362). Furthermore, protest camps can become spaces that prompt an ecological perspective, in which activists experience the dissolution of binaries and become entangled in protest actions and tactics. As much as these are questions of collective reckoning, they also concern subjective transformations where there can be a radical shift in what protesters believe is violent or non-violent, and what they are willing or unwilling to do.

Protest action ecology

No set of codified descriptions or training workshops asking if we want to be 'arrestable' can capture the lived ambiguities and transformations that protesters undergo when engaged in ongoing struggle, particularly from the temporally and spatially unique site of a protest camp. Over time at an encampment – as at a counter-summit convergence space, or at an ongoing squat or social centre – people must sort through their own feelings and the feelings of others with whom they are protesting and living. This often occurs in situations where participants are living and protesting in very close proximity

3.2 Climate Camp in the City at the G20 meeting in London, 2009 – Ian Tomlinson, a bystander, died after an unprovoked attack by the police, who were heavily criticised for their excessive use of force

both to each other and to the police, often under conditions of intense surveillance and harassment. Within these lived spaces of protest, tactics are not abstract or hypothetical, but rather entangled in each other's feelings and ideas.

In addition, emotions and affect are also bound up with people's experiences of, and orientations towards, the different kinds of objects involved in protest actions and tactics. People come into the camp with pre-existing ideas about whether they can use hammers, locks, legal notepads, glitter eyeshadow or handkerchiefs. They enter with notions about what using these things will make them feel, or do, or look like. Maybe you have a fear of heights and tripods look dangerous, or maybe you love amusement park rides and can't wait to climb up one. Maybe you get cold easily or hot quickly and this limits what you feel capable of doing on a crisp frosty morning or out in a desert. Maybe you have bad memories of really needing to urinate or are used to fasting and feel you could go hungry for days at a time. Previous experiences and understandings of ourselves are always multi-layered and always linked to our surroundings (Ahmed 2004).

Our orientations towards particular protest tactics are also shaped by our previous encounters with the state and police – and different bodies encounter these forces in very different ways. There will be some at a protest camp who are regularly stopped and searched, others who have been dragged away from numerous blockade lines, and many others whose encounters have been limited to asking for directions or following traffic signals. There will be differently abled bodies, bodies who are accustomed to different levels of verbal and physical harassment, bodies that can be killed by a bruise, and bodies that regularly come home from sport or training sessions covered in bruises.

In all of these ways, and more, our feelings and ideas about tactics are complicated. We have what Avery Gordon has called 'complex personhood', always 'beset by contradictions', always more than the social categories deployed to define us (Gordon 1997: 4–5). As such, our orientations towards actions are never as neatly aligned as the categories of violence/non-violence, smashy/fluffy or spiky/hippie try to describe them as being. A better approach for understanding how protest actions play out is to look beyond binaries, and to do this we take an ecological approach. Viewing the protest camp as an ecology, we are interested in the entangled ways in which objects, people and environments come together in protest action.

As we have discussed, protest action infrastructures involve patterns of dynamic human and non-human interrelations and groupings. Common examples of human and non-human elements coming together in actions at a protest camp might include: bolt cutters–fences–hands;

locks–arms–bladders; police horses–pavement–badge numbers; lemon juice–water–tear gas; hot tea–tired legs–hugs. In each protest camp, in every different location, how and when such objects and bodies come together will vary. Take for example, Stavros Stavrides' description of 'collective inventiveness' at Syntagma Square in Greece in 2011:

> People in the squares devised ways to make decisions and to defend themselves against police aggression, which established new forms of direct equalitarian democracy. Just after one such incident – a brutal police charge in which the people had been chased, hit, and tear-gassed – the square of Syntagma was peacefully re-occupied: people formed long human chains that transported, from hand to hand, small bottles of water to clean the square from the poisonous tear gas remains (Stavrides 2012: 590).

In Stavrides' recounting of this incident, police and people are brought together in conflict, in the violent contact zone of the square. Yet they are more than a collection of bodies. Accompanied by batons, tear gas, gas canisters, water and pavement, it is the ways in which these elements of protest come together that create what Stavrides describes as 'new forms of direct equalitarian democracy' (ibid.: 590; see also Tsomou et al. 2011).

In the only discussion of protest ecologies we have found in social movement literature, Alex Foti introduces the idea in a reflection on the protests that took place in Heiligendamm, Germany, during the 2007 G8. Foti argues that an 'ecosystem of protest' was formed by the many forms of both black bloc and playful, 'pink' protests he encountered at the G8 protests – from the actions of the Clown Army to the samba band and Pink Rabbits who alerted the Rostock camp when the police arrived on site:

> Black resistance and pink blockades go hand in hand, and pink clowns were defended by black anarchists when the police roughed them up during the actions and demonstrations: pink and black are complementary and not substitutes, like many, including myself, were led to believe in the past few years (Foti 2007).

Beyond advocating 'diversity' as an act of tolerance, Foti emphasises the tactical interplay, flexible collaboration and militant alliances that can form between pink and black bloc tactics. This kind of ecological reading offers a space for thinking about how forms of resistance at a protest camp do not simply compete or coexist, but are also co-generative, as the energy and outcomes they produce feed back into each other.

Our approach sees tactics as always and inseparably tied to their surroundings. When it is combined with thinking on protest infrastructures and tactics, this idea of a protest action ecology helps reorient discussions away from the binaries of violence/non-violence, symbolic/direct and spiky/fluffy that have come to dominate debate within social movements. Thinking about protest action from this vantage point enables us to move beyond such binaries to consider how the protest camp becomes a space of experimentation, of insurrectionary imagination where people adapt and expand not only their tactics but also their understanding of each other and of what their bodies can do – and of what they need to be able to do.

Protest action ecosystems

In an effort to offer a different way of reading the complexities and conflicts of protest actions from the approach of a protest action ecology, we now look at a series of examples from the space of the protest camp. We want to ask what else might we uncover or excavate if we begin from an ecological perspective? This shift in viewpoint can help uncover the feelings and objects that often get lost in abstract debates on tactics and strategies. To organise our discussion, we look at particular entanglements in which protesters, environments, structures and objects (and sometimes animals) are brought into contact with each other. Each example shows how protesters, from the site of the encampment and its surroundings, construct and negotiate a distinct set of infrastructures and practices. To work through each of the examples, we begin from emblems of activist resistance: fences, trees and street fights. Following Latour, we try to get these objects talking, 'to offer descriptions of themselves, to produce scripts of what they are making others – humans and non-humans – do' (Latour 2005: 79). We use these examples to show how debates about tactics cannot – and should not – be contained within violence/non-violence and corresponding binaries, as well as to highlight the role of the protest camp as a laboratory of tactical innovation.

Fences Both protest camps and the places protest camps target are often surrounded by fences and walls. We find protest camps near places where people are contained within fences: detention centres (Woomera), refugee camps (Calais), militarised borders (Palestine, Mexico) and other ghettoised geographical enclosures. We also find protest camps by fences erected to protect the mobile neo-fortresses of elite global gatherings and trade summits, such as G8 and G20, Free Trade Area of the Americas (FTAA) and WTO meetings. Whether serving as boundaries to keep protesters out, or barricades to shelter protesters behind, fences at these locations form part of the distinct territoriality of the protest camp; we discuss these in Chapter 5. Here, we are interested in the way fences provoke, entice and make action. As both symbols and physical technologies of control and containment, fences are often prominent objects in protesters' actions. Sometimes fences are targeted as objects in themselves, drawing attention to their function as oppressive containers. At other times they are torn down as a means of accessing whatever is on the other side. (And, in some situations, they are put up by protesters themselves, as reclamations of space and refusals to allow access to others.)

At Greenham Common, the fence served as a physical barrier forming part of a sophisticated security network and functioned as a symbol of state and military violence. It was legally regarded as a piece of property, protected by the interests of various authorities and officials. At the same time, as in many other protest camps, the perimeter fence marked the space of the encampment and the site of protest action. Former *Guardian* newspaper defence correspondent David Fairhall wrote in his book on Greenham: 'To a remarkable extent, it was the physical nature of [the fence] that determined the protest' (Fairhall 2006: 105). By considering the fence in relation to women's action at Greenham we can better understand how and why physical objects and, in particular, physical perimeters matter in protest ecologies. It also allows us to think through the affective dimensions of both the debates about tactics and the objects (such as fences) that comprise the geographical and symbolic space of a protest camp.

At Greenham, women used a variety of methods to cut down the fence at different points. The largest fence-cutting came with the 1983 Halloween action in which 2,000 women – many dressed as witches – took down four miles of the nine-mile perimeter fence surrounding the military base. 'Armed' with bolt cutters and broomsticks, this action played on both the reclaimed feminist figure of the witch in opposition to the patriarchal order and the commercialisation or Disneyfication of the witch, recoded here as an anti-nuclear activist. While the police and soldiers were prepared for a mass action, they were not prepared for *this* action. The majority of officers were located inside rather than outside the fence, making it difficult for them to physically stop the women from cutting through the wire by standing between protesters and the fence. As the soldiers and police lost control of the situation, violence was used against the women. Many women took baton hits to the hands and arms, leaving a number of women hospitalised and some with broken bones (Roseneil 2000: 211–14). The police arrested 187 women at the action.

The fence actions at Greenham also brought to the fore intersections of race, gender, age and ability, as they cut across questions of violence and vulnerability. The protester–fence action assemblage gives rise to what Sara Ahmed calls 'the differences that matter' as bodies are oriented to practices (Ahmed 1998). Amanda Hassan documented her participation in a fence-based action at Greenham:

> I was holding onto the fence along with some other women (all white), and from nowhere a big burly policeman gave me a chop on my arms and sent me reeling into the mud. None of the other women who were also holding onto the fence got this treatment. When I commented on this, a woman said: 'Well, you're only picked on because you're so short' (I'm under five foot). Couldn't they see it was because I was Black? (Hassan 1984: 7).

3.3 Police violence often reveals the race, class and gender oppressions that operate in protest camps

Thinking of Amanda Hassan as part of a protest community raises questions about how Greenham, as a collective space, revealed differences between women. Readings of violence as institutionalised or systematic rightfully situate brutality as a problem at the level of the collective. However, manifestations of this violence are carried out through individual people or small groups. The incident Amanda recalls parallels many similar cases documented at North American and European protest camps within the time period we looked at. Acts of racialised violence were often either dismissed or seen as a problem for the individual protester rather than for the collective protest. When the ways in which bodies differ are not taken into proper consideration, this impacts on other connections in the protest camp and the function of the camp as a homeplace in which people can feel part of a community of resistance together.

As women at Greenham sorted through their own feelings and the feelings of others with whom they worked and lived, a concern about each other's 'comfort zones' guided their interactions. Many women believed that resistance tactics had to be specific and situational, as well as flexible to different people's realities and capabilities. Questions about experience, collectivity, autonomy and trust therefore surrounded women's considerations about cutting the Greenham fence. In the following two excerpts, we look at how fence-cutting is discussed in relation to the violent/non-violent binary of action, as well as at how differences of age, political ideology, class and previous experience are articulated with regard to tactical decision-making. While each woman narrates her own story, she also positions herself as a participant in Greenham's protest ecology, where people with many different experiences met and became entangled with new objects, emotions and environmental surroundings. As each woman shares her views, she speaks of being interdependent with other participants and with the objects of protest, anticipating possible reactions.

Jane, an older protester at Greenham, offered her perspective on fence-cutting in an issue of the camp's *Green & Common* newsletter:

> I am 60 years of age, a war widow, a mother of 6, of CND, END and the labour party. I went to Greenham because I was disillusioned with all party politics ... When the question of cutting fences arose, I was filled with horror. I had been an antique dealer, and had a great respect for property. I felt cutting fences was

criminal vandalism. I spent agonising weeks, worrying about this.
Then I got angry. I realised it was my right to cut the fence. It
was my way of saying no … We are challenging the establishment,
threatening their authority over us, because they are threatening us
with their war machine … I tell you it's a very liberating experience
even if you have to go to prison for it. Think how terrified all
governments would be if this mentality caught on. TRY IT!

In Jane's description of how she went from condemning fence-cutting
to celebrating it, she cites 'getting angry' as an emotion linked to
the shift in her views. As Bradshaw and Thornhill discuss (1983),
non-violence at Greenham involved finding creative uses for anger.

When women constructed analyses that viewed the fence as a
symbol of illegitimate authority, cutting the fence could become,
simultaneously, both an emotional release and an effective, direct
demonstration of women's anger at the system. In her story of fence-
cutting, Jane mentions her age to emphasise a difference between her
perception of herself and her view of younger campers, who she did
not feel shared her hesitations or anxieties about cutting the fence.
At the same time, Jane's writing attempted to forge a connection
between herself and other older women who might also be reluctant
about fence-cutting. For Jane, engaging in this action helped her form
an analysis of the fence as part of the 'war machine'. She ended her
piece with an invitation for other women to 'TRY IT!' This marks a
reorientation of her body with the object of the bolt cutters and the
infrastructure of the fence, expanding or transforming the horizon
of what her body could do.

Long-term camper Rebecca Johnson's account of the fence-cutting
debate talks explicitly about the ways in which the ideology of non-
violence came to be understood as flexible. She argues that it was
important to consider fence-cutting both as a tactic for achieving a
political aim and as a symbolic act that would generate affect. In
an essay that was reprinted in a number of Greenham-based and
Greenham-related publications, Rebecca wrote:

At first I thought the division between violence and non-violence
was easily identifiable. Violence hurts or injures, so you don't
do it if you believe in non-violence. I felt good that we decided
not to cut the fence on New Year's Day. But during that time we
have talked and thought a lot about it and I began to realise it

wasn't that simple. Cutting the wire and taking down the fence is
damage to property. Is that violence? Where do you draw the line?
A carpenter takes a piece of wood and cuts and planes and shapes
it into something else: a house, a bed or a child's toy. The wood is
cut, but we don't call that violence. We do this all the time: cutting
wheat to make bread, melting metal to reshape it, burning wood on
our camp fire. We are transforming things for our purposes. That's
what creativity is about ... With our own hands we pull down the
fence, making a huge door to the base. Only a few people can
climb up a ladder and over the barbed wire, but thousands of
common people can walk into the base through the door we have
made into the common land. Where is the violence? That whole
fence and its purpose is violence, against us and against the land
(Harford and Hopkins 1984: 41).

In this personal essay, Rebecca repeatedly discusses fence-cutting as
a collective issue, using 'we' and 'our' to situate the practice in relation to Greenham as a protest community. She wrote that dialogue
and debate with other women transformed the ways in which she
thought about cutting the fence. Rebecca formulated her position,
in part by reflecting on a previous protest event. At the silo action,
women climbed over fences on to the base, ran up the silos built to
store missiles, and danced and sang at dawn in front of an array of
press cameras and bewildered authorities. For the silo action, women
decided not to cut the fence. Whether women felt it was violent, were
intimidated by the thought, believed it was tactically or symbolically
ineffective, or feared legal repression, enough women were hesitant
that a decision was made to climb over the fence using carpets and
ladders rather than clip through it with bolt cutters. In conversations following the action, some women suggested that if the fence
had been cut down for the silo action, it would have been possible
for more than 40 women to take part. Here, Greenham, as a place
of ongoing protest, provided the space–time for reflections on and
developments of tactics.

Rebecca constructed her argument in support of fence-cutting
by first acknowledging that, normatively, fence-cutting is an act of
property damage. Once the fence is cut, however, it becomes a 'door'
and the question of damage no longer even applies. This analysis shifts
attention from the act of cutting to a question of what that cutting

creates. As the cutting creates a situation in which more people are able to participate in an ethical, responsible protest against violence, it cannot, she says, be considered violent. In this case, both the ethical and tactical dimensions of the violence/non-violence debate are contextualised in relation to Greenham as a particular protest community, made up of interactions between people, objects and environments. Rebecca's argument is both analytically sophisticated and, in Ann Seller's terms, demonstrates 'intelligent feelings' (Seller 1985). Moreover, Rebecca's discussion highlights the many entanglements of the fence, and, perhaps most importantly, the possibility of transforming it into a doorway to other possible worlds.

This possibility shows how protesters' collective production is based on the notion of power as capacity, the 'power to' or *potenza* of Hardt and Negri (2000) and Holloway (2002). Starhawk (1987) developed a similar concept that furthers the notion of 'power with', which we will discuss in Chapter 4 in more detail. But here we can already grasp that what is individual 'power to', the horizon of 'what our bodies can do', is greatly enhanced in the collective setting of the protest camp. Two further brief examples of fence-based actions at protest camps again draw attention to the need to think beyond binaries and to consider the entanglements of objects and emotions at the site of protest action.

In 2002, an action generated out of a NoBorders camp saw another transformation of fence into doorway, enacting – though briefly – a world with freedom of movement. The NoBorders solidarity camp was held outside the Woomera detention centre, a detainee prison in a remote part of south Australia, well known for numerous human rights abuses during its operation from 1999 to 2003. During a day of solidarity action, nearly 1,000 migrant rights campaigners gathered around the fence surrounding the Woomera complex. Using primarily their bare hands, the fence was torn down by those both inside and outside. A description of Woomera offered by Luther Blissett[2] reads: 'The Woomera detention centre is all dust, tin sheds, riot cops and razor wire, but it still looks like an armed enclave, a roman camp' (Blissett 2002). Blissett's scene shows the interlinking of people and technology in a protest ecology, an assemblage of resistance. On the

---

2 Luther Blissett is a pseudonym used by an Italian collective of writers and in Australia by artists and social activists. Blissett was a well-known footballer.

website antipopper.com, Ben, a protest participant, describes this coming together:

> The wonderful kind of limited engagement that happened at Woomera was like a *deus ex machina* plot twist that happened at the beginning (rather than at the end) of the play that was our mutual action. *God out of the machine.* It seemed to just *arrive*. Hundreds of people, ready to do what it took to challenge the fences (and what they stood for), on both sides – whether it was breaking the law or … providing a network of support. A general and uncanny resolve (http://antipopper.com/papers/an-engagement-with-the-real/).

In this interview about Woomera, Ben and another protester, Claire, draw attention to both the importance of the collective management of camp infrastructures and to the role of affect in protest action. Claire reflected:

> I don't think people were crying at the fences/border because they were intellectualizing that they had nothing to gain from the deten-tion of those inside. I will never give up a politics which creates the space, or at least attempts to, for people to cry, get angry, outraged and upset, because this politics is real. It engages not only with our everyday lives but our humanity and our collectivity (http://antipopper.com/papers/an-engagement-with-the-real/).

Nowhere in Ben and Claire's reflection is a discussion of property damage to fences, of whether this was a violent or non-violent strategy. Instead, their understanding of how tactics played out at Woomera is about what they call 'resonance' – sympathy, compassion, the ability to feel and act in the moment with others. Taking down the fence was a collective reorientation of what these bodies, inside and outside the fence, could do. For those outside the fence, it arose out of their proximity to the violence of 'living in a country where people who come to us for help are locked up in cages' (Claire at http://antipopper.com/papers/an-engagement-with-the-real/).

Trees A large number of protest camps have taken place around, and often in, trees. These camps have developed intricate and highly sophisticated re-creation and action infrastructures that allow protesters to travel between trees, lock on to them, and sleep, cook and go to the toilet metres above the ground. For activists confronting security forces and police who will not kill them, the threat of 'it's me or the tree' physically prevents – or in many cases hinders and makes incredibly expensive – the cutting down of trees. The protester, made vulnerable to the machine, is entangled with the tree, creating a tactical assemblage that draws on a long history of daring and innovative tree-based tactics, often earning protesters the label 'tree huggers'.

The term 'tree hugger' originated not as an insult but as a protest tactic. It is said to date back to 1730, when a village of Bishnois in India sacrificed their lives to save their sacred and resource-rich trees from being cut down to build a new palace for the king. This act of hugging a tree to defend the livelihood of the land was popularised nearly 250 years later when another group of Indian villagers, living in the Himalayas, brought together an ecological understanding of the effects of deforestation and Gandhian principles. In the early 1970s, the women villagers embracing trees to stop loggers from cutting them down were termed the Chipko movement, *chipko* meaning 'hugging' in Hindi (see Jain 1984; Shiva 1991). This turned into a national movement against commercial logging, and inspired indigenous and environmental activists outside India, particularly activists at the Clayoquot protest camp. The Clayoquot activists blockaded commercial deforestation in the 1990s in British Columbia, Canada, and explicitly referenced the Chipko movement in their internal and external communications (Moore 2011). More than 12,000 people took part in blockades at Clayoquot, with hundreds sometimes staying at the protest camp on site. Anti-roads activists in Britain were also inspired by the Chipko movement (Brian Doherty personal correspondence, 19 October 2012).

An early tree camp emerging out of the German environmental movement was established in 1980 to protest against the construction of an airport runway in Frankfurt. As protesters assembled for actions and demonstrations in a forest near the runway construction site, many began to stay overnight; over time, an elaborate encampment developed. German protesters constructed a 'hut village' that served as a base camp and as a direct prevention of deforestation (see http://autox.nadir.org/archiv/chrono/startb_chro.html). Most of the hut village was built at ground level, but there was also a tripod and a low-rise tree house. Within the German Green movement, site occupations had developed as a tactic to protest against nuclear power plants in the mid-1970s, and the hut built in the Frankfurt airport protest resembled the hut built in Wyhl in 1975.

At the time of the Frankfurt camp, tree-climbing as a form of protest was not common, but a decade later many tree blockades left ground level and the 1990s saw tree platforms built high up in tree branches. This development came with advancements in climbing safety equipment that led to a popularisation of climbing as a recreational activity. In the mid-1980s, summer camps and recreational facilities in North America and Europe started featuring the sport, and climbing gear became more widely available in camping stores (Waterman and Waterman 2002). These innovations reoriented protesters' engagements with the trees as tactics, sending encampments up into the skies. By the mid-1990s, when protest camps swept through the UK to target the building of new motorways, tree-climbing had reached high levels of sophistication. The first of the anti-roads camps appeared in Twyford Down in 1992, and soon protest campers were occupying treetops up and down the UK. The rapid growth of these protest camps led to widespread media coverage; as *The Economist* reported in February 1994, 'Protesting about new roads has become that rarest of British phenomena, a truly populist movement drawing supporters from all walks of life' (Economist 1994).

At blockade camps preventing the cutting down of trees, protesters often spend days, weeks or even months at a time entangled in trees. Here, not only do protesters develop a close relationship with each other, with loggers and with security and the police, they also develop a relationship with the trees. In a reciprocal and interdependent bond, they protect the trees, and the trees protect them, offering shelter and security. At these blockade camps, the infrastructures of action and re-creation are made up of the same materials, and protesters, in a sense, live both *in* and *as* their tactics. As a protest camper explains in their recounting of a first tree sit-in at the Minnehaha Free State encampment:

> My first night in a tree sit was incredible. I climbed up the rope ladder with some instruction, then I was left to my own devices … words cannot convey what I felt in that tree, but those first hours in the tree expanded my understanding of the interconnectedness of the entire ecosystem (Egan 2006).

This intimate intertwining of protesters and trees has led to many imaginative protest tactics, as the forest encampments became 'laboratories of insurrectionary imagination'.

Tree sits were just one among many tree-based tactics that protesters in the UK anti-roads movement developed and adapted. At many anti-roads camps, defending trees involved the creation of complex protest action infrastructures including tree houses, walkways, climbing equipment, methods for bringing food up into the trees and waste down from the trees, including tactics for 'how to pee in a harness', and instructions about what to do when ropes were cut by security forces or when faced with cherry pickers (mechanical elevation vehicles for fruit-picking that were repurposed to remove protesters from tree branches). Tactics from tree spiking to building rope walkways were meticulously collected in print and online handbooks such as the UK-produced pamphlet *Road Raging*, which documents and details tactics with step-by-step instructions, images and reflections on implementation and context from experiences in the British anti-roads movement between 1992 and 1996 (see Road Alert 1997; www.eco-action.org/rr/ch9.html#tree).

Many of these tree tactics involved learning processes, including reading training guides as well as attending training workshops and skill-sharing sessions at the camp. In the Newbury bypass camp, professional climbers came down from a club in Sheffield (Merrick 1996). However, climbers were also brought in to remove protesters from trees, which illustrates the broader ways in which resources (training manuals, strategy reflections, books such as this one) and people (informants, provocateurs) can move between activist and security networks.

The time and space that protest camps can offer for exchanging skills and knowledge make them fertile ground for tactical innovation. Describing the lock-ons at Newbury, Merrick recalls:

We built a lock-on at the bottom of each tree: we dug a tunnel diagonally down between the roots of the tree, then set half a metre of drainpipe in concrete in the hole, the top of which was flush with the ground. There was a piece of metal to clip on to down at the bottom of the pipe. We made bracelets of steel cable with a snap-shut clip on. So, the eviction comes, someone wearing one of the bracelets puts their arm down the pipe and clips onto the metal. The tree can't be felled until the person is moved. The

Abseiling

Great fun. Although bear in mind that abseiling has caused more serious injuries on tree campaigns than anything else. Really, I mean it, get someone to teach you properly. Anyway, this is how you abseil with a figure eight.

1. Find a climbing rope that is firmly attached to a tree and which reaches all the way to the ground.

2. Tie your hair up and tuck your necklaces in.

3. Unclip your fig 8 and hold it this way up.

4. With the rope in your right hand, if you are right handed, push it through the large hole from the front.

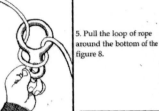

5. Pull the loop of rope around the bottom of the figure 8.

6. Attach the bottom of the fig 8 to your main carabiner. Do-up-the-screwgate-and-undo-it-half-a-turn.

Now this allows you to slide, in a controlled fashion, down a rope ONLY provided that you hold the protruding rope DOWNWARDS.

If you let go of the rope then you will fall.

If you go too fast, then you may burn your hand, let go of the rope and fall (avoid this by wearing a leather gardening glove).

And if you have any stray locks of hair or necklace type things near the fig 8 then they will be magically sucked into it and make you very unhappy.

SO the first time you abseil, it is as well to get someone to hold the bottom of the rope, slackly, so that if you yell, they can pull it downwards and slow you down. You can also try passing the rope under your bottom and holding it with your other hand, or wrapping it loosely around your lower leg and gripping it between your boots.

Don't hold onto the rope above the fig 8.

Got that? Ready?

3.4 Kate Evans' abseiling handbook

person can't be moved until the concrete is carefully drilled out and the drainpipe cut open. We put rubber in the concrete to repel hammer action drills, and broken glass to make drilling unsafe. That's a lock-on. They've been successfully used at numerous other road protests in recent years, and there's always new clever little bits of refinement in the design being thought up all the time. Think clever. One step ahead (ibid.).

At Newbury, some other tactical 'refinements' included activists moving from climbing ropes to steel cables after bailiffs started cutting them down.

Passing on knowledge in protest camps is not a neutral activity; power relations in the camp are produced – and reproduced – by who is seen as an expert, what bodies are presumed to use what tools, and what kinds of techniques of voice, gesture and demonstration are engaged to share skills. UK anti-roads camps were criticised by many women in the wider movement for their machismo and reproductions of gender norms and practices. As one anti-roads protester reflected: 'Camps can be too easily dominated by macho ego-warriors, complete with harness codpieces, who create an intimidating atmosphere, especially after a few cans' (Do or Die 1999). In relation to tree tactics, these observations often centred on methods that involved climbing trees. In another article written for UK magazine *Do or Die*, a woman involved in the protest camps wrote:

> I recall once sitting up an ash tree that I had lived in for the last two months when a reasonably experienced male climber visited the site and was pottering about in the walkways, passing by my tree. He took one look at my abline and quickened his pace. 'Oh dear,' he said, 'how long have you been abseiling on that?' – just that brief sentence was enough to make my eyes roll into the back of my head, and take a deep breath before proceeding with my somewhat short answer. Before I knew it he was involved with untangling the line of the various branches, tutting to himself about the unsafety of my present line, and about how everyone did it this way these days. Fair enough, at this stage I was grateful for his advice. That would not have been so bad if not an hour later some other 'dashing knight in shining harness' was to come ambling past only to re-tie the abline using the previous knot. I threw my hands up in disbelief and left them to it, but admittedly felt somewhat stupid because I had not listened to myself. I should have been able to say that the line was fine as it was, that I had done it myself and I knew it was okay – but my confidence was challenged by these men, and I believed at first that they genuinely knew better (Do or Die 1998).

It is not surprising that the harness became a focal point for people's ideas and emotions involving gender. Strapped to the body around the waist and upper thighs, the harness fits snuggly and frames the crotch. Putting a harness together, rigging up ropes to trees, and positioning the body for climbing all involve physical extensions of the body that are infused with vulnerability and risk – 'not doing it right' can lead to serious injury. As with athletic pursuits more generally, people encounter the climbing harness in a culture that defines the capacities of different bodies in particular ways (Young 2005).

An important intervention in tactical knowledge-sharing came with Kate Evans' book *Copse*. Inspired by her time as a child at Greenham Common, Evans set off for Newbury. Released in 1998, Evans' book visually detailed the how-tos of tree tactics and depicted an array of bodies and close-up detailed sketches of climbing techniques and tools. In it she pokes fun at the machismo associated with particular practices, explaining a method to climb down trees without branches 'for wussy girls' and offering practical tips for abseiling (for example, 'Tie your hair up and tuck your necklaces in') as well as explaining in (literally) graphic detail 'how to pee in a harness' (Evans 1998). Rather than blaming either tools or bodies for 'not fitting' (Ahmed 2004), Evans' book, like many of the innovations of Greenham women, reconfigured ideas about tools and how protesters can use them. It offered a reorientation for those not fitting the white, male body and masculine norms, familiarising them with the objects and practices of tree protest action from an alternative perspective. Such reorientations are a crucial part of tactical innovation; and bringing them from peripheral conversations and designated 'spaces' (women's, queer, people of colour) to the centre of a camp's knowledge exchange practices can help build a community of 'power to' where skills and capacities are shared.

The tree tactics developed at the UK anti-roads camps were widely shared both nationally and transnationally. Yet, as the authors of *Road Raging* point out, they could only directly translate into other contexts where the police were unlikely to use severe tools of repression:

> Bear in mind that a lot of the tactics [in this guide] will only be viable whilst they don't want to kill us. To readers outside Britain, where rubber bullets, water cannons and guns are routinely used to suppress protest, these tactics may seem naive (Road Alert 1997).

During the mid-1990s, protesters in Clayoquot and in the anti-roads camps in the UK exchanged knowledge and techniques for blockading, tree house-building and climbing. For example, a Canadian activist visiting the Faslane Peace Camp for its nineteenth birthday first saw Kate Evans' book *Copse* and later borrowed a copy from a friend to create a zine with key images and instructions; this was reproduced and circulated via Black Cat Distro, and now by AK Press (Evans 1998). The 1998 Minnehaha Free State encampment in Minnesota also adopted lock-on and tunnelling tactics from the UK. These tactics continued to be mobilised in battles to block deforestation in the early 2000s; tree protests appeared in campaigns including the Shepton Mallet Anti-Tesco protests, which saw 90-foot tree platforms in 2006; the Borsbeek camp in Belgium against the expansion of Antwerp airport in 2005; the Save Titnore Woods campaign in the UK; and a 2008 treetop camp in Frankfurt against airport expansion that also drew on previous experiences of the early 1980s hut village camp in Germany. In 2012, Europe saw its biggest direct action camp against airport expansion swell to 40,000 with La ZAD (Zone A Défendre) protests. In the 40 years since airport construction plans were announced, protesters held meetings, wrote to legislators, and later squatted the land. They built houses, gardens, wind turbines and other ecological living infrastructures as part of their resistance. The campaign gained momentum in 2009 after a successful Climate Camp brought new people and new ideas into the movement. This again highlights how infrastructures travel, creating and shaping movement cultures and protest action. In the past few years, La ZAD protesters have utilised Indymedia, critical mass bike rides and Reclaim the Streets parties, showing how the protest camp as a homeplace becomes a hub of tactical exchange and innovation.

Street-fighting assemblages While Britain's tree camps are a fruitful example to use when thinking about how protest camps can become 'laboratories of insurrectionary imagination', Tahrir Square offers an insight into the collective 'power to', showing how affect and working together transform tactical possibilities. Published stories of protesters' experiences defending the square relate how feelings of individual and collective power arose through protesters' close encounters with each other and with the violence of the police state. From the entangled bodies, objects and environments of the street fight, we can see how protesters deploy an improvisational militancy (Feigenbaum 2007) against the heavy machinery of state force. We can also see how infrastructures for re-creation not only 'support' those defending the square but were interdependent in their actions. They provided the sustenance – emotionally and physically – that allowed the battles to go on for days, and created the affective bonds between friends and strangers that formed in the streets, enabling protesters to take on the police and their government.

On what was seen as the first day of the '18 days in Tahrir Square', 25 January 2011, people came together to protest about a public holiday commemorating the police. Organisers were involved in campaigns relating to the young man Khaled Said, who was beaten to death by police after being dragged out of an internet café by two undercover police officers in 2010. Said was not the first person killed by the police, nor was 25 January the first protest against police violence. From the late 1990s and throughout the 2000s, mini-uprisings targeted police stations in which there were incidences of police violence (Ismail 2012: 446). These uprisings responded to specific cases of violence, as well as ongoing abuses and harassment by the police including falsified drug charges, bribery, intense surveillance, stop and searches, torture and beatings. Ismail described the invasiveness of the police in people's everyday lives:

> Ordinary citizens' encounters with police take place in outdoor markets, on roads and highways, in public transport, in alleyways, and in their private dwellings. Very often, these encounters involve violence and humiliation.
>
> As the spaces of everyday life become spaces of police violence and humiliation, people come to have affective dispositions such as anger, disdain, and revulsion toward the police (ibid.: 437–8).

While many who participated in the uprisings in Egypt were adherents of principled non-violence, and non-violent teachings and training manuals were circulated among protesters, the complexity of the tactics that emerged in Cairo's violent contact zones cannot be made sense of within a binary logic of violence/non-violence. By making moral judgements about protest action within these binary confines we simplify the complex realities of the protest, distorting history and retracing the circular path of the violence/non-violence debate.

Rather, accounts from those defending the streets of Tahrir show another perspective. By looking at a small sample of these accounts, we want to draw attention to what it meant for people not just to occupy the square but to defend it. To do so, we focus on what happened when bodies, entangled in the objects and environments of the urban street, came to reorient themselves in the moment, engaging in street-fighting tactics. Importantly, the accounts we draw on here are only from men who were not regularly involved in battles with the police, and for whom this kind of direct, militant engagement in protest was new. Much of the action they describe themselves improvising took place alongside others in the uprising, such as football fans called the Ultras, who were more accustomed to both police abuse and street fights (Mehrez 2012; Ismail 2012). These perspectives are therefore incomplete, but they illustrate clearly how affective transformations arise and move through place-based protest spaces. In a republished diary account of two days defending the square, one protester writes:

[Wednesday 2 February] I spend the night helping fighters at perimeters of the square by bringing them rocks and stones from within the square and by banging stones loudly on metal fences. We are creating the drums of war! In fact, this has the most posi-tive impact on all of us. With our small stones we manage to beat them – because we believe in our cause whereas these paid thugs do not ...

[Thursday 3 February] We are exhausted this morning. We have had no sleep and very little food. We are so happy, though, to see the people arriving in Tahrir since early morning, bringing in food, medical supplies, blankets and water. One of them is a boy, no older than 14 years old, who has come on his own from the Pyramids area carrying two huge bags of baked goods. It is a dangerous thing for him to do. He left his home at 6 a.m., arriving in Tahrir four hours later. God, I love these people. We deserve a better country and these young people deserve a better future (Mehrez 2012).

Part of the street-fighting assemblages were infrastructures for medical care. As those fighting police and soldiers on the streets were injured, they were trolleyed back inside the square and nearby repurposed buildings for medical care. There were also field pharma-cies set up with first aid equipment, and many on the streets carried vinegar-soaked handkerchiefs, water and Coca-Cola to combat the effects of the tear gas being fired at them constantly by the police.

In another account, a middle-aged man reflects on his participation in the street fights and recalls his feelings after protesters found a truckload of weapons in a police vehicle they had stopped that was shooting gas at protesters:

> There was a big argument on what to do with these weapons.
> In the end the older people, and I among them, convinced the
> younger crowd it would be best if we threw all the weapons in
> the Nile, which we did. Later that night, I regretted the decision.
> That night, the police were using live ammunition against us ...
> There were many injured people and an ambulance came through
> and we let it through thinking they were there to get the injured
> people, but they didn't take anybody and a few minutes later
> the ambulance was gone. The police started firing again, so that
> ambulance must have been carrying ammunition; can you imagine?
> ... I remember at that time, we were organised in a very random
> way. Nobody was managing us, but some were hitting iron fences
> to make noise, others were breaking up the sidewalk for stones,
> others were carrying the stones and still others were throwing the
> stones. Automatically and without previous organisation, if anyone
> got tired throwing, he would be replaced and so on. Random but
> organised (Rushdie, in Mehrez 2012).

In comparison with actions experienced in other camps, the street-fighting assemblages of Tahrir Square stand out for many reasons. But what unites the accounts of 'tree-hugging' campers and Egyptians fighting for their rights is the role played by the camp's action infrastructures in enabling their collective potential, a notion of power that we discuss in more detail in the next chapter. It certainly seems to be the case that to be in action together directly impacts on the ability to self-organise in collectives; importantly, this organisation was without formal management. Along with makeshift hospitals and other auxiliary spaces, for example coffee shops providing care for protesters, Tahrir Square functioned as a base camp. It offered street fighters a space of collective energy, a place for rejuvenation, where the one became many. It empowered people to start to speak up, voice their opinions, speak freely. It created a community of resistance, a place to find justification and motivation to dare to challenge the powers that be. In this sense, Tahrir Square stands firmly in the tradition of other protest camps, and has greatly expanded our understanding of the role protest camps can play in revolutionary uprisings.

Conclusion

An understanding of the action infrastructures of protest camps must move beyond the frequently used but conceptually facile binaries of symbolic and direct action, of violent versus non-violent protest. Moreover, looking at how protest action unfolds in protest camps complicates the dominant notion of a diversity of tactics. As we have argued in this chapter, protest camps create spaces where the logic, patterns and repression of these old divides seem to break open again. To this end, we see such binaries as continuing to serve those who want to suppress protest. Rather than providing useful functions for activists, they are frequently encouraged and enhanced by forces that defend the status quo. In this chapter we have discussed how black bloc tactics arose in response to police violence against new action forms. Those new action forms were non-violent, but they were able to challenge the state authority and question the logic of the status quo. As protesters occupied building sites, they disregarded the due legal process in which the nuclear power plants had been approved. They disregarded the rules of the game, but they did not harm anyone, nor was that ever their intention. In a variety of contexts, rule-breaking has been an important and powerful tool of activists: whether Indian tree huggers or the protest campers they inspired in Britain and beyond; whether Gandhian independence fighters, Resurrection City dwellers, or women at Greenham Common, protesters act in defiance of rules and of the law. In many instances the state responded with violence to these peaceful but uncompromising tactics, and when, under brutal and sustained assault, people started to defend themselves, politicians called those people violent.

Sure enough, protesters did respond to the binaries, and often reaffirmed them. In camps, as we have tried to show, an environment exists for protesters to develop a shared understanding of protest tactics. The camps are places of discussion, exchanges and transformations. They form action ecosystems of bio-political organisation where tactics develop within and out of the entanglements of protesters, available objects and existing environments. This does not mean that questions of what constitutes violence are left undiscussed. Rather, in practice such discussions unfold in the context of actual strategic and tactical situations where people live in close proximity, needing each other's support and relying on infrastructures that provide care. Protest camps are ecological systems in which people must learn to trust and care for each other in order to succeed – and, at times, to survive. Together, protesters must discuss how best to approach a given situation. Within the confines of a violence/non-violence binary, conflict will often override innovation and mutual understanding. Looking at histories of protest camps, we can see moments when this binary dissolves and tactics take on successful new forms. The ways in which protest campers conduct their discussions and how collective decision-making takes place at protest camps are explored in the next chapter.

Moving out of the tent in the morning I recall the actions of last night, the running battles with the police, the thrill, the fear, the fun. I move to the central marquee of my neighbourhood. Here is breakfast, coffee, bread, muesli and some smiling faces. The kitchen volunteers are already up, have cooked porridge, and are offering it to the arriving, yawning activists. As I settle with my breakfast at one of the tables in the kitchen marquee, the plenary starts by filling in the rota for volunteering over the next two days. Appreciating my warm meal, I agree to cook porridge the next morning. The meeting continues to discuss police violence against the camp. Positions need to be taken in respect of demands from the police to enter the site. A discussion starts over breakfast. Paralleled in a dozen more neighbourhoods where a similar process takes place. Later the consensus decisions taken from the neighbourhoods will be exchanged in the spokescouncil and an attempt will be made to find a decision based on a consensus between all camp participants. Will it be an endless debate or will we, like on the previous day, somewhat magically reach a decision that is not a compromise nor the position of only a few, but an expression of our collective will? (Kingsnorth protest camp, UK, 2008)

Introduction

The Occupy movement has perhaps, more than any earlier protest camps, led to a diffusion of knowledge about horizontal decision-making (HDM) procedures. Even Fox News and CNN debated (and often mocked) the attempts to organise without hierarchies and leaders. Protest camps might appear to naturally organise with consensus process, wiggly fingers and working groups, but not all protest camps are run in a horizontal, democratic fashion. While many protest camps adapted and adopted such tactics as their basis for governance, the convergence between protest camps and horizontal forms of decision-making in camps such as Occupy needs careful examination and explanation. In this chapter we look at the development of infrastructures of governance and organisation in protest camps

AGREE   UNSURE   DISAGREE   BLOCK

POINT OF PROCESS   POINT OF INFORMATION   I HAVE A QUESTION   WRAP IT UP

4.1 The hand signals of consensus decision-making popularised by Occupy

to raise questions about how both procedural and spatial practices shape and underwrite camps.

In particular, we ask how protest camps afford, enable and encourage specific kinds of organisation. We ask how the study of protest camps might allow us to draw conclusions about broader questions of organisation, and the political questions this evokes relating to autonomy, power and management. Infrastructures of governance and organisation include procedures of decision-making, often drawn out in constitutions, handbooks or agreed regulations, but – importantly – are also represented and realised in architecture and what we call here antagonistic spatial practice. In protest camps, these include ways of decision-making adopted in the camp, the layout of the campsite and its construction, as well as more practical tools and conventions, like the by-now famous 'jazz hands' or 'wiggly fingers' to show agreement in the consensus process.

Beyond such formal elements, there are also other, more implicit forms of organisation, which relate to relationships between people in the camp. Trust, reciprocity and affective ties built through previous social movement connections and friendships often exist among some participants of a protest camp before the camp starts. However, as the camp is spatially and temporally limited, new ties are generated and existing ones transformed, as affective attachments strengthen and weaken. As products of specific social movements, themselves subject to social, political, environmental and media contexts, protest camps are subject to the histories and cultures of activism. These implicit forms of structure have an influence on the governance, and indeed on the workings, of the camp.

In turning our attention towards the history of protest camping and experimentation in creating governance infrastructures that foster horizontality, we describe firstly how encampments lend themselves to the experience of organic horizontality among participants. Even in camps with more formal modes of organisation and governance, for example the Scout movement, forms of organic horizontalism or 'communitas' emerge. Resurrection City serves as an example of the emergent tensions between traditional left-wing organisational structures and the horizontalism of the new social movements. We then move into a discussion of the 1970s anti-nuclear movement in West Germany and the US to show how mass occupations of building sites develop features of protest camps as they begin to create infrastructures for sustaining daily life and protest within the space of their occupations. Here, the specific camp-like features of occupations, including a clear antagonism and a spatially and often temporally confined character, enhance experiences of organic horizontality. We show how these experiences led to attempts to formalise organic horizontality in the US, attempts that had both successes and setbacks.

The development and spread of peace camps in the 1980s bring another set of crucial innovations. For many such camps, their space is deliberately utilised to induce organic horizontality for political reasons. In the following decades, protest camps become a common form of political practice. Several camp governance infrastructures appear, such as the use of 'talking sticks', neighbourhoods, spokes-councils and the like. Many protest camps formalise their organisation and governance processes, whether in fixed procedures and rules or in their territorial layout. Partial organisation is achieved both through formalisation of decision-making and through architecture. In the final section of the chapter, we look at more recent examples of protest camps. Here, it becomes clear how protest camps now use procedural as well as spatial practice to develop partial organisation, and we identify how spatial and procedural practices of governance develop certain dynamics. We end with a look at the advanced stage of development of governance infrastructures in the Occupy movement, where experimentation with organisation and governance reaches unprecedented levels, as well as new limitations.

We look at this range of examples from different protest camps in order to develop three arguments. First, we examine how governance has worked at specific protest camps. We argue that the key to understanding such structures lies in refining our understanding of HDM and organic horizontality. Second, looking outside the protest camp, we argue that protest camps have played an important role in the formation of formal governance infrastructures, and particularly HDM, during the last 40 years of social movement history. Finally, we argue that beyond the development of processes and procedures of decision-making, protest camps also allow for experimentation with the spatial practices and architectures of governance infrastructures. In particular, we highlight sets of characteristics that enable and enhance the experience of organic horizontality, and we also try to tease out some of the infrastructure patterns that can inhibit such an experience.

Organic horizontality and partial organisation

Before we move into a historical analysis of protest camps in this chapter, we first want to disentangle some of the terms we use to describe social movement structures, introducing the concepts of 'organic horizontality' and 'partial organisation'. We find these concepts particularly useful to the study of governance and organisation in protest camps as temporally and spatially limited spaces of political activism. In protest camps, spatial organisation practices consist of the ways in which camp tents are physically organised around communal areas and what processes are used to determine where a speaker talks from at a meeting. These are often intentionally developed into governance infrastructures that operate in combination with formalised processes and procedures of HDM. As a consequence, the tensions created between these processes and procedures mark protest camps as 'spaces of experimentation', where forms of governance and organisation that move beyond the limits of the existing social order are often tested.

To elaborate this claim, we first need to examine what we mean by organisation and governance in theoretical terms. From a reading of the wider literature on the topic, it is clear that organisation is both a very 'natural' phenomenon for human beings and something that can be abstract and planned. Ahrne and Brunsson describe organisation as the ability to make decisions for oneself and also on behalf of others. The elements of organisation they describe are all connected to the capacity to make decisions: membership defines for whom the decisions are being made, and a hierarchy defines who makes those decisions. The way in which decisions are made is described in advance, and, through monitoring and sanctioning, organisations make sure that everybody follows the rules and adheres to the decisions taken (Ahrne and Brunsson 2011). All these elements of organisation are areas in which most modern organisations, the state perhaps as the best example, exercise domination over their members. Often associated with modernity and bureaucracy, organisations need to be managed and governed and therefore give rise to a managerial class, controlling a meta-level of structure. There is, then – to some extent inevitably – a hierarchy that seems to come with organisation.

Networks and organisations In literature that attempts to explain protest movements in the West over the last 40 years, a general observation is that these groups tend to reject the structures of traditional social movement organisations such as trade unions and political parties. New social movements are characterised by the search for new forms of organisation (Böhm et al. 2010; Calhoun 1992; Crossley 2003; Offe 1987). This shift has been described as the emergence of 'prefigurative politics' (Breines 1989). In this view, the way of doing politics, its *processes*, are considered crucial to allow it to work effectively towards social change. This change in focus emphasises the development of new organisational forms and more participatory processes of decision-making aligned with the political aspirations expressed in left-wing politics (Cornell 2011). In pursuing organisational forms such as HDM, and in attempting to reach consensus rather than majority decisions, new political movements have increasingly attempted 'to change the world without taking power' (Holloway 2002). Their aim has been to create new forms of organisation from the bottom up that can replace the existing structures, considered to be undemocratic or not democratic enough.

While this drive towards horizontality predates the 'network society' paradigm (Castells 1996), it has retrospectively been discussed in the context of this shift. New social movements, accordingly, are now often considered as networks rather than as organisations (Routledge et al. 2007; Hardt and Negri 2000; 2004). And, indeed, social movements have also increasingly used the term 'network' to describe their own structures. The use of the network metaphor was, of course, propelled by the spread and extension of new media technologies, which are particularly successful at enabling horizontal, non-hierarchical structures beyond local community and real-time proximity. The internet, listservs and – in the last five years – social media have played a central role in popularising the term 'network' to describe social movements.

However, the popularity of the idea that networks are somewhat better and more advanced structures than the traditional hierarchically and formally structured organisation extends beyond the realm of social movements. In corporations, ideas such as 'lean management' and 'teamwork' have prevailed in the last 40 years. In more general terms, this is reflected in an anti-bureaucratic drive underlying continuous attempts at restructuring that are characteristic of the (post-) modern organisation. In the past decade we have seen calls for 'open leadership' coming from top corporations and government agencies, and over two-thirds of all offices have become open plan (NBBJ Architects cited in Cheek 2012). In political and management theory, these discourses around openness and network models of leadership have also been mobilised to support neo-liberal arguments against the state (Boltanski and Chiapello 2005). In short, a move to the idea of the network as a better alternative to traditional organisation is not necessarily the progressive endeavour that some claim it to be (see Rossiter 2006). Instead, the ubiquity of the concepts of 'network' and 'openness' have led to an increasing imprecision in definitions. It is therefore worthwhile to attempt to disentangle what kinds of organisational forms we see protest camps as taking, from the large body of literature that now exists on networks.

Organisation is different from networks because it is 'not emergent, but the result of the intervention of individuals or formal organisations which can and do make decisions not only about their own, but also about the behaviour and distinctions of others' (Ahrne and Brunsson 2011: 90). The link between organisation and governance here is crucial. If a network is seen as something open, fluid and without any organisation, then there would be no need to make decisions, or for those comprising the network to govern and be governed. Moreover, networks, when used amorphously to describe the open and fluid, do not have boundaries. As protest camps have spatial and temporal limits, they are not entirely fluid spaces. They require systems for attending to people's everyday needs, as well as for planning campaigns, actions and various policies and practices to guide camp life.

As Paolo Gerbaudo (2012) has recently argued, much of the scholarship on social movements and networks forsakes the physical space of the action and of the protest camp to theorise about the networked space of the movements. From this perspective, it does not make much sense to describe the place-based protest camps simply in terms of networks. While protest camps have some network char-acteristics – they can build on relationships, affective ties and existing trust between people, for example – these are not the only features to consider. Protest camps pursue certain aims, and sometimes make decisions on behalf of their participants. They consciously decide on the way in which they do politics, and as a result they develop a structure. At the same time, the horizontal and fluid elements of the network structure are not eliminated, nor would this be desirable. Instead, a tension arises between the network structure and more traditional managerial methods of organisation. When establishing infrastructures of governance, protesters often find themselves in a balancing act: trying to find a reasonable level of organisation while maintaining network characteristics.

Partial organisation Rossiter (2006) suggests calling such attempts 'organised networks'; however, we find it more useful to operate with Ahrne and Brunsson's (2011) notion of 'partial organisation' to account for such phenomena. Critically, one may argue that all organisation is partial and neither pure networks nor full organisation actually exists; everything could be described as partial organisation. We would argue that it still makes a difference whether certain elem-ents of organisation can be avoided or whether they have to be decided upon. For Ahrne and Brunsson, partial organisation constitutes the existence of some elements of organisation, which they define as 'membership, hierarchy, rules, monitoring and sanction' (ibid.: 86). Where there is formal or full organisation, all these elements have to be decided, whereas in partial organisation the elements to be adopted have to be chosen by organisers.

When a network becomes organised, elements of organisation, such as decision-making, do not have to follow a pre-arranged or formalised procedure. To use an example from Ahrne and Brunsson, in a group of friends, the decision to go to a restaurant means that the group becomes organised – in theoretical terms, the network becomes partially organised. However, it is unlikely that the friends will devise a formal system of decision-making to reach a decision about which restaurant to pick. Perhaps some people have strong opinions about the choice of restaurant and others are happy to go along; perhaps someone takes the lead and the others follow. No formalisation is needed here, because group members already know each other and have a level of trust towards each other; or it could be that some of them do not find the issue particularly important.

In a social movement, the introduction of elements of organisation into the network is also often based on trust and affective ties that already exist between people. Discussing the issue of power in anarchist networks, Gordon (2010) describes this phenomenon through the concept of 'power with', which is borrowed from activist writer Starhawk (1987) and by extension from Holloway (2002) and Hardt and Negri (2000). 'Power with' is differentiated from 'power over' (*potere*), the logic of power as domination, and 'power to' (*potenza*, the notion of capability that enables both other forms) (ibid.). Crucially, in 'power over' people can make other people do what they do not want to do. Coercion, authority, violence and manipulation are modes in which 'power over' occurs.

In contrast to this traditional managerial model, Gordon argues that the organisation in many anarchist groups operates differently. People are not coerced, manipulated or forced into doing things; instead, we find a terrain of 'power with' where they 'influence each other's behaviour in the absence of a conflict of wills and interest' (Gordon 2010: 45). This describes the situation of the group of friends who become organised to go to a restaurant, and it can also describe how many political groups, in particular affinity groups, get organised. This notion of 'power with' may also be thought of as a rejection of the much-referenced duality between 'power to' and 'power over' as a binary opposition.

Gordon, along with many other social movement participant re-searchers, argues that despite the absence of domination, there are numerous power issues that can arise in a 'power with' setting. For

Gordon, these issues have to do with the individual resources and individual capabilities ('power to') that different members bring to a group. Gerbaudo (2012) has made a similar argument and has indicated that hierarchies tend to arise despite attempts to 'stay true' to horizontal logic. These informal hierarchies that may occur are based on control of resources, information or social capital (ibid.). Because of such differences, leaders and elites may evolve in these groups and end up effectively exercising 'power over' the group while being 'hidden' because there is no formal acknowledgement of such roles. Such hidden structures of power are often described with reference to Freeman's 'tyranny of structurelessness' of the 1970s. This, for Freeman, is the 'tyranny' that can result from not having a formalised set of roles, responsibilities and accountabilities (Freeman 1982). This can, for example, lead to some protest camps replicating the patriarchal structures of the outside world through the unequal distribution of power; this can affect decision-making spaces and practices through speech, gesture and tone (Kanngieser 2012). But before we discuss the conflicts and tensions that emerge out of governance infrastructures seeking to facilitate a 'power with' model of organisation and decision-making, we begin by offering an overview of the experience of 'power with' as it often manifests in protest camping, an experience we call 'organic horizontality'.

Organic horizontality The experience of organic horizontality is not limited to a protest camp, but can be found in a group of friends, or an anarchist affinity group, as well as in much larger social contexts, for example at a music festival. Perhaps most vividly described by Victor Turner (1977), people may experience the social as 'communitas', a sociality where hierarchies and social roles, class differences and other structures that separate people from each other are dissolved in moments of liminality. People meet each other as equals. For Turner, the experience of communitas takes place mostly in cultural contexts; however, it unquestionably has political implications. According to Turner, the experience of communitas enables the questioning of the existing social order; it is like a break from the normal that allows a reconsideration of organisation. This experience of organic horizontality is not limited to rituals or festivals. As David Graeber (2011) has concisely argued, many of our daily interactions, from language to forms of exchange and co-operation, depend on what he calls 'baseline communism'. Here, neither hierarchy nor cut-throat competition but the principle of mutuality – from each according to their abilities, to each according to their needs – defines our interactions. While not discussing protest, Cohen (2009) connects this idea to the camping experience to make a case for socialism as a preferable and achievable model of society:

> You and I and whole bunch of others go on a camping trip. There is no hierarchy among us, our common aim is that each of us should have a good time, doing, as far as possible, the things that he or she likes best (some things we do together; others we do separately). We have facilities with which to carry out our enterprise ... And, as is usual on camping trips, we avail ourselves of those facilities collectively: even if they are privately owned things, they are under collective control for the duration of the trip (ibid.: 3f).

In political contexts, experiences of organic horizontality are not confined to small groups of activists who know each other well; they can also occur in mass contexts such as the Argentinian uprising in December 2001. What we need to emphasise here, however, is the role of exceptionality in organic horizontality, something that is clearly highlighted by Turner's notion of liminality. Pointing to exceptionality does not mean questioning the permanent role of 'baseline communism' in human interaction, but rather highlighting the fact that there seem to be specific points when it is experienced and practised by many people as the most obvious mode of human interaction.

In Argentina, on the basis of the cry 'All must go!', a popular movement formed out of existing movements of unemployed and recently de-classed middle classes, and also pulled in broad sections of wider society. According to the vivid accounts of the revolution provided by Sitrin (2006), horizontality grew out of people meeting each other in the streets and in front of banks:

> When you went out with the *cacerola* [a pan – people banged their pans in protest at the beginning of the uprising] on the 19th [December 2001] you saw people also *cacerolando* [pot banging]. And you said: how crazy! Because I never speak to that person, or we see that one in the street and only say good morning, or not, and here is my neighbour and [he] is also banging a pot! ... The feeling of community began with this: let's share our problems (ibid.: 28f).

Crucial for the newfound communality was the total breakdown of trust in the existing institutions. The 'All must go!' rallying cry of the Argentinian horizontality experience of 2001 points to a further important condition of organic horizontality in political contexts: antagonism. People are connected because they commonly reject and oppose. Holloway (2002) calls this experience 'anti-power', a cry of negation. In Argentina, horizontality emerged as the most obvious and practical way to organise the resistance. Neighbourhoods formed assemblies that took over the organisation of all aspects of social reproduction, including factories, childcare and food supplies, on the basis of 'power with' rather than 'power over'. We witness these same phenomena at many protest camps. But, as indicated earlier, 'power with' comes with its own power issues.

While organic horizontality can be experienced in both small and very large groups, in social movement spaces problems often begin to emerge when numbers grow and newcomers need to be accommodated. Moreover, if a social movement wants to pursue broader coalitions or a particular action or campaign, decision-making will become more contested. Hidden structures might be brought to the surface and challenged, or people may decide to leave. The aspiration to maintain horizontality in more organised forms of social movements over time often prompts efforts to create new procedures to allow for more formal, if partial, structures of organisation. In the history of new social movements, looking at these junctures when formal organisation and organic horizontality are negotiated can help explain the political innovations in movement participants' efforts to create other possible worlds, or to manifest what is often termed 'prefigurative politics'.

Horizontal decision-making In terms of governance and organisation, key innovations in participatory forms of decision-making emerged in US social movements in the 1970s. Together, these sets of practices, operations, guidelines and sensibilities are termed horizontal decision-making (HDM). HDM is not a unified practice, and it is therefore unhelpful to try to describe it without looking at specific contexts. However, what unites different approaches to HDM is the attempt to nurture organic horizontality and to create conditions in which organic horizontality can flourish for the purpose of organising large groups and coalitions without resorting to 'power over'.

Returning to Ahrne and Brunsson's (2011) framework for the definition of organisation, we can identify the elements – membership, hierarchy, rules, monitoring and sanction – at work in the enabling conditions of HDM. Pertinent questions are who takes part in decisions? Who oversees the rules and procedures? Who monitors and perhaps sanctions or holds members accountable? The parallels between HDM and more traditional modes of group organisation illustrate how HDM works as a specific tool of organisation, but also, importantly, how it does not work.

First, in relation to membership, endless debates can be held over who can rightly take part in HDM in a given context (be it in a squat, a neighbourhood organisation or a protest camp). In principle, no one can be rejected for membership based on an organisational model that aims to be fully inclusive. Yet this problem arose in a number of protest camps we studied, from Resurrection City to Greenham, HoriZone and Occupy, where campers faced difficulties in figuring out how to balance issues of inclusivity, safety and wellbeing. Furthermore, hierarchies often inevitably emerge in practice when, in theory, they should be avoided. For example, they can surface over time as people become experienced camp organisers and develop knowledge or gain control of resources – money, accounts or equipment – which place them in de facto leadership positions. In addition, and often as a direct result of this, such people can sometimes be seen as being in a stronger position to question the wisdom of contributions and ideas from newly arrived campers. Media attention – even unwanted attention – can also bestow leadership labels and authority on individuals (Gitlin 1980). Thus, even if people in horizontal networks do not wish to become leaders or present themselves as such, they can possess many of the qualities even without the title. Ultimately, the development of 'power over' forms of governance and organisation is always limited by the fact that 'power over' is based on the power to enforce decisions (see Gordon 2010). But voluntary, free associations, as seen in social movements and protest camps, cannot physically enforce decisions on participants and members as they wish. People associate freely, and if they do not like what is going on, in most cases they can leave. That said, such movements and camps can and certainly do enforce decisions through cultural codes and practices.

In trying to grow and sustain experiences of organic horizontality, social movement activists have spent a considerable amount of time experimenting with infrastructures, adopting certain elements of organisation while avoiding others. In these attempts, we argue, protest camps play an important and often overlooked role. In the remainder of this chapter we look at protest camps in a variety of political and cultural contexts to show how they are particularly well suited to the experience of organic horizontality and how they provide – at the same time – a specific context that allows for attempts to create more formalised modes of organisation.

The organised camp and organic horizontality

Modern organised camping was developed with blueprints from the military. This is perhaps most evident in the founding of Scout camping in 1907 by Robert Baden-Powell. Clear hierarchies exist in the organisation and governance of Scout camping, with leaders on all levels, drawing from Baden-Powell's time as a Lieutenant-General in the British Army. This extends to the metaphysical levels, with the allegiance that Scouts had to swear to God and the monarchy. Political youth camps of the early twentieth century, often modelled or drawn from the Scout movement, used clear-cut hierarchies as well. However, from the earliest camps, we find reports of organic horizontality emerging within them. Research has shown how the Scout camps developed somewhat parallel experiences of organic horizontality beyond their formalised modes of decision-making (Mills 2011; 2012). This includes the transgression of social boundaries between participants, the formation of strong ties and affect among participants, and communality without hierarchy. Despite being organised on a meta-level as highly hierarchical organisations, organic horizontality emerges in Scout camping. And, indeed, such was the intention of the founder of the Scout movement, Lieutenant-General Baden-Powell, who was aiming, among other things, to transgress class differences in Britain (with the intention of mobilising the working classes for the imperial project) (Rojek 1993). However, over the years there were often tensions between organic horizontality and a more formal meta-level of organisation in the camp as a social form. This included conflicts about communists in the Scout movement emerging in the 1950s (Mills 2012), as well as about the role of girls in the Scouts, as they were initially banned from the movement (Mills 2011).

Resurrection City and anarchitecture

Similar tensions between hierarchy and horizontalism to those discussed above were evident in Resurrection City in 1968. Designed by a committee that included professional architects from local universities, Resurrection City had its own city planners. As such an intentional protest camp project on this scale had never before been attempted, the 15-acre encampment was modelled loosely on army camps and camps for migratory workers. The parkland was divided into a series of subsections or 'community units'. While this way of organising shelters into 'scaled-up' units worked well for traffic flow and resource allocation, it perhaps also contributed – in addition to existing practices and cultures – to the self-segregation by race that took place in the camp. This made the dining hall and other major service centres important spaces for interracial exchange and solidarity-building. Tensions also surrounded the splitting of Native American and some Hispanic and white participants, who took up residence in the nearby Hawthorne school. As they had a more fortified shelter, regular hot meals and showers, this created a sense of inequality and disaffection in those in the outdoor encampment, becoming a heated topic of debate in both protest habitations (Wright 2007; Fager 1969).

In addition, some elements of the City's planning were not undertaken in a centralised fashion – partly a necessity, as a number of the initial plans did not materialise. There were no washing facilities in place and participants had to be bussed to showers during the duration of the camp. Such hiccups in the planning process led to improvisation on the ground. More importantly, planning became more democratic in the course of the building of the camp. As one of the members of the planning committee, Wiebenson (1969: 407), recalled:

> Those from large cities seemed to have more experience in working together, and they built rapidly in teams. The New York crowd, for example, was able to put up shelters at a rate of about one unit per fifteen minutes per three-man team.

The duality found here in the planning of the space seems to have applied equally to the governance of the camp. Organised in a strictly hierarchical manner, the governance of the camp was supposed to be controlled by the leaders of the Poor People's Campaign (PPC) and the foremost Southern Christian Leadership Conference (SCLC) leader, Reverend Ralph Abernathy. However, the Resurrection City leadership, including Abernathy, did not stay at the camp but rather off-site at a black-owned motel in the neighbouring area (Chase 1998).

On the ground, grassroots organising took hold, and increasingly led to a more autonomous character within the City. For example, the SCLC had arranged for 'marshals', urban black youth who would act as a special volunteer security force to keep the camp under control (Wiebenson 1969). What might have started as a legitimate precautionary measure to keep security in the encampment became more and more contested in the course of the protest. When camp organisers failed to sufficiently address the complaints of campers, a new security force was established inside the camp by a group of people from Detroit:

> [The] Tent City Rangers solved some security problems, and they provided other services, such as rush transportation, as well. But, there was more a sense of competition than of cooperation between the Marshals and the Rangers, and, amid occasional announce-ments from City Hall that the Rangers would soon be disbanded, security continued to be a problem (ibid.: 409).

Interestingly, Wiebenson's take on the power structures that de-veloped within Resurrection City considers them to have been of no great importance or influence. The 'town meetings' that took place had merely the character of forums, while decisions were made outside the city by the SCLC leadership. He overlooks the fact that these spaces and forums, as well as the experience on the ground, allowed for a development of organic horizontality in Resurrection City. This is observed and valued in Chase's (1998) assessment of the internal power processes in the camp. Structures were in place to provide representation for the camp participants based on elec-tions, and they were designed to represent the ethnic diversity in the camp. These structures, though nominally fixed, became rather fluid in practice as camp participants dropped in and out over the period of the six-week-long camp experience. Indeed, while these structures also constituted a formal arrangement of governance, it was the specific spatiality that rendered them more like expressions of organic horizontality (see Wright 2008).

The fluidity of people coming in and out of the camp and their increasing familiarity with others within the City led to a diffused leadership. This sentiment is captured by one volunteer, who remarked:

> All the people engaged in leadership decisions, formally or informally, had the implicit acknowledgement all the time that this was a class problem. And that race and class were mixed in together (quoted in Chase 1998: 1).

This active involvement in decision-making may be interpreted as being a result of the affective ties that developed because people lived together. Further, it points to the implications and role of political camps in enabling political convergence and coalitions: 'It was an incredibly grass-roots effort in politics. Leaders were developed by general agreement. A consensus,' reported Maggard, another participant quoted in Chase (ibid.: 1). She went on to say: 'The Committee planned daily demonstrations on a real democratic basis. We had included everybody's needs from blacks, to Indians, whites, and Mexicans.'

Organised camps, then, seem to bring with them a propensity to develop organic horizontality, and this is linked to their spatially and temporally confined character. This, of course, is nothing new. Corps spirit in army or Scout camps, or among ships' crews, is a well-known phenomenon and – from the perspective of formal, managerial organisation – a central problem. Perhaps we could argue that the highly formalised and hierarchical meta-level of organisation we find in the military has its precise purpose in suppressing the organic horizontality that naturally emerges in spatially limited communities.

As an organised camp, Resurrection City prefigured the protest camps yet to come. The experience of the month-long tent city suggests that, in a temporally and spatially confined place of protest, there is an organic development of a sense of political affinity between participants, particularly when there is a shared antagonism. Despite the many differences in culture and ethnicity present in the Resurrection City encampment, participants formed ways of becoming a community, even when faced with persistent rain and knee-deep mud. At Resurrection City, organic horizontality emerged and challenged the meta-level organisation of the organisers. While the experience of this phenomenon in Resurrection City did not directly lead to the creation of more political camps, it left an idea in people's imaginations. Largely seen as a failure both by the media and by many movement participants, Resurrection City was forcefully evicted by the police over a three-day period ending on 24 June 1968. However, not much later, and to some extent unintentionally, social movement activists returned to the form and strategy of the protest camp as they developed direct actions targeted at occupying building sites.

Anti-nuclear occupations

In Europe in the 1970s, protest camps developed in the occupations of the emerging anti-nuclear movement. The lower Rhine valley, a borderland area encompassing parts of Switzerland, eastern France and the south-west German region of Baden, remains today a largely rural area dominated by agriculture and tourism. The Rhine River, however, provides one central resource for nuclear power production: a large cooling capacity. In the 1970s the area became a focal point – after the oil crisis – for the nuclear expansion plans of the Swiss, French and German governments. From the beginning, these plans were met by local resistance from large and diverse sections of the community.

The broad resistance, which began with protests, demonstrations and interventions in the planning process, expanded to the occupation of proposed building sites. The first anti-nuclear occupation of a building site occurred in Switzerland, in Kaiseraugst, in April 1974. The occupation lasted for six weeks and the police and authorities were totally unprepared. It proved to be a significant step towards abolishing plans for Kaiseraugst nuclear power station a few years later. Activists from France and Germany had joined the Swiss activists in their resistance, and so when France announced plans for the building of a massive four-block nuclear power plant in the town of Fessenheim, the co-ordination and organisation between initiatives and movements in the region continued. The resistance against Fessenheim halted the construction of two of the blocks but could not stop the other two. However, tactics and approaches were shared in the resistance and the cross-border movement grew. In summer 1974, transnational grassroots initiatives occupied the building site of a chemical plant on the French side of the Rhine, which was subsequently stopped as well. In the winter of 1974 and 1975, a nuclear power plant on the German side, near the town of Wyhl, received planning permission and in February 1975 transnational initiatives occupied the building site of this plant. A few days after a first eviction, a large demonstration of

30,000 people led to a new occupation of the building site. This time it lasted for eight months, and the occupiers left only on the basis of a 'peace agreement' between them and the state government of the German region. The peace agreement included concessions from the state government to stop building and to reopen the planning process in exchange for the ending of the occupation.

The second occupation of Wyhl was the largest and longest instance of this new emerging tactic of using the protest camp as a form of direct action. Although not initially intended as a protest camp, the contours of modern protest camping emerged distinctively. Participants recalled the 'spontaneous architecture' of the occupation, where infrastructures such as fireplaces, windbreaks and roofs were built as needed (Mossmann quoted in Baer and Dellwo 2012: 27). A 'friendship house', made in the form of a Sami yurt, was built in the centre of the occupation to house protesters and to accommodate meetings and social activities. A kitchen shed, next to the friendship house, was also built, as was the 'Volkshochschule Wyhler Wald', a 'people's university' that housed presentations and talks on nuclear power and alternative energy, among other themes.

In terms of governance, it is important to note that the political strategy of the movements against Wyhl was co-ordinated by a coalition of grassroots groups based in the surrounding villages. Political and strategic discussions did not take place centrally on the occupied building site. This external infrastructure also influenced the governance and organisation of the camp. At the occupation encampment, no infrastructures of formal decision-making were put in place; there were no plenary meetings or assemblies. Two different groups contributed to the running of the occupation. First, there were the occupiers who lived on the site. Many of the occupiers were students and the majority of them came from the neighbouring city of Freiburg. The attendance of occupiers was generally fluid, with many people coming only for weekends and smaller numbers taking up permanent residence.

Second, there were the residents of neighbouring villages who did not stay at the camp, but visited regularly and provided food, wood and other supplies needed to sustain the camp. This dual structure effectively meant that the running of the camp was based on an informal agreement between locals and occupiers. The latter were invited to stay on site to protect the occupation in exchange for the provision of food and other supplies from the neighbouring villages. The occupation was therefore a highly instrumental element in preventing the nuclear power plant but had little aspiration, as a social space, to become a place of alternative governance or decision-making. Wyhl, while it was not originally planned as a protest camp, unlike Resurrection City, and therefore did not have its infrastructures planned to the same extent, did develop into one.

Despite Wyhl having separate spaces of governance (off-site) and occupation (on-site), organic horizontality emerged in the encampment. As a consequence, this led to a number of significant results that impacted on the strategy and tactics of the growing anti-nuclear resistance movement. The occupation, as a convergence space, enabled encounters between local farmers and conservationists, as well as communist and environmentalist students and middle-class professionals from the cities. As such, it spatially represented and embodied a potential organisational structure for the developing Green movement. In order to bridge differences in ideology, participatory approaches to democratic debate were needed to facilitate the formation of these emerging coalitions. The participatory approach of the grassroots initiatives dated back to the time before the occupation. However, the occupation created a semi-permanent example showing that these processes could work not just to organise action, but to organise collective life more generally. In this way Wyhl enabled the experience of partial organisation through spatial practice that allowed social movements made up of diverse participants to pursue a successful campaign together. After a long row of legal battles and a series of reoccupations, the state finally abandoned plans for the Wyhl power plant in 1984. The early occupations were key to this success, both in physically preventing the building and in enhancing the partial organisation of the grassroots initiatives.

After the experiences of Wyhl, politicians in France and Germany realised the potential of this new strategy and focused on preventing any further occupations with brute force, as we discussed in the previous chapter. Importantly, by blocking people from living together on the building site, the state managed to prevent participants from diverse backgrounds and political convictions overcoming splits and building trust. In the meantime, the cross-continental inspiration behind certain types of action and, in particular, new tactics led to the diffusion of site occupations as a means of protest in the US.

The development of formalised consensus decision-making

In 1977, the Clamshell Alliance mobilised for a 2,000-strong occupation of the building site of the planned Seabrook nuclear power plant in New Hampshire. This occupation (as well as two smaller occupations preceding it) was inspired by the actions in Wyhl in 1975. While the occupation was evicted quickly, there was a subsequent collective imprisonment of over 1,500 of the occupiers over a period of two weeks. The imprisoned had decided to refuse their bail conditions and were then kept in National Guard armouries in New Hampshire (Downey 1986). During this time, the imprisoned protesters successfully self-organised their defence, and the governor, frustrated by a unified front of prisoners, decided to release all of them, dropping all charges.

While there are conflicting views about the protesters' actions in the armouries – some attributed the governor's frustration not so much to the advanced negotiation tactics of the protesters as to the prevailing chaos of the mass incarceration – doubtless the events sparked broad enthusiasm in radical movements in the US and a heightened interest in the ways in which the Clamshell Alliance had managed to create what some saw as the 'incredible clamshell solidarity' (ibid.: 361). This solidarity was based on a newly developed form of decision-making. Drawn from methods used by anarchist self-organised collectives in Spain in the 1930s and by the independence struggle in India, the Clamshell Alliance, together with activists from the Movement for a New Society (MNS), had developed a formalised version of consensus HDM to enable larger groups to operate within the realm of 'power with' (Cornell 2011; Downey 1986). According to Cornell (ibid.), the MNS and the Clamshell Alliance had combined three distinct elements of organising: affinity groups, spokescouncils and consensus process.

Affinity groups are small units of activists, effectively mirroring, in organisational terms, a group of friends, as discussed earlier. In an affinity group, decision-making is based on organic horizontality and consensus is the condition of every decision. As in our group of friends, if one participant strongly opposed going to a particular restaurant, the whole group probably would not go there. In the consensus process the attempt is to operate with a large number of affinity groups to come to widely shared and accepted decisions. Therefore, the spokescouncil is introduced.

In the spokescouncil, delegates from each affinity group meet and report the decisions and interests of their respective group. Delegates from the affinity groups deliberate until there is a consensus, enabling the search for a consensual decision among all participants. With the development of HDM, the Clamshell Alliance and the MNS had developed a model of decision-making that mirrored organic horizontality but enabled it to work in large groups over time. Across the US and Canada, people were keen to learn the method. The MNS developed handbooks and gave training courses, arguably playing a central role in the diffusion of HDM across the US, as Cornell describes: 'After Seabrook, MNS trainers travelled throughout the country training anti-nuke organisations in consensus and the spokes council model that had worked so well in New Hampshire' (Cornell 2011: 37f).

The MNS set out proposals to formalise and put into practice certain procedures for organising their collectives democratically. These procedures were aimed not simply at enabling large-scale direct action, such as occupations, but more broadly at building 'counter-institutions' to facilitate radical challenges to the political status quo in the US. In many ways it was a pragmatic intervention, allowing for the creation of a wide range of left-wing alternative structures beyond event-oriented and exceptional activism and protest, to include housing, childcare, work and education-related institutions. These terrains offered themselves as laboratories for new modes of social reproduction, as well as practical solutions to the needs of the members of the group. Rather than working in jobs 'in the system', labour could be increasingly de-commodified, waged labour replaced and more time spent on leisure and political activism (ibid.).

Cornell and his interviewees argued that the MNS was resolutely opposed to what they saw as 'alternative institutions' such as communes, organic food stores and alternative schools, which tended to be incorporated within a new consumer lifestyle. Consequently, the MNS was explicit in its desire *not* to be a commune or to partake in 'lifestyle anarchism'. Rather it believed in the need to develop 'counter-institutions' to organise political resistance against existing societal institutions. In line with this perspective, the MNS never viewed HDM as simply a way to reach decisions, but instead saw it as a situation-specific, pragmatic approach to certain problems of collective organisation (ibid.). Indeed, some members of the MNS itself retrospectively criticised the fetishisation of HDM that – they claimed – played a significant role in the demise of the group.

Consensus and HDM seemed to be highly practical solutions during the earlier processes of group formation, when the MNS participants developed their ideas and concepts. At a later stage, when the group had reached a national level of organising, HDM became increasingly limiting. As the origin and the contested practice of HDM in the MNS indicate, HDM is best understood as a situated practice that poses as many questions as it answers. Considering our earlier reflections, it is intriguing that Cornell and others who have reflected on the formalisation of HDM in the US anti-nuclear movement did not consider the spatially and temporally limited experience of occupations in their evaluation of HDM. Arguably, the experiences of living in a de facto prison camp with 1,500 people for two weeks led to the successful training of activists in these forms of collective governance. This success facilitated the adaptation of HDM in social movements in the US in the years following, often outside the context of spatially and temporally limited spaces. Attempts to reproduce organic horizontality in partial organisation by using HDM, for example by providing training and writing handbooks, led to a number of problems, namely the abstraction of the process as a model for all situations and contexts. But, interestingly, in the 1980s protest campers in the UK succeeded in re-creating organic horizontality, not through procedure but through spatial practice and architecture.

Horizontality without formal horizontal decision-making

We discussed earlier that organic horizontality in political contexts often comes with antagonism. The case of the Argentinian uprising in 2001 served as an example of how people organised their neighbourhoods horizontally after the total breakdown of trust in the existing institutions and on the basis of a radical antagonism against the ruling elites. Political collectives and heterogeneous coalitions are often enabled or enhanced by a clear antagonism, a shared opposition. Putting their differences aside, fighting a shared enemy or focusing on a shared target helps overcome problems of governance and organisation. The women protesters of Greenham Common shared their rejection of the military and of the use of nuclear weapons. But the antagonism on which Greenham was based went further than that, for the military was considered an expression, and perhaps a particularly poignant one, of what was wrong more generally with the political and social status quo. The protesters considered the military as the

4.2 The first Climate Camp in summer 2006 in Yorkshire – antagonistically against the status quo

pinnacle of patriarchy, and, in the camp – a women's camp for most of its existence – an alternative was created. The camp space offered itself as a place in which to form this alternative; even though it was not intentionally planned in such a way, the camp therefore resulted from a bordering practice that created it as an alternative world, standing in opposition to its surroundings. We call this 'antagonistic spatial practice', and, as we will show, this encompassed a range of practical and architectural arrangements that facilitated a governance structure based on 'power with', yet without the need to resort to procedures such as HDM.

At Greenham, the antagonism was not simply a matter of shared opposition but affected the creation of the distinct space of the camp. In this sense, the effect of the shared antagonism was stronger than in other antagonistic settings; indeed, its impact was not simply on the easing of negotiations between divergent groups. Rather, it enabled protesters to 'step' into the antagonism, to tangibly feel it. As a result, organic horizontality could be maintained among a large number of women without formal systems. In comparison to the procedures of HDM in the US, which by this time were highly formalised, the women in Greenham were 'unorganised' and processes of decision-making emerged casually and accidentally, rather like the camp itself.

For Starhawk (1987), who came to the camp with her US experience, the 'informality' of decision-making at Greenham Common caused something of a shock:

> For me, participating in decision-making with the Greenham Common women brought culture shock. In contrast to our West Coast [US] style of consensus, involving facilitators, agendas, plans, and formal processes, their meetings seemed to have no structure at all. No one facilitated, no agendas were set; everyone spoke whenever she wanted to and said what she thought. Where we valued plans and scenarios, they valued spontaneity, trusting in the energy of the group and the moment. Instead of long discussions about the pros and cons of any given plan, those women who wanted to do it simply went ahead, and those who didn't, did not participate.

The 'shock' expressed by Starhawk reinforces the point that governance systems and structures differ from camp to camp, even within similar movements. This raises questions about how and why infrastructures of governance travel internationally, sometimes repeating their form (or formality) and sometimes taking on new forms.

In Greenham, the use of spatial practice to deal with issues of organisation and governance did not merely consist of the antagonistic positioning of the camp to the outside. Internally, Greenham also resolved issues of organisation and governance through spatial practice. As Roseneil (1995) reports, Greenham was characterised by its diversity; women from a variety of political, class and cultural backgrounds took part. This diversity was reflected in a specific way in the structure of Greenham Common, as we detailed in Chapter 1. Greenham Common consisted of a large range of interdependent encampments at the different 'coloured' gates of the airbase. The different camps, at the different gated entrances surrounding the base, had very distinct characters, as could be seen in their outlooks on action, decision-making and cultural preferences.

Perhaps it was, in part, the affinity shared by those in the different camps that meant there was less of a need to have formal decision-making procedures involving the whole camp. Having multiple campsites allowed for small groups with highly specific preferences to coexist within a broader coalition structure. Roseneil argues that 'the establishment of a number of gates served to create physical and discursive space for the management of differences between women at Greenham', which strengthened the camp. Yet, at the same time, it 'opened up lines of fracture within the camp, above all between Yellow Gate and the rest of the camp' (ibid.: 82). Despite these adverse effects, Greenham endorsed the principle of decentralisation; this is central to anarchist political theory, because it enables horizontal decision-making in large groups (Bookchin 1995). At Greenham Common, this was developed into a spatial strategy that, we would argue, served at least in part as an inspiration for the specific neighbourhood structures we find in many of the British protest camps emerging after the 1980s.

Greenham's success inspired women across the world to adopt the protest form of the camp, and protest camps sprung up across six continents in reaction. In Seneca Falls in 1983, 150 women started a protest camp near a US airbase; the camp lasted for nine years. The organisation differed greatly from Greenham Common, both in the approach to the land used for the camp and in the decision-making procedures put in place. In Seneca Falls, the land used for the camp was purchased by camp organisers. Moreover, paid activists lived in the camp and were the cornerstone of the maintenance of the infrastructures (Costello and Stanley 1985). Other women participants joined for larger actions following mobilisations and organised themselves in the camp in an affinity group structure. The consensus decision-making system developed by the MNS was usually the preferred method of operation in such camps.

The mixture of formal procedures of decision-making with spatial practice is reflected in the West German Hunsrück women's peace camp. Founded in 1983, the camp took place annually in the summer for nine years. The first one was planned one year in advance in a series of meetings by a variety of loosely connected women's groups, including affinity groups in larger German cities. While the Hunsrück camps were inspired by Greenham, some Hunsrück organisers had been to the Seneca Falls camp and the organisational model adopted at Hunsrück can be seen to closely follow the US procedural forms of HDM.

Protest camps are spaces in which to explore forms and models of governance. As such, the Hunsrück women experimented with these different inspirations and – over the course of the first two camps – developed a model that effectively combined elements of procedural HDM with a conscious use of spatial practice to enhance

4.3 A map illustrating decentralisation – different neighbourhoods in the 2008 Climate Camp in Kingsnorth

those elements. Leidinger (2011: 292), in an insightful account of the camp, explained:

> In the Hunsrück, collective relationships based on trust did initially only exist among those women who came from city-based affinity groups. Institutional arrangements were needed to ensure adherence to decisions; and that the structural arrangements and

obligations were trusted. Beyond those mentioned in the handbook, there were other organisation principles that were at work in the Hunsrück camps: the consensus principle, the block (veto), the structure of affinity groups (first based on city affinity groups and later organised territorially around kitchen tents) and, from 1984, decentralised decision-making on action forms and the spokes-council system [our translation].

Both a description and an interpretation, Leidinger's insight offers a record of the use of guidebooks in the protest camps; these were used to explain the camp's governance process to newcomers. Also of note is the deliberate use of territorial sub-units, organised around kitchen tents.

As at Greenham Common, decision-making was decentralised around smaller units, but rather than emerging from the specific geography of the contested site (as in Greenham with its many gates), here the organisation into subgroups was deliberate and part of the overall governance infrastructures. As Leidinger argues:

> The procedures of discussion commonly developed or chosen
> ... helped ameliorate well-known problems and conflicts in the
> women's movement: not to listen to the other person, knee-jerk
> reactions, verbal attacks and fights. These procedures brought
> 'moderation' into tense situations and enabled more constructive
> debate [our translation] (ibid.: 296).

Beyond these procedural arrangements, Leidinger also interprets what we call organic horizontality with a particular and perceptive twist. Leidinger focuses especially on the physical proximity that allows and necessitates the development of relationships and the building of affective ties. In this regard, the camp is exceptional in that spatiality and temporality enable the women to develop an 'atmosphere of eroticism'. The erotic, not understood sexually but rather as an intensity between women, was an important aspect of the emerging feminist circles of the 1970s and 1980s, and the atmosphere of cohabitation in the camps is described and remembered explicitly as erotic in this sense (ibid.). Roseneil (2000) also deals with similar themes, looking at how Greenham embraced messiness and diversity.

With this account, we can see a combination of factors that explains the role of protest camps in the development of new forms of governance and organisation. Beyond their part in the development of procedural forms of HDM, protest camps allow for horizontal governance as spatial practice. This is firstly because camps enable the development and strengthening of affective ties and become places where relationships can be built. Secondly, antagonistic spatial practice enables the camp participants to enter a zone of antagonism and difference in which their diversity is respected. Thirdly, the spatial practice of decentralisation inside the camp is developed as an additional element of partial organisation.

Spaces of experimentation

In the diversity of protest camps that has occurred over the past 45 years, protesters have often reinvented these infrastructures and practices, using some of them but not others, and adapting existing organisational forms to the specific contexts in which their encampments have emerged. In the remainder of this chapter we try to tease out the dynamic relationship that exists between spatial and procedural practices of governance. Not only does this help to explain some of the successes and setbacks of specific camps, it provides a more general understanding of the crucial role protest camps have played in the development of governance in social movement activism.

We discussed earlier the limits of procedural attempts to copy organic horizontality, as exemplified in what MNS activists called the fetishisation of HDM. By 'fetishisation', they referred to the use of HDM regardless of context and as a blueprint for better, more advanced organisation and governance. Unsurprisingly, antagonistic spatial practice also has its limits. Where protest camps base their horizontality on a clear-cut antagonism to the outside, their organisation will depend less on formal procedures. To this extent, the women in Greenham Common did not need to use HDM. Likewise, the protest camps erected in revolutionary contexts, for example in Tahrir Square in Cairo in 2011, were based on antagonistic spatial practice, the revolutionary demand of system change that united their diverse supporters despite their differences and enabled shared political action. The procedural infrastructures of horizontality were not needed to achieve a level of organisation that respected the diversity of heterogeneous groups joining the camp. Activists created the antagonism, which, in turn, developed into a protest camp.

In a very different political context, at the 2005 Gleneagles G8

Summit and the anti-G8 protests built around the HoriZone protest camp, the antagonism of the camp proved to be a limiting factor. While to some extent the result of external factors (the camp was in a field bordered by a river and penned in by police lines), the isolation of the camp was also due to a limited ability to open the antagonistic spatial practice of the camp (that is, a representation of the political rejection of the G8 as a body of global governance) to more moderate but potentially sympathetic social movements, unions and media (Turbulence 2007). Similarly, smaller camps often show a certain level of isolation from the outside, as has been the case with some of the longer-term land occupations in Britain, in particular following on from the anti-roads movement in the 1990s. Some long-term camps have led to the formation of distinct 'activists' identities' with dress codes, music and dietary styles. This is a problem that extends beyond the context of protest camps (Chatterton 2006) but is amplified in some examples of antagonistic spatial practice in protest camps when the dichotomy between the inside and the outside becomes excessively pronounced. Politically, such a fixation on identity makes it easy for opponents to discount protest movements as 'merely cultural', outsiders, marginal. In the context of the described dynamics between spatial and procedural practice, it is highly significant that forms of organic horizontality in camps based on antagonistic spatial practice tend to produce more strongly those hidden power structures and elites that threaten the democratic ideal of 'power with' (Gordon 2010). This is particularly concerning in cases where gendered power relations come to the fore when 'fighter' subjectivities are created that replicate militarist and often male-coded notions of struggle, undermining the ecology of action we described earlier.

Antagonistic spatial practice is therefore a delicate matter and needs to be carefully employed; we discuss instances of violence that occur within camps in relation to this problem in the next chapter. However, we would argue that antagonism itself is central, as is perhaps underlined by the experience of protest camps where the shared antagonism perishes. A prominent example of such an occurrence, in our view, might explain why the British Camp for Climate Action, organised every year from 2006 to 2010, decided not to pursue national mobilisations for a Climate Camp after 2010. One key problem here, as others have pointed out, might be Climate Campers' increasing loss of a shared antagonism (see Saunders 2012), as well as perhaps an overt focus, resulting from this lack of a clear antagonism, on common-sense politics, on applying scientific rationalism as political ideology (Schlembach et al. 2012). Without an antagonism, the space of the camp in some ways may have appeared to simply mirror the status quo as a place of political debate that happened to be in a field surrounded by police. Openness and horizontality in the Climate Camps looked increasingly like a liberal space of deliberation, akin to a coffee house or a salon.

Without antagonism, protest camps lose their raison d'être to some extent. In contrast, procedural forms of HDM do not seem to be a necessary component of a protest camp. Instead, as we see in the next chapter, protest camps may address the limits of procedural notions of governance, understood as a differentiated level of management and organisation, through antagonistic spatial practice.

However, antagonism comes in different shapes and forms: for example, Occupy Wall Street perhaps contrasts with Climate Camps, and also with Tahrir Square or the Argentinian uprising of 2001. Occupy started off with a well-developed and inclusive antagonism, the 99 per cent (against the 1 per cent of the population that effectively controlled the political system). But despite being inspired by the Tahrir Square protests in Egypt, the Occupy movement was never based on a clear antagonism in the same way as Tahrir. For Occupy, there was no common cry that 'They all must go!'; there was never 'one demand'. And while Occupy's choice of location – Wall Street – symbolically indicated the contestation of concentrated domestic and global financial power, Occupy did not amass the numbers or collective will to significantly block or interrupt the workings of the financial industry. Instead, the Zuccotti Park Occupy camp was open to a broad range of people with various grievances, financial and otherwise. In fact, Occupy deliberately rejected any specific demand in the name of openness and inclusivity. To aggregate power as 'power with' in partial organisation, Occupy Wall Street therefore still employed largely procedural modes of organisation. It is therefore not surprising how widely the procedural forms of HDM that Occupy employed to reach partial organisation have been reported in mainstream media outlets.

Despite the sarcastic scorn that it received from hostile reporters and commentators, HDM was badly needed, because the 99 per cent were not willing to unite over a cry of resistance, a notion of immediate exodus or revolution that could have, for example, demanded that the American president step down. In order to allow the greatest openness, HDM was supposed to produce horizontality as partial organisation where relatively little organic horizontality could emerge from such a clear demand or antagonism. In our view, this explains the visibility of HDM within the Occupy movement. It has been argued that Occupy fetishised the procedural approach through its deployment of HDM as a blueprint of better organisation, independent of the specific context and situation (see N+1 2011). And, indeed, this constitutes a serious limitation to any attempts at producing partial organisation, as the founders of the first widely shared blueprint of HDM had already experienced in the 1980s (Cornell 2011). But, for us, what remains impressive about Occupy is the vivid attempt to organise horizontally on an unprecedented scale – and, considering the scale, with unprecedented success.

Conclusion

This chapter has discussed governance and organisation infrastructures in protest camps to show how camps have played a crucial role in the development of forms of (partial) organisation that operate on the basis of 'power with' in many social movements over the last 40 years. They allowed social movements to organise their networks in order to aggregate political demands beyond local contexts, without needing to resort to full organisation and the implicit structures of domination that full organisation brings. Protest camps therefore constitute an important and largely overlooked laboratory of prefigurative politics. In particular, the development of procedural forms of HDM has been strongly influenced by the experiences of anti-nuclear occupations in the 1970s.

Protest camps fulfil this role because they have a propensity to produce organic horizontality. In spatially and temporally confined collectives, affective ties may grow between participants, lessening the need to connect people through abstract organisation. But politically inspired protest camps play a special role here because they translate political ambitions for a better, more democratic social order into spatial practice. This is illustrated by a variety of protest camps that operate without HDM and yet induce the questioning of the political status quo. Spatial practice to reach partial organisation in protest camps consists of an antagonism that is expressed in the camp as a tangible experience, an oppositional position (and a show of opposition) you can walk into (and out of) – an antagonism, therefore, that is constituted without always needing to resort to formal organisation. In some protest camps, organisation and governance may operate without procedural HDM and yet express the ambitions of diverse groups of participants; they can become partially organised without having to resort to 'power over', although this seems to be limited to the initial stages of their existence.

Beyond antagonism, protest camps can also use spatial practice to organise partially by design. The construction of neighbourhoods and barrios in some protest camps since at least the 1980s is a conscious attempt to implement decentralisation within a framework of partial organisation. Understanding spatial practices therefore requires an approach that is conscious of the camp's design and evolution. There is a variety of factors that may influence the spatial practices of a camp, for example the ability to plan a camp in advance. This may influence governance procedures as well as the accumulation and use of available resources (individuals, skills, material, legalities, terrain). Of interest for future work, then, are differences in the spatial practices between protest camps planned in advance and those that are more spontaneous. Another important factor influencing spatial practices is the duration of the camp, not least because – as we have pointed out – governance structures may emerge and develop in a protest camp over time. Moreover, authorities may react differently to camps that are (or present themselves as being) temporary in nature compared with those that embed themselves for the long haul. Related to this, we must not assume that the spatial practices of protest camps are static, but rather we should commit to studying them over time and paying particular attention to how specific governance decisions or incidents such as police raids or threats may alter these practices.

In this chapter we also showed that procedural and spatial practices of achieving partial organisation in protest camps relate to each other, and produce a dynamic that allows us to discuss individual camps in various political and cultural contexts. This enables protest camps to become spaces in which organisation and governance are experimented with. It also means that every protest camp is unique, even if they are informed by past movements, actions or camps. Whenever blueprints are drawn from the experience of one camp and carried forward to the next one, they are also transformed and adapted to the specific cultural, political and environmental context and to the unique history of activism. We showed how this applies to both procedural and spatial practices.

In the next chapter, we look more closely at antagonistic spatial practices in the context of re-creation. Protest camps seem to aspire to re-create alternative worlds, claiming autonomy from the existing world, but at the same time they are entangled in and limited by it.

5 | RE-CREATION INFRASTRUCTURES

I am arriving at the border of the camp, and there is a wall of police. Officers overlook as prospective camp participants have to open their bags, kneeling, forced to unpack their private belongings. An intelligence police team is filming, some legal observer is trying to give the police a hard time. It makes me angry to see how the police indulge in what feels like an intended humiliation, like the real purpose of this procedure, being inflicted upon my fellow protesters. Opening your bags, searching wallets, pockets and purses, asking intrusive questions, all in the name of security. While I am waiting to take my turn, memories come up: border checks on the way to Berlin, east German border police searching cars, keeping us waiting, showing their strength. Entering this protest camp feels like crossing an international border. But it is not only the police with their check point that cause this impression. Once I am through the lines, on the other side, there is a welcome space, staffed with volunteers. Our side of the border. I am greeted warmly, there is a map with the neighbourhoods, a booklet that contains basic information about the camp, its programme, the way it's run, where the toilets are, what is expected of me. I am in friendly, familiar territory. It's the climate camp Kingsnorth and I have crossed the line. (Kingsnorth Climate Camp, Kent, 2008)

Introduction

This chapter is about infrastructures of re-creation in protest camps. In the most general sense, re-creational infrastructures are in place to shelter, feed and protect campers. The infrastructures we listed as re-creational in Chapter 1 include tents, mobile kitchens, toilets, border markers or defences, as well as childcare, facilities that cater for the disabled and other spaces and structures for well-being. Some of these infrastructures are shared between protest camps and other kinds of camps, for example refugee, military or Scout camps. Re-creational infrastructures point to camps as forms of temporal architecture with diverse global histories, ranging from the hunter-gatherer origins of humanity to contemporary music festivals; from old to more recent nomadic cultures and people on the move. In this chapter we shift from delineating these infrastructures to raising questions about the wider processes and practices at stake in creating and operating a protest camp as a site of re-creation. The central argument we make is that protesters animate these infrastructures with their struggle and labour, moving them beyond merely functional facilities to enable protest as an expression of autonomy vis-à-vis the status quo.

Re-creational infrastructures create the camp as a 'world', a micro-city or micro-village, a sociality on its own. As in the example above, the protest camp is often separated, in some marked way, from the outside. Autonomy is a contested feature of this 'world', but not in the individual sense we discussed in the previous chapter (individual autonomy in the collective), but rather in the sense of autonomy of the protest campers' collectivity in relation to the status quo. In earlier writing about protest camps we have called these infrastructures 'domestic' (Frenzel, Feigenbaum and McCurdy forthcoming) to indicate how their functions are related to 'home-making'. But to call these infrastructures 'domestic' is problematic in two ways. Firstly, the association with the domestic sphere of the house evokes a history of gendered relations. The domestic sphere and its infrastructures are read as concerning women and as being private (and hence non-political). But the 'home' the camp creates is not a private home. As we have discussed in Chapter 1, the 'homeplace' of the protest camp is a community of resistance, and a site through which both social movement politics and the politics of everyday life are exposed. This 'home', in the sense of the Greek notion of '*oikos*' (which forms the linguistic root of the term 'economy'), is a socio-economic sphere of social reproduction. In this sense, re-creational infrastructures constitute the 'political economy' of the protest camp. Seeing the home as a socio-economic sphere allows us to ask questions about how labour and struggle are socially reproduced at campsites, which we do at length at the end of this chapter.

Secondly, protest camps often share the infrastructures discussed in this chapter with other camps; however, in protest camps different meanings are given to their function, and, at times, different strategies are used to animate them. The protest camp is never merely a camp of necessity (i.e. for disaster relief) or a camp of leisure (i.e. a tourist camp). Rather, in the case of protest camps, re-creational infrastructures are employed in ways that signify a break from the

5.1 Education is a central area of social reproduction pursued in protest camps

norms of the everyday, in ways that point beyond it. Unlike an exclusively needs-based camp or a purely recreational campsite, a protest camp's re-creational infrastructures are established and enacted explicitly as politics. They are built as political expression, to expose existing systems as deficient, 'broken' or 'in crisis'. In some instances, particularly those of a refugee camp turned protest camp, a homeless tent city turned protest camp, or, from a different angle, an eco-village poised against over-consumption and land waste, the camp itself highlights the inability of existing systems of social reproduction to care sufficiently for people. The protest camp often re-creates the world when the outside is considered unable to adequately provide (Resurrection City) or acknowledge the pre-existence of (Aboriginal Tent Embassy) a socio-economic 'home'. In other cases, such as No TAV or the Shell to Sea Rossport Solidarity Camp, re-creation is a strategy both for maintaining well-being and care for those engaged in these ongoing protests, and for amplifying the voice of the land with which people's livelihoods are intertwined.

For us, the 're-' of re-creation signifies the political relationship between the alternative world of the camp and its surroundings. Of course, such a break of the routine of going along with the status quo may also be pursued through other protest strategies, for example by a demonstration or a strike. But a key feature of the protest camp is that it attempts (at least temporarily) to replace the basic workings of the status quo through acts of re-creation. Unlike the demonstration, march or ongoing strike, the site of social reproduction of a protest camp is largely the site of the protest itself. This place-based shift in the site of politics, as we discussed in relation to 'media stages', exposes the activist life of the camp. The inner workings of the camp's political economy become highly visible and often highly contested. In addition, as contact zones of violence and vulnerability, protest camps are places of ongoing affective intensity and bodily care. This makes questions of territoriality (bordering, inclusion, 'membership') and of social reproduction (divisions of labour, care work, security) a unique challenge that protest campers often attempt to engage in opposition to the cultural norms and practices of the status quo.

This chapter looks at the ways protest campers employ, understand and render political their re-creational infrastructures in spatial and reproductive, bio-political practices. It examines how protest campers relate to their 'outside', and how they often claim autonomy from it. We are not suggesting that all protest camps do this explicitly or intentionally, and we have chosen to highlight those camps in which a politics of autonomy is clearly articulated in contrast to the status quo. We approach this discussion from the notion of the '(im)possibility of autonomy' (Böhm et al. 2010), an issue that has gained increasing attention in social movement studies. As Böhm et al. (ibid.) have claimed, social movements seek autonomy in at least three domains: autonomy from the state, from capital, and, in the case of the global South, from development as defined in neo-liberal terms. Autonomy, however, as Böhm et al. (ibid.) point out, is not easily achieved. In all three domains, discourses and practices associated with autonomy are integrated into the workings of the status quo. They conclude that autonomy cannot be understood in absolute terms, but that its configuration depends on a set of specific conditions in which the demand for autonomy becomes possible or impossible. We find it significant that social movements' increasing focus on autonomy and autonomous politics coincides with an increasing visibility of protest camps as an organisational form.

In this chapter we show that protest camps are an ideal place to study the (im)possibilities of autonomy that social movements seek in practice. This is largely because protest camps' claims to autonomy are contentious and provisional. As we argue, protest camps may present themselves as autonomous political entities and often signify this idea in their names. However, the autonomy of the protest camp is always limited and contested, and protest campers are often involved in struggles to substantiate their claims to autonomy. For those movements in which camping is embedded in countercultural politics and identities, it can be asked to what extent some protest camps differ from the music festivals with which they can be compared. If they are 'merely cultural' (Butler 1998), they might be seen as fully integrated into the workings of the status quo. Their autonomy, therefore, would be an illusion, ultimately in support of the political status quo. What makes the alternative world of these protest camps different from a festival, from a holiday camp or from a rainbow gathering?

For other protest camps, where actions often extend far out into the streets and existing infrastructures of the city, the camp itself can fade into the background. It can be overlooked as an insignificant element of support work. It can be perceived as being there simply to refuel the movement, a rest stop on the highway to change. In these cases, the camp is not seen as the revolution or uprising – this belongs to the demonstrations, marchers, political meetings or street fights taking place. The questions to ask here are the following: how are the re-creational infrastructures and practices of the camp bound up in the production of alternatives, of other possible worlds? What is the relationship between the uprising and the attempt to reproduce, but in a different way, socio-economic life and sociality?

The chapter starts off with a discussion of the development of re-creational infrastructures in the diverse history of the formation of the camp as a temporary, nomadic architecture. The analysis of re-creational infrastructures in relation to ideas of nomadic life and its hybrid practices, transversal meaning and cross-cultural genealogies helps us point out common features of the global spread of protest camps. Exceptionality and its political role are discussed next. Penal and tourist camps have both been described as 'exceptional spaces' with important political implications. Theories of exceptionality have emerged to discuss these two types of camp but have rarely considered protest camps in relation to notions of exceptionality. Secondly, we use this chapter to discuss how protest campers render re-creational infrastructures into claims of and for autonomy.

We pick up the notion of spatial practice from the last chapter and discuss and analyse protest camps' use of bordering infrastructures and soundscapes to mark their territories, and how contentious claims to autonomy and its limits arise in these practices. We then look at issues relating to the social reproduction of the camp, both politically and economically. As in the previous chapters, throughout our argument we discuss why we think that looking from the vantage point of protest camps may change our perspectives and understandings of social movement politics. Here, we are interested in particular in the limits of performed or prefigurative autonomy, as well as the politics of the commons and re-creational politics.

Nomadology

As discussed in the introduction, we owe the word 'camp' to the temporary housing of Roman armies in the 'field', the Latin translation of field being '*campus*'. From here, the word developed a range of meanings in various contexts in European history. However, while the etymological roots of the word 'camp' point to a European history, looking at the infrastructures of re-creation opens up a broader view. The re-creational infrastructures of the camp relate to a diverse set of global histories, with frequent cross-cultural transformations. The tent is perhaps the most universal example, bridging cultures and contexts, often in contrast to the stable, permanent and localised architecture of the house (Cowan 2002). The relationship between the tent and the house is mirrored by the relationship between the camp and the city, and, more generally, between nomadic and sedentary cultures and people. These aligned binaries are subject to a range of sociological and philosophical discussions stretching back to the considerations of Ibn Khaldoun, a sociologist of fourteenth-century north Africa.

Ibn Khaldoun developed a theory of transmutation of nomadic and settled cultures that moved beyond the binary nomadic/settled. For him, this relationship was not one of essential cultural difference. What is pertinent to the study of protest camps is that Ibn Khaldoun charted the relationship between nomads and city-dwellers as a political relationship. He argued that, historically, nomadic societies progress to urban societies. However, when they become urbanised, the former nomads lose their social cohesion or solidarity (*abasiya* in Arabic) and weaken. Eventually, urban civilisations are bound to collapse under the assault of new nomads, who are still in possession of their *abasiya* and therefore stronger than the urbanites. It is important to note that Ibn Khaldoun does not refer to 'nomads' in an essentialist sense. *Abasiya* results, rather, from an organisational logic in which there are no permanent social hierarchies. Leadership is of a charismatic nature, and organisation transient and, at best, partial. The concept of *abasiya* resembles the notion of 'organic horizontality' we discussed in the previous chapter. In Ibn Khaldoun we find a political reading of the relationship between nomads and settled peoples, between camp and city, between tent and house.

The political reading of the use of re-creational infrastructures such as the tent that we find in protest camps might therefore be substantiated by a much older history, as described in Ibn Khaldoun's nomadology. This is certainly what Cowan (ibid.: 108) suggests in his consideration of the Aboriginal Tent Embassy in Canberra, Australia:

> In the Western world of the late twentieth century, tents and
> collapsible architectures have also become familiar features in
> the context of protests and demonstrations, increasing with the
> global activism of the 1960s ... The connection between these ways
> of employing tents in the West, and the vernacular uses of tents
> by nomads, is not a coincidence, but rather that each relates to
> architecturally significant features of the tent (ibid.: 109).

These 'architecturally significant features' of the tent are, according to Cowan, its indeterminate, mobile, temporary and rapidly deployable nature. He adds with regard to protest camps: 'The tent is a choice of architectural strategy which is not merely pragmatic. Ideological reasons also underpin the uses of these kinds of structure, contributing to their significance as architecture' (ibid.: 109).

In this most basic sense, the protest camp uses re-creational infra-structures to challenge the existing order. Perhaps it is not surprising, in this respect, to find evidence for an early Roman 'protest camp', a practice of commoners leaving the city and camping outside, called the 'secession of the plebs'. The protesters threatened permanent withdrawal from the city state to negotiate more favourable terms of social distribution with the Roman aristocrats (Graeber 2011: 230). Graeber understands this as a middle strategy between two existing ways of protesting in antiquity: revolts in Greece and mass exodus in Egypt and Mesopotamia.

Questions arise over how nomadic practices become protest. What, for example, is the relationship between Ibn Khaldoun's 'nomads' and the concept of 'new nomads' in Hardt and Negri's *Empire*, a concept that has often been mobilised in social movement literature and commentary over the past decade? Hardt and Negri write: 'A *new nomad horde*, a new race of barbarians, will arise to invade or evacuate the empire' (Hardt and Negri 2000: 213). Hardt and Negri draw from Deleuze and Guattari's philosophical nomadology, which is in some ways an extension of Ibn Khaldoun's. But Hardt and Negri argue against territorialising strategies of place-making, which they associate with nationalism. Hardt and Negri's nomads, it is reasonably safe to assume, are not building camps. Countering such rejections of localisation and place-making, in his study of Occupy LSX, Sam Halvorsen (2012) argues that the protest camp uses territorial strategies to ground its politics in place, to delineate control over a specific area, and to exert influence through the taking and holding of space. 'In opposition to Hardt and Negri's "multitude"', the protest camp 'uses fixity and territory as a weapon' (ibid.: 431; see also Invisible Committee 2009).

In line with Halvorsen, we see protest camps as arising from inside the global capitalist system, yet their acts of re-creation occur in a deeply territorial way. The aspiration, then, to build a new place, to re-create home, emerges, in part, from the hegemony of settled architecture (Cowan 2002) as it embodies the structures of inequality and injustice, of the status quo. But how does the new place escape the limits of territoriality, the danger of re-creating the problems of the status quo? Protest camps attempt this through what we discuss as a 'politics of exceptionality'.

Theories of exceptionality

When reflecting on the re-creational infrastructures used to create protest camps, the politics of exceptionality need to be considered. What purpose and consequence does exceptional re-creation have? How do protest camps succeed in challenging the status quo, and when do they merely confirm or reproduce the status quo? We argue that analysing the use of re-creational infrastructures by protest campers may help shed more light on the theoretical debates outlined here and lead us to advance our understanding of the politics of exceptionality and the (im)possibilities of autonomy. Before doing this, we offer a brief overview of the theories surrounding exceptionality and camps.

While exceptionality has not been discussed much in relation to protest camps, many other kinds of camp, from countercultural festivals to tourist and penal camps, have been studied extensively with regard to their exceptionality and to its political role. In this section we look at how other types of camp have been thought of as 'spaces of exception' in order to ask where the protest camp might fit into these territorial understandings of political spaces of re-creation. A very influential political reading of camps as spaces of exception has focused on penal camps, following Agamben's (1998) theory of exceptionality. Considering that his empirical starting point is concentration camps, it is not surprising that exceptionality, for Agamben, illustrates primarily the autonomy of the sovereign state to ignore and violate human rights within its territory. Agamben's camp is a space where civil and human rights are systemically stripped from the inmates, who become *homo sacer*, naked, bare life. Pointing to the role of exceptionality beyond totalitarian regimes, Agamben alludes to the parallel between the 'bio politics of modern totalitarianism on the one hand, and mass society of consumerism and hedonism on the other', indicating that his notion of 'bare life' and the camp applies equally in the 'total meaninglessness of the society of the spectacle' (ibid.: 21).

Following on from this remark, Agamben's theory of exceptionality has been extended beyond penal camps. Diken and Laustsen (2005) use Agamben's notion of the camp to describe tourist enclaves in places such as the island of Ibiza in Spain. They see the exceptional space of the 'tourist camp' as politically highly problematic. On entering these places, tourists may feel that the normal rules of the status quo no longer apply. A sense of freedom and autonomy prevails, as people are encouraged into excessive celebrations and transgressions. Exceptionality is used to mark the liberation from the routine found in tourist enclaves as a delusion. Exceptional space has an anti-political role: 'In the holiday camp, the rules are suspended rather than destroyed … Transgression does not suppress but suspends the rule' (ibid.: 104). The 'party animals' of the island strip off their legal and social personas and become naked, bare life. Like Agamben, Diken and Laustsen understand this 'becoming naked' as constitutive for modernity and, equally, as undermining autonomy.

In the concept of 'rational recreation', Rojek (1993) develops an historical analysis of the leisure industry as producing exceptional experiences to affirm and strengthen the political status quo, functioning like a safety valve to release social pressure when people are unhappy. Theorists of the cultural industries go even further in their critiques of exceptionality. They argue that in modern capitalism, leisure and recreation have transmuted from having a cultural and political function in maintaining the status quo into becoming a predominant sphere of capitalist production and exchange. The recreation industry and the 'experience economy' are considered 'post-industrial' industries. In their early critique of these new industries, authors from the Frankfurt school criticised the development of modern leisure practices. Adorno (1991) notes the difference between 'free time' and 'freedom proper', in which the former is part and parcel of the cultural industries' functionality within capitalism. As in Agamben's theory, here the exception ('free time') confirms the rule ('labour').

The critique of capitalism by the Situationist thinkers, most prominently in Debord's (1968) *The Society of the Spectacle*, focuses more explicitly on the spectacle as the new festival-like composition of capitalism. As media events and entertainment become a permanent feature of the society of the spectacle, it is increasingly difficult to see them as exceptional. Rather – according to Debord – capitalism is now based on selling the idea of breaking free from the constraints of the everyday, a concept that is picked up in the psychological critique of consumer capitalism as 'forced enjoyment' by Lacan and others (see Cremin 2007). Importantly, however, the Situationists also develop the notion of the 'situation', an exceptionality that allows a questioning of capitalism in its new configuration. Exceptionality as 'situation' may therefore enhance autonomy, a view that has inspired a range of political activists and interventions in the context of creative resistance (Duncombe 2007; Grindon 2007). Equally, cultural geographers have pointed out the political potential of marginal spaces (Cresswell 1996; Pickerill and Chatterton 2006; Pusey 2010). In this sense, Cresswell has argued through his analysis of Greenham Common as a 'space out of space' that exceptionality creates a vantage point for the critique of the status quo. Significantly, he also highlighted that women were 'marginalised' in Greenham Common, and that it was the status quo through hostile media and Conservative politicians that banned the women into an exceptional space. He omitted the fact that the women were actively pursuing exceptionality, an antagonistic spatial practice, as we discussed in the previous chapter, even if this was initially accidental.

Activists and academics involved in protest camps build on this notion of an exceptionality that can be tactically and strategically employed to advance political quests for autonomy. De Angelis, for example, provides a view of exceptional territoriality with reference to protest camps in his discussion of the HoriZone camp, which he also attended.

> The Stirling camp during the anti-G8 action in Gleneagles in July 2005 was a temporary autonomous zone, a temporary time–space commons ... The experience in this commons can be useful in measuring the daily practices on the upside-down common of global markets ... the Stirling camp became a place in which other values were dominating social cooperation, or co-production (De Angelis 2007: 19).

In earlier writing, De Angelis had already envisioned this spatial articulation of a radical critique of the status quo:

> The space of alternatives to capital has to go through the opening up of counter-enclosures, of spaces of commons. The alternatives to capital pose a limit to accumulation by setting up rigidities and liberating spaces. In a word, alternatives, whatever they are, act as 'counter-enclosures'. This, of course, opens up the question of capital's co-optation of alternatives (De Angelis 2004: 73f).

The notion of 'counter-enclosure', qualified as 'time–space commons' with regard to HoriZone, points to a political exceptionality based on territorial practices that place a limit on capital, and at the same time indicate a social logic of co-operation based on values other than capital. Territorial boundaries are combined here with alternative value practices, unproductive labour and the social co-operation of the protest campers.

Exceptionality as spatial practice Following the work of Mezzadra and Neilson (2008), borders and bordering practices can be studied to understand political geographies. Mezzadra and Neilson are primarily interested in the border strategies of states. Their argument is that borders are not fixed lines in the sand, but rather flexible tools that exist in time and space and that move according to diverse sets of policies of inclusion and exclusion. Putting this challenge to traditional border thinking to use in our study of protest camps, we suggest that protest camps engage in strategies of exceptionality to define their relationship to the status quo.

Protest camp borders are not 'lines in the sand' and protest campers are not simply defending territory through barricades. Instead, we find a broad range of what we previously described as antagonistic spatial practices, combined with reproductive practices, when re-creational infrastructures are employed to mark the camp as exceptional space. This often happens in a very material, territorial way; examples can be found by looking at the barricading practices that we often see in operation at protest camps. However, borders are also drawn through a range of other means, as protesters engage in symbolic and political/ legal battles, create signage and sculptures, erect welcome tents, and employ cultural markers such as dress codes and music styles. In most protest camps, a mixture of strategies of exceptionality can be found, as we discuss in the following section. In looking at protest campers' territorial strategies of re-creation, we focus on the nature of the relationship between the camp and the status quo. We look at the use of re-creational infrastructures such as the tent and the barricade, as well as at some of the communicative practices and processes protest campers use to make territorial claims in order to gain autonomy. We argue that in re-creating the world, protest camps come to constitute an exception to the status quo, a place from which the status quo can be questioned and reformed. To make this argument, we once again turn our attention to the site of the protest camp itself. In all of the examples we look at, important differences exist between protest camps in the way in which they relate to the outside, make claims to political autonomy, and implement those claims.

Strategies of (re)territorialisation In looking at how protest camps claim and produce space, one remarkable phenomenon is the way in which some camps claim to be autonomous political entities or 'free' states and republics. Protest camps, more often than not, claim territory. Doherty (1998) recounts the way in which anti-roads pro- testers in Britain in the 1990s found inspiration in the 1949 Ealing Studios comedy *Passport to Pimlico*. The comedy is set in London, where post-war austerity bites. An ancient document is uncovered that shows that Pimlico is not actually part of the UK but of Burgundy.

5.2 The occupation of Alcatraz marked the island as Indian land

Suddenly the laws of Great Britain are no longer valid in Pimlico. The citizens of Pimlico start to run their neighbourhood through a council and realise their own ideas for city development, among them a swimming pool that was previously rejected by the planning authorities of the city. But in austerity London, Pimlico suddenly also functions as a free trade zone where late-night drinking is permitted and trade is unregulated, prompting the government of the rest of the UK to introduce border controls.

The satirical take of the comedy on political geography and territorial sovereignty inspired protesters decades later. According to Doherty (ibid.: 372), road protesters in the London anti-M11 campaign in Claremont Road referred to the film when they created a series of 'free states' in houses they squatted along the planned motorway route. But the film was not the only inspiration. Doherty also refers to:

> an earlier Free State declared by London housing activists in the late 1970s and of counter-cultural Free States such as the Orange Free State in Amsterdam which, like that at Claremont Road, was intended to provide a place of artistic expression and an experiment in showing how an alternative community could work (ibid.: 372).

'Free states' were also declared in the German anti-nuclear movement in the early 1980s. In rural Wendland, where successive German governments planned to create a nuclear waste site, local resistance groups declared their own 'Freie Republik Wendland' in the early 1980s. Famous for its lax approach to soft drugs and indoor smoking, the free state of Christiania in Copenhagen, founded in the early 1970s, was a further inspiration for claims to independence and autonomy by protest campers.

In the US in 1998, the Minnehaha Free State was declared in a Minneapolis anti-roads protest driven by the efforts of indigenous activists, locals and environmentalists from Earth First! The campers took inspiration from the occupation of the island of Alcatraz in 1969, a landmark protest action by campaigners for the rights of indigenous Americans that lasted for two years, in which protesters renamed (or, perhaps, unnamed) the island, changing the existing 'United States Property' arrival sign to read 'United Indian Property'. Below and above the sign were messages reading 'Indian Land' and 'Indians Welcome'. Again, claims to independence and political autonomy were central in these acts of territorial protest.

In the 2007 Climate Camp at Heathrow near London, campers

5.3 A large installation of a plane invites people entering the 2007 Climate Camp at Heathrow to 'exit the system'

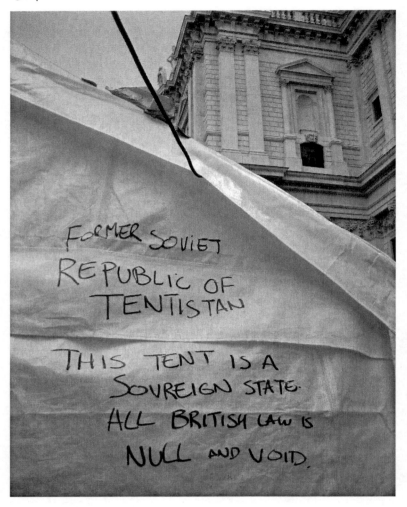

5.4 A playful take on secession at Occupy LSX, 2011

were greeted with a big plywood sculpture in the shape of an aeroplane, which invited newcomers to 'exit the system' as they passed through it.

Most recently, in Occupy LSX, a sign on a tent claimed the camp's independence: 'All British law is null and void'.

It is important to note that these claims of 'free' republics are antagonistic gestures, not necessarily aiming at the establishment of actual state republics. In fact, they are often articulated sarcastically to expose the limit of the state form itself. An example is this road protesters' manifesto from Britain in the 1990s:

> This is the Independent Free State of Trollheim ... we have no allegiance to the UK government ... We do not recognize history, patriarchy, matriarchy, politics, communists, fascists or lollipop men/ladies ... We have a hierarchy based on dog worship ... Our currency is to be based on the quark barter system. We do not recognize the Gregorian calendar: by doing so this day shall be known as One ... Be afraid, be afraid, all ye that hear. Respect this State (Griffiths 2000: 145).

However, the playfulness and theatricality of these articulations do not detract from their material enactment of territorial practices. Each sign bearing the name 'free state' accompanies acts of claiming and bordering space. The theatricality of the protest camp mirrors – and uncovers – how every nation state was made. Contestation over land (as it is entangled with people's livelihoods and well-being) marks protest campers' politics of place-making vis-à-vis the status quo.

Productive borders Strategies of exceptionality around place-making emerged from the Egyptian revolution, which, in its first days in January 2011, centred on the capture of Tahrir Square (Ramadan 2013). The 'liberation square' had first to be liberated from a police force that had been instructed to prevent this by all means necessary. Tahrir Square was already imbued with revolutionary meaning from various popular movements and struggles stretching back to the beginning of the twentieth century. In order to claim it, protesters had to battle and struggle for three days, after which the sheer mass of dedicated people finally overran the police. Once the square was 'liberated' and occupied, its autonomy was declared. In their interpretation of the Tahrir Square protest camp, Keraitim and Mehrez report how the square was transformed into 'The independent republic of Tahrir':

> Together protesters set up the new boundaries surrounding Tahrir: checkpoints that ensured the safety of those within the square, forms of political and cultural expression and mobilization that animated it and sustenance of daily life for the massive sit-in of thousands of protesters camped in the *midan*. Setting up checkpoints to protect the revolution and using their bodies as well as all available

materials to set up barricades, the independent republic of Tahrir was bordered to its outside in a permanent fashion (Keraitim and Mehrez 2012: 28).

In addition to the barricades of the camp, an exceptional time/space of the encampment also emerged in cultural terms. As Keraitim and Mehrez (ibid.: 36) argue, Tahrir Square became a 'festival of the oppressed'. An inclusive atmosphere dominated the protest camp, relating to the traditional celebration of the *mulid*. In Egypt, *mulids* are regular celebrations of the birthdays of religious figures, often regulated as public holidays; for years, as Keraitim and Mehrez argue, they were also a source of oppositional agitation beyond state control. In their view, the protest camps on Tahrir Square became a politically charged *mulid* where the Egyptian nation was reborn, a festive as well as painful process. While it may seem that barricades and cultural markers of difference are at odds with each other, the cases we have discussed here show how they coexist in protest camps. The festive atmosphere of the protest camp often exists alongside the battle atmosphere, and this contradiction is part of what creates its exceptionality – and why, as we discussed in Chapter 2, it is difficult for the mainstream media to capture it.

Just as in Tahrir, barricades also characterised the occupation of Oaxaca in Mexico in 2006, becoming a powerful symbol of this protest. The encampment in Oaxaca was initially a teachers' protest; however, it drew in larger and more diverse constituencies when the teachers' protest camp was violently broken up in June 2006. Groups formed the Popular Assembly of the Peoples of Oaxaca (Asamblea Popular de los Pueblos de Oaxaca or APPO) and effectively took over the running of the city for the whole of the summer of 2006. The APPO asserted its power through the construction and fortification of barricades at strategic points in the city in order to prevent a crackdown on the movement. The barricades – according to Gustavo Esteva – marked a politicisation of the urban movements that had become part of the struggle:

> The barricades arose spontaneously as a popular response to the governor's attacks on the APPO encampments, and rapidly took on a life of their own, to the extent of becoming autonomous focal points for social and political organization. Long sleepless nights provided the opportunity for extensive political discussions, which

awakened in many young people a hitherto nonexistent or inchoate social consciousness. The new graffiti manifested this aroused awareness. On the barricades, new forms of anarchism – in both ideological and lifestyle applications – began to appear. The collectives on the barricades defended their autonomy ferociously and sometimes with a level of hostility that was hard to channel. Some groups occupied abandoned public buildings and began not only to live in them but to convert them into centers of cultural and political activity. The children and youth of these groups played a significant part in the movement, especially in confrontations with the police, which many of them were used to (Esteva 2010: 2).

Strategies of territoriality mentioned here include building barricades, squatting, creating visual landscapes and engaging with countercultures. The birth of a protest coalition and movement on the barricades also, of course, harks back to the productivity of borders that Mezzadra and Neilson described. But here it is not the state that bio-politically manages a populace into different categories of legal and work-based integration. Rather, the barricades become an enactment of the autonomous production of subjectivities of resistance and liberation in struggle.

Strategies of exceptionality and the law Another set of territorial strategies of exceptionality and the production of autonomy can be seen in relation to engagements with the law. In the case of the Australian Tent Embassy in Canberra, Australia in 1972, Aboriginal protesters claimed land that belonged to the Australian state. They used a law that allowed everyone to camp on common land. This strategy exposed the fact that the land had belonged to them in the first instance before it was taken away by the Australian settler state. Here, the Aboriginal Tent Embassy protesters claimed a legal exceptionality. If the government was not going to recognise the land rights of Aboriginal people, then the people would grant themselves the right to use the government's land. In this example, the Tent Embassy itself posed as an 'other possible world' to the settler (and settled) Australian nation. The territorial strategy of erecting and operating a Tent Embassy exposed the foundation myths of the Australian settler state by peacefully re-enacting the occupation of land.

Indigenous protest in the United States has also used existing laws

5.5 Climate Camp at Heathrow, 2007 – tripods are used to secure squatted land

to make claims for autonomous spaces. For example, in the occupation of Alcatraz, activists mobilised a US federal law that provided for the return of federal land to the tribes from which it had been taken if it was no longer in use. After the prison on Alcatraz was closed, the protesters claimed the land back. While they lost the legal battle, the claim helped enable the defence of the camp for the 14 months it lasted.

Legal boundary-making is always contested. Under English law, protest camps have often relied on 'squatters' rights'. Until recently, occupying land that was privately owned was therefore not an offence, and the owner rather than the occupier needed to seek a court injunction, based on claiming their title to the land, in order to evict the occupiers.

While the full implications of the change in the law relating to squatting in the UK are yet to be seen in the context of protest camps, the case can be made that the Occupy LSX camp might not have come into being under the new law. As Occupy LSX tried to establish itself on private land in the city, the police stopped evicting the camp when the custodian of St Paul's cathedral stated that he tolerated the occupation. In the future, with squatting as a public offence, the police will have the right to evict a camp even if the owner of the land asks them not to. The epic legal battles over Occupy LSX shaped the tactical outlook of the camp. Trying to keep the church onside, protesters mobilised a distinctly 'Christian' repertoire and frame, even at one point erecting a banner reading 'What Would Jesus Do?'

Protesters carved out territory on the cathedral grounds, in part by creating a visual landscape that, alongside media adaptation strategies, could respond to and intervene in ongoing debates on whether the Church of England would continue to tolerate the camp. In a legal context, the camp also started questioning the political and juridical constitution of the City of London Corporation, which became one of its main adversaries. This antagonism emerged not because of the particular aims of the encampment, nor because the City of London Corporation was initially chosen as a protest target. Rather, it was through creating the territorial space of the Occupy encampment that the City of London Corporation came to embody the status quo campers sought to challenge. Eventually, Occupy LSX lost the long-running legal battles to allow the protesters to stay.

In other contexts the law might be less flexible, or less available, as part of protesters' strategies of re-territorialisation. The protesters of Tahrir Square had no chance of attempting a legal strategy considering the political character of Egyptian law. Moreover the legal protection that is provided in Western settings is always limited, because the state may use violent force legally in the (self-declared) state of emergency. Fundamentally, the executive power of the state supersedes human rights or any other legal framework, as Agamben (1998) has shown concisely.

The use of force in the dissolution of some Occupy camps in the US illustrates this clearly. For example, a judge who had ordered the city of New York to stop evicting Occupy Wall Street was removed from the case and her order subsequently revoked by a new judge assigned to it (Ross and Connor 2011). While it might be more difficult for US police to gun down protesters (particularly when those protesters constitute a white majority), it is not the law that protects them, but the persuasive, material powers behind the law: media coverage and public opinion, or, in other words, people defending the right to protest.

Culture against the status quo In addition to legal strategies, many protest camp movements engage extensively in cultural production as part of their re-territorialising practices to create and claim collective autonomy. The Thai Red Shirt protest camp in Bangkok stands out as an example of the extent to which cultural production can be intertwined with more traditional physical practices of taking up space in protest. From March 2010 to a bloody crackdown in May 2010, Red Shirt protesters gathered in a protest camp in the Thai capital to demand that the government stepped down and that new elections were held. A decisive conflict over the political future of Thailand had begun when in 2006 the elected prime minister and billionaire Thaksin Shinawatra was ousted in a coup.

Conflicts occurred between the Red Shirts, largely urban and rural poor who supported the ousted prime minister, and the Yellow Shirts, urban middle classes who rejected the populist policies of Shinawatra. Shinawatra was accused of corruption and fled into exile to avoid prosecution in Thailand. The dynamics of the conflict are complex and have changed over the years. While the Red Shirts were accused of being bought off by the absent Shinawatra in order to take part in demonstrations, many observers seem to suggest that the three months of protest in the capital in 2010 were a genuine people's movement for democracy. Its crushing by the Thai military in May 2010 left over 80 people dead and hundreds wounded, among them journalists and bystanders, and was condemned internationally. Elections were finally held in 2011 and delivered a majority for the parties representing the Red Shirt movement.

The protesters' camp moved through the capital, first taking in the politically significant spaces around Ratchadamnoen Avenue and later moving to the middle of Bangkok's international business district and shopping centre. Initially the camp was bordered not so much in terms of external borders and barricades, which went on to dominate the final weeks of the camp, but instead by camp participants wearing red shirts, red hats and other clothing that signified their support for and participation in the movement. In this way, participation in the camp was a matter of a change of clothes, as described by the BBC journalist Rachel Harvey:

> I remember one woman, who was wearing the uniform of the office worker – smart skirt, high heels and make-up – but in her open shoulder bag, a neatly folded red T-shirt revealed her true allegiance (Harvey 2010).

The camp was also extraordinarily well organised, providing for protesters' autonomy with free food, massage and toilet facilities.

Beyond these re-creational infrastructures, the camp presented itself as a cultural phenomenon, claiming its space through the use of bordering atmospheric soundscapes (Tausig and Doolan 2012). While a large main stage was set up to broadcast the speeches of movement leaders and to play folk music, many participants in the protest brought their own music and sound systems, creating a pluriverse of sounds, characteristic of a festival. Ben Tausig has argued that the music played signifies a bordering strategy for the campers that helps identify who is in and who is not. At the same time, the many different sounds underline the diversity of the protest movement itself, despite being united under one banner or one idea in a central camp. The Red Shirt campers were united in their attempt to speak out in the capital and they were united in their demand for 'real democracy', and they presented this through their excessive use of sounds, among other things. For Tausig, the Red Shirts prefigured the diversity that would characterise the protest movements and camps of 2011.

Decades before, the bordering practices of anti-roads camps in Britain in the 1990s also created alternative worlds, in this earlier case through a combination of blockading tactics and the development of

5.6 The cycle-powered Rinky Dink sound system at the Climate Camp at Heathrow, 2007

'imaginary communities of resistance' (Routledge 1997). These were often based on countercultural identities and lifestyles (Cresswell 1996; Hetherington 1998) and 'tribal politics' (Bauman 1992). Places such as Pollock Free State in Glasgow were explicitly posited against, and constructed as autonomous from, the surrounding polity (Seel 1997). The 'free state' was meant to stop the building of a motorway, but it equally became an attempt to rebuild society in a better way. Resistance culture meant, as one participant stated: 'We are living it, rather than just talking about it' (Routledge 1997: 371).

Protest camps in Britain at this time were strongly influenced by countercultural developments; the use of lifestyles to denote political dissidence was central in this period. The free festivals of the 1970s had a profound influence on the making of protest camps by providing infrastructural innovations such as the 'bender' and mobile kitchens. The peace movement linked up with what was left of the free festival culture in the early 1980s, a process of overlap well described by Worthington (2004) and Hetherington (2000). In the United States, 'tribal' movements that grew out of the counterculture included the new age Rainbow People in the 1970s. The Rainbows' mobile

5.7 Protecting nature – the protest camps against aluminium smelters in Iceland, 2005–07

lifestyle took inspiration from indigenous people to claim a radical new existence in accordance with the needs of nature. They created re-creational strategies that were at times contentious as they appropriated elements of indigenous culture, leaving the context behind. While 'Rainbow politics' have been questioned on this and other counts, their appropriations of indigenous cultures and their influence on direct action environmentalists can be traced in a range of tactical mash-ups, with strategies such as the 'talking stick' making its way from the north-west of the US into the Occupy Ottawa encampment (Feigenbaum, McCurdy and Frenzel 2013).

Overlaps between the cultural and political forms of camping, as well as with outdoor festivals, and appropriations of indigenous, tribal cultures and celebrations of nature existed well before 1960 in the Western context of leisure camping. As we argued earlier, this overlap can be traced back through the history of modern leisure camping to the early countercultural movements of 'Wandervögel' or 'summer camps'. It is interesting in this respect that a number of organisers of the UK Climate Camps had, as children, been part of the Woodcraft Folk camping movement. (The Woodcraft Folk had split off from Scout camping in 1925 because of the latter's open militarism.)

Merely artistic? These links between festival and countercultural movements and protest camps have been critiqued more recently, with such countercultural attempts of 'exiting the system' often rejected by more political campaigners and movements organised primarily around antagonism. In Marxist and anarchist writing, those engaging in countercultural strategies for producing autonomy were often seen as 'lifestyle' anarchists (Bookchin 1995). This view is mirrored to some extent in the analysis of the 1960s protests as being driven by 'artist critique' rather than 'social critique', prioritising personal freedom and expression over social justice (Boltanski and Chiapello 2005).

We do not agree with this divide. Our evidence from the study of protest camps' territorial practices and strategies of exceptionality shows that artistic and social critiques cannot be separated. Rather, they tend to come together in the re-creation of the protest camp, as our discussions of Tahrir, Thailand and the anti-roads movement show. Moreover, camps that engage 'lifestyle' elements do not do so in a void, where no other strategies are developed or deployed. As we have discussed, the strategies of exceptionality that go into the

f a protest camp's unique space–time involve hybrid uses
cal barriers, legal strategies, visual landscapes, soundscapes
,untercultural demarcations. In addition, as we have argued,
is perhaps most unique about protest camps is that they provide
the space to socially reproduce. Their attempts to claim autonomy
are found in their care, as well as in their politics and culture. In
attempting to sustain a living space and daily action, they expose
how such sustenance of a longer-term movement might work (or not
work); this is an area we address in the next section of this chapter.

Social reproduction

Protest camps' re-creational infrastructures do not deal only with
spatial practices of territorialisation but also with social reproduction.
As we argued earlier, care work and re-creational infrastructures are
often strongly gendered and rendered 'private'; they are often made
or kept invisible from the centre of a social movement's politics. As
exposed and vulnerable places of politics, protest camps make visible
reproductive labour and the infrastructures in which this labour takes
place. The social and biological becomes political. In this section
we discuss infrastructures and practices of social reproduction in
relation to claims to autonomy and exceptionality. We offer only a
brief overview of some of the major points of contestation around
social reproduction. This discussion is focused in particular on the
development of well-being practices in the protest camps of the global
North, as they have been touched and shaped by the transnational
movement of ideas and practices that extends beyond national borders.
An entire book could be written on each, and they deserve more time
and consideration than we can provide here.

Following Foucault, we can consider the employment of re-
creational infrastructures as 'bio-political'. While Foucault is mainly
interested in the ways in which the state has attempted to regulate and
exercise power in this bio-political fashion (for example in prisons and
hospitals), his ideas can – and have – been mobilised to understand
the bio-politics of political life, or what feminists have long termed
the importance of the 'personal as the political' in democratic strategy.
The assumption that results from applying the idea of bio-politics
to the work of social change and anti-capitalism draws from authors
such as Federici, who has indicated the way in which capital exploits
the 'free' reproductive labour of women. In her work on the ACT UP

movement, Federici argues that political movements need to – and can – move beyond symbolic protest by re-creating structures of solidarity and social care (Federici 2004).

The majority of discussions about care and social reproduction in social movements come from indigenous, feminist, ecological, queer and anarchist literature. Indeed, it was these approaches that were among the first to question the blind spots of critical theories in relation to care and social reproduction, including the traditionally Marxist analysis of society. Framing this in terms of a bio-political struggle, we could say that the focus here is on the expansion of basic human relations. In protest camps, tensions between bio-politics and emancipatory politics come to the fore. In the past 50 years of protest camp history – as it has run alongside post-1968 women's liberation movements in many countries – we have seen an increasing (if not always consistent) level of attention paid to questions of care. While the protest camp has been home to experiments and innovations in how care is perceived and organised, this has not come without contestation.

Bio-politics in protest camps In the 1970s and 1980s, feminist modes of consensus decision-making, an emphasis on the importance of having childcare, and critiques of gendered divisions of labour in tasks such as cooking and cleaning were mobilised in many social movements. The international women's peace camps of the 1980s arguably emerged, in large part, from women's desire to take part in autonomous separations that claimed space for women to organise themselves apart from the men who had dominated their movements, workplaces and home lives. Inviting women to engage in the making of a protest camp, the handbook of reflections from the Puget Sound women's peace camp opens by telling readers:

> The title of this book [*Ordinary Women*] distils the essence of our work, which is to demystify political action – any woman who can plan a gathering of friends can plan a political action (Participants of the Puget Sound Women's Peace Camp 1985).

It goes on to describe the ways in which their feminist politics came into contact with direct action, and with indigenous and ecological perspectives, and draws attention to practices of well-being and care:

> The Puget Sound Women's Peace Camp is based on the principles

of non-violence and of feminism. A non-violent, feminist way of living seeks cooperation, not domination, and includes respect for people's physical and spiritual well-being and a love of the earth and her creatures. We strive to hear and include each of our voices equally in group decisions and to provide a supportive place for women to learn new skills (ibid.).

In the 1990s, in UK anti-roads protests, divisions of labour and questions of well-being were often pushed to the sidelines. Re-creational concerns were often superseded by the 'real work' of direct action and of maintaining oppositional territories through extensive barricading and tunnelling. This came to the fore in protesters' attempts to carry the tactic of protest camping into the city of London. In 1996, drawing inspiration from the anti-roads movement, people squatted unused land to create a commune based on the Diggers' ideals. The Pure Genius occupation sought to make land common and create autonomous re-creation infrastructures based on permaculture practices. The encampment lasted for over five months, but, according to Doherty (1998), faced numerous challenges relating to how to provide care for participants.

> The eviction stimulated much discussion about the site, much of which focused on its internal problems: articles by John Vidal and George Monbiot in the *Guardian* of October 16 concentrated on 'how few pissheads it takes to wreck a site'. It is accepted that the site itself had serious problems ... At the same time it becomes easy for people to be scapegoated as the reason for the problems of the site and for the attention to be deflected away from ambiguities in the formation and conceptualisation of the campaign (Featherstone 1997: 56)

Was it possible that the 'pissheads' were people in need of care that others in the camp, focused on its political aims and objective, were unwilling to provide?

In a number of accounts of protest camps published in the Earth First! journal *Do or Die* in the 1990s, protest campers reflected on similar problems (see issues 6–9). Of particular interest is a piece in issue 6 on the Newbury bypass protests. One section of this article, subtitled 'Personal problems get in the way of campaigning', is preceded by an editor's note:

> The following two paragraphs put across ideas that members of the idiotorial [sic] collective heavily disagreed with. Rather than not include the piece, or edit it so that it 'conformed', we decided to print it with a reply at the end. We hope this aids discussion and debate.

This exchange highlights the reflective processes that many in the anti-roads movement, and in the wider autonomous social movements of the time, were working through. The article's author goes on to argue that:

> Whether you call them dime-bars, energy vampires, lunch-outs, or whatever, it is undeniable that personal problems can often seriously hinder the effectiveness of a campaign. The free-living, utopian lifestyle of protest camps attracts all sorts of people (and rightly so), but sometimes for the wrong reasons. There can be a conflict between the view that everyone should be free to live their own individual life, and the right for a community to exist free of disruption. This conflict should not exist: a road protest camp is not a community centre to deal with people's problems – it is neither desirable or feasible (Do or Die 1997).

Here, the author rejects the notion that re-creational infrastructures and practices for care and social reproduction have any place in a direct action camp. Claims to autonomy come purely from the antagonistic gesture, not from the collective effort to create alternatives to the status quo.

Objecting to this view, the editors respond in a section entitled: 'If we can't sort out each other, how are we meant to sort out the world?' They write that the author:

> Seems to suggest that we should leave our emotional baggage at home and if we begin to crack up, leave the campaign – effectively, we are discarded when we are no longer 'productive'. But I would argue that the primary aim of campaigns is to rebuild communities and create a movement that can really transcend industrial capitalism as a whole. The rather minor effect we have on industry is less important than the way in which our campaigns affect us and our movement. In a socially fragmented world, the mad arena of campaigning is, frighteningly, one of the few opportunities we have for 'group therapy' and individual and collective evolution (ibid.).

This discussion shifts the debate by placing questions of care and support at the centre of the autonomous project of the protest camp. It destabilises, or to return to Sara Ahmed's terminology, it reorients the 'mad subject' and the protest camp in such a way that neither is seen as failing. Rather, the failure – the place where more work must be done – concerns our alignment of questions of individual wellness, community well-being and antagonism towards the state. Here, we start to see an articulation of an emancipatory bio-politics.

In attempts to draw together these movement debates and critiques, while offering practical advice, the handbook *Road Raging* devotes a full chapter to 'Sustaining yourself and the campaign community'. Listed under this category are the topics: tolerance, mutual support, burn-out, gender issues, living communally, maintaining personal stamina, common camp ailments, and 'natural additions to your first aid kit'. This range of concerns demonstrates the integration of feminist, spiritual, well-being and health issues, which were coming together in autonomous social movements and direct action campaigns during the 1990s. In *Road Raging*, these issues remain largely relegated to a category of support work, rather than being positioned as central practices of autonomous and emancipatory politics. However, their articulation in conjunction with each other illustrates increasing efforts to politicise the bio-politics of protest camp life and ongoing protest action.

By the early 2000s, counter-summit, NoBorders and World Social Forum encampments were learning from the previous decades by pulling together strategies from existing feminist, indigenous, queer, ecological and anti-capitalist organising. As part of a broader alter-globalisation politics, those building these encampments worked to create infrastructures and practices for well-being and care in a territorial form. Childcare, communal cooking and well-being spaces were commonplace. At the same time, issues of sexism, sexual violence and aggression were taken up in meetings and workshops. In some camps, collectives of queer people of colour and women of colour created autonomous projects and sometimes tent spaces, while generating analyses and actions that further influenced and shaped meetings and their movements more generally. Disability activists challenged dominant ways of thinking about 'ability' in their fight for accessibility, both within the spaces of their movements (such as protest camps) and against the state. Mental health, alternative medicine, herbal gynaecology and menstrual politics were articulated in these encampments, as skill-shares and educational networks came together at, and grew from, many of these counter-summits and convergence encampments. Throughout the 2000s, these protest camps began to emphasise more and more strongly their bio-political exemplarity.

In the British context, the evolution from HoriZone's eco-village to the Climate Camps highlighted the influence that social reproduction interventions had had on the organisation of protest camps. For example, active in HoriZone and carried over into Climate Camps and future counter-summits was Activist Trauma Support (ATS). The ATS formed after the Evian G8 protests in which, among other acts of violence and harassment, police cut the cords of two protesters suspended from a bridge; they then plummeted to the ground and sustained serious injuries. Reflecting on, and bringing together, concerns about the emotional well-being of protesters involved in the violent and vulnerable contact zones of counter-summit actions, ATS founders wrote:

> A lot of people drop out, disappear, stop being active, feel excluded because of their fear or because they are suffering from post-traumatic stress disorders (PTSD). Even after obvious incidents like the Diaz school in Genoa [a violent police raid including beatings on sleeping protesters], there was no emotional support set up for the victims. A lot of them suffered more from the emotional consequences than the physical injuries.

In the years before Evian, discussions had begun to circulate around the need for 'partially organised' strategies and spaces able to respond to protesters' care and re-creational needs. After the 1999 Anti-World Trade Organization in Seattle, Washington, anarchist medial group Black Cross wrote and distributed a pamphlet for Prague in 2000. Likewise, drawing on 1980s and 1990s methods for dealing with 'activist trauma', Starhawk circulated materials post-Genova in 2001. These efforts came together, alongside work from queer and disability communities, in the formation of the ATS.

In addition to the development of the ATS, in Chapter 1 we discussed the influence of 'permaculture' as a political approach that connects care for nature with the development of re-creational infrastructures. In permaculture, an emancipatory approach to bio-politics is attempted. The sheer diversity of infrastructures that developed

5.8 Re-creating life in sustainable ways – renewable energy in protest camps

within this context, and that continued into the Climate Camps, is remarkable. In these encampments, teaching and learning infrastructures were provided, as well as childcare facilities, well-being spaces and mediation, and the camps were openly described as 'alternative worlds'.

The idea was to create life as example; to manifest and make visible alternatives to capitalism through the social reproduction of the movement within the space of the camp. Describing the autonomous practices of the Climate Camp, Stuart Jordan writes:

The Camp gives you a chance to experience an alternative to the world of wage labour and commodity markets. The things we consume at camp (the tent space, sanitation, food etc.) are to a large extent products of our collective labour. We do not grow the veg or weave the tent fabric (for this we rely on the capitalist market place) but for the duration of Camp the work is collectively shared and the product of that work is held in common. We do not operate a money economy or buy and sell these products. We are not given money in exchange for the time we spend 'working'. Our daily needs are satisfied by the collective work of the community and so commodity markets are unnecessary. We find that it is not necessary to compel people to work with the threat of poverty. On the contrary, the split between work and leisure which is a feature of capitalist society is broken down and work becomes enjoyable and satisfying. As we work together, human relations are formed quite easily and we have a new appreciation of each other as striving towards a common end: the life and wellbeing of the camp ... We relate directly as human beings, reliant on each other for our sustenance (Shift Magazine and Dysophia 2010).

While Jordan celebrates the exceptionality of the Climate Camp, he indicates the limitations of its autonomy, pointing out the inability to autonomously produce or source raw materials and food supplies. Later in the piece he explicitly acknowledges the contradictions many in the movement feel regarding their temporally bound actions.

The actual construction of alternative infrastructures always comes with a variety of limitations. For example, HoriZone provided compost toilets but still had to rent chemical toilets as well. While food was supplied all the time, a lot of participants nipped to the local supermarkets on various occasions to stock up. Famously, the Heiligendamm G8 protest camp in Reddelich in 2007 was erected next to a meat factory. The local businessman decided that some of his produce might go down well with protesters and so he erected a sausage stall by the entrance to the camp. The organisers in Germany, aware of the anti-meat and anti-capitalist tendencies of some of the camp participants, appealed to them to leave the meat stall alone, and suggested to vegan campers that they should camp in one of the other camps. In Reddelich, however, the sausage stall was a huge success.

Another limitation or (im)possibility of autonomy experienced at protest camps involves re-creations of security. For example, while a tranquillity team and legal working group were active on site in Climate Camps, occasions still arose in which the police were called on site to deal with physical disputes and thefts. This reliance on the police causes tension among many protesters. Yet, as can be seen in examples spanning from Resurrection City to Occupy Toronto, self-managed security systems raise a number of further issues around violence and mediation. In an interview with the media co-op, Toronto occupier Taylor Chelsea discussed these re-creational issues encountered at the encampment:

the kinds of people who were like 'ya I want to marshal all night' drew people that they themselves needed to be de-escalated at

5.9 Climate Camp in the City in Bishopsgate, London, 2009

times. Also, having so few people taking on the responsibility of safety for the entire camp created a lot of stress for those few people. So on the third day or the fifth day or the second week, we had very tired people trying to perform the same action, getting yelled at a lot, trying to mediate conflict. And those people are becoming low at their wits' end and their nerves' end, so they are actually quick to go off themselves. And that's not something to be criticized, that's just something to observe as indicative when you ask a small group of people to mediate and be responsible for the safety of a very large group of people (http://toronto.mediacoop.ca/story/interview-security-and-community-occupy-toronto/8810).

Drawing on issues relating to exhaustion, collective responsibility and stress, Taylor's reflections again show how re-creational infrastructures and practices of the protest camp are bound up in the desire to enact an exceptionality of well-being and care. The aim is to produce a system of security that does not mirror, but rather challenges, that of the status quo. Yet in their attempts to run an autonomous security system, protest campers are drawn into larger questions of conflict mediation, collective responsibility and the reproduction of violence.

This again points to the importance of paying attention to how basic bodily care – such as the need for sleep – is always entangled in more complex issues about how to re-create autonomous practices.

Protest camps, particularly when they are located in urban centres, can come to take on these care roles. They may find themselves serving as makeshift shelters, drop-in clinics and on-call group therapy sessions. Again, this is why we argue that the protest camp is a site of exposure of the state's inadequacies in providing care. It also highlights the protest camp's struggles with autonomy. For critics, the failure of protest camps to deal with social care is proof that the camps are savage and reckless spaces, unsafe particularly for women and children. The contradictions inherent in the endeavour to create an alternative logic of reproduction within the camp may have been at their most striking in the city-based camps that were part of the Occupy movement. In Occupy encampments, as well as in those of M15 in Spain and housing-related protest camps in many Israeli cities, large numbers of people came together in the camps who were in need of a wide range of care. This was contingent on the current economic recession, on the urban location of these camps, and, in some places, on the weather and time of year. As campers addressed the many levels of care needs at these encampments – from getting and cooking food for thousands, to dealing with drug addiction and alcoholism, mental health, trauma from police abuse and exhaustion – a number of differences and difficulties arose.

In the case of Occupy, incidents of sexual assault and rape occurred in several camps, and were sensationally picked up by mainstream media outlets. Sexual assault and rape in social movements is not, of course, a new phenomenon. Sexual violence has been documented at Resurrection City, Greenham Common and in the British anti-roads movement, among others. At Occupy, campers were challenged to respond both to the media coverage of these events and to the sexual violence that occurred in the camps. They did so in a variety of ways. One way was building women-only spaces, such as those in Occupy camps in, for example, New York, Toronto and Washington, DC. Occupiers also tried to develop internal mechanisms for dealing with sexual violence. In many camps, people reflected on how to police sexual assault. However, these initiatives also faced challenges. At Occupy LSX, the women-only space had a man enter in the middle of the night on more than one occasion, and at Occupy

5.10 Struggles for de-colonisation and anti-racism were prominent in many Occupy camps, as shown here at Occupy Toronto

Baltimore, campers were heavily criticised for suggesting in a leaflet to victims of sexual assault that they should talk to the camp's own security team before alerting the police. Critics from women's shelter organisations felt that such advice might lead to victims not pursuing the perpetrators of sexual violence.

The attempt to build alternative structures of care and security often reached its limit in cases of sexual violence and other serious physical assaults. At the same time as many sought to intervene in camp-based violence, critical voices pointed out that the sexual and other forms of physical violence occurring in camps reflected the level of violence that occurs every day. Just as protest camps can expose the poor conditions of homelessness, lack of land rights, failures of public education and erasure of common space for people to gather in, so too can they draw attention to the inadequacies and failures of our efforts to intervene in, respond to and prevent gendered and racialised violence. While protest camps often strive to build alternatives to the status quo, the spheres in which they cannot achieve this alone highlight those areas in our wider social contexts – and particularly in social movements – that require more attention and responsibility.

Many of the struggles that accompany the re-creation of everyday life were captured and discussed in the Occupy movement pamphlet *Mindful Occupation*. As an instructional collection and movement reflection that emerged out of a collaboration between mental health groups such as the Icarus Project and MindFreedom International, as well as individuals in and around the Occupy movement, *Mindful Occupation* focuses on many of the broader issues in social movements and everyday life under global capitalism as they crystallise in the protest camp. The booklet starts by drawing attention to Occupy's many human and non-human entanglements: 'Occupy is an evolving movement, affected by the forces of passion, time, police, government, corporations, tactics, weather, creativity, and the growing pains that all activist movements experience.' Explicitly positioning Occupy and well-being as matters of bio-politics within global capitalism, the authors write:

> When corporations that prioritize productivity over community are culturally and politically sanctified, challenging the status quo seems all the more difficult. However, through social protest – whether with Occupy or radical mental health – we take a step against the accepted paradigm to reclaim our humanity and community. Given that we are putting our real selves on the line, we may become stressed. We may be hurt. We may be traumatized. That is why it is important to learn how to give and take care of ourselves, through mutual support and community. It's fundamentally important to try to match our process in doing this work with the product that we are collectively seeking.

Here, *Mindful Occupation* articulates the main argument we seek to make about protest camps' re-creational practices and strategies of exceptionality more generally. It illustrates protest campers' collective struggles to challenge the status quo through building re-creational infrastructures and practices that can make autonomous claims against the state and corporations.

Conclusion

In this chapter we have discussed how the re-creational infrastructures and practices found at protest camps engage strategies of exceptionality. These strategies are often engaged to claim autonomy from the state, and at the same time to challenge the political status quo. We argued that the nomadic character of camps, charted by Ibn Khaldoun and reflected in the 'nomadology' of Deleuze and Guattari, can help make sense of the protest camp in relation to the settled norms of the state, or, in other words, of how protest camps confront or sustain the status quo. Focusing on protest camps as temporal and spatial zones of exceptionality, we argued that protest campers intuit this conflict as it becomes an issue in creating the camp as an exceptional space through the employment of re-creational infrastructures and practices. Some of the key ways in which protest campers re-territorialise space include cultural, political and legal strategies that create exceptionality. By looking at protest camps, we found that more 'material' and confrontational border strategies are often intertwined with legal and cultural struggles. This finding poses a challenge to those seeking to separate antagonism from 'merely cultural' politics.

This approach to the protest camp as a space of exceptionality is linked to infrastructures and practices of social reproduction as they are bound up in (im)possible struggles for autonomy. Protest campers' attempts to care for each other – as well as their failures or reluctance to care – show the (im)possibilities of autonomy both in the space of the protest camp and in social movements more broadly. At the same time, protest camps expose the inadequacies of the capitalist state's ability to care for its people. Approaching autonomy in this way – as a territorial formation of shared struggle and labour – we see the protest camp as being engaged in attempted autonomy. It is therefore not the product – the protest camp – that is autonomous but its production, in the sense that people co-operate to make it happen. It is not the compost toilet or the women-only space or tranquillity tent that provides the alternative to the status quo; it is the fact that people build it together because it needs to be built.

6 | ALTERNATIVE WORLDS

Introduction

In this final chapter we offer a summary of the central arguments made in *Protest Camps*. We reassert the importance of examining protest camps as distinct organisational forms that share key infrastructures. The study of politics and social movements has too long overlooked the microcosm of protest camps as spaces where democratic action is experienced and experimented with. Protest camps are places of learning, where participants often work to increase human autonomy and freedom in an inclusive and socially conscious way. They are also sites of creativity and innovation, further characterised as the product of co-operation and solidarity. We also believe that protest camps are a rich, and largely uncharted, area of empirical study, and an important subject for sociological and activist reflection. Seen from this perspective, our book is a call to action in the hope that insights from the study of protest camps can offer material to reflect on, stories to share and ideas for future camps.

We begin this last chapter by discussing some larger themes relating to alternative world-making, revolutionary politics, utopias, heterotopias and the commons. From there we revisit the arguments made in the previous chapters to show how our infrastructural analysis can shed light on the position of protest camps in relation to these more general ideas and debates around processes and practices of radical social change. Finally, based on these discussions, we offer a way to think – or rethink – about the 'successes' and 'failures' of camps, looking more conceptually at the relationship between protest camps and wider social movement politics.

Alternative worlds

As we have argued throughout this book, protest camps are political spaces of high intensity, where democracy can be experienced and experimented with in a living form. Often, camps are set up instrumentally only to support action in remote locations; sometimes they occur spontaneously without a plan. But even in such cases, we can identify the emergence of four infrastructures: communications, action, governance and re-creation. Concurrently, we often found evidence of the development of strong collective identities within the camp, which shaped and were shaped by the creation of internal democratic processes. These processes come with many challenges, and are not always pleasant. The dynamics of a camp may create insider and outsider dichotomies between different participants, depending on their level of involvement, political backgrounds and other experiences and notions of identity. But these internal divisions and conflicts are also key to understanding protest camps as alternative worlds and places of radical democratic experiences.

This is mainly because experiences of such intense democratic process cannot often be felt in the mainstream political arena, where the pains and potentials of participation are limited by institutions that formalise and make distant the decision-making process. Even in reasonably democratic societies, politics is a highly professionalised field that leaves little more for the normal citizen to do than approve or dismiss political parties in electoral cycles. In other words, politics is institutionally separated from the life of the vast majority of people. Protest camps enable all their participants to experience political processes as they re-create life by developing alternative ways of housing, feeding, entertaining and living together, alongside innovations in political action as intervention and democratic process. This is why protest camps are more than just ephemeral places or instrumental strategies of particular social movements. They are laboratories of radical, tangible democracy that can help to imagine and build blueprints for alternative worlds.

Utopia and heterotopia As alternative worlds, protest camps relate to a whole range of social practices that can be discussed as utopic or heterotopic spaces. Utopia, in particular, was first evoked by Thomas More's famous novel as a place that is at the same time a good place and nowhere. Criticising the transcendental notion of such an ideal world, far removed from reality, has been the stuff of both activists' interventions (in the name of claiming the good life in *this* world) and political theory. Perhaps most intriguing is Foucault's (1967) concept of heterotopia, the notion of a space that is entangled in this world and yet extends beyond its limits. Foucault's heterotopia mirrors the status quo and at the same time points beyond it. However,

Foucault's discussion of heterotopia is really too short to warrant any conclusions of the kind that claim that protest camps are in fact heterotopias. We would argue instead that a utopian politics aimed at radical alternatives to the status quo often inspires protest campers, since their practices are – without doubt – located in the here and now (see More and Duncombe 2012).

As we have argued and shown throughout this book, protest camps come into being because they border themselves against the outside, but they also remain entangled in and related to this world. Protest camps are partially organised, attempting to influence their environment through a strategy aimed at extending autonomy. But without a radical gesture of break, an antagonism that rejects the status quo at least implicitly, the space of the camp does not seem to come into being easily. With the negation of the status quo come the inspiring ideas that propel many social movements and activists. These ideas of an alternative world are indeed often so far removed from our present experiences that any path there seems to depend on a radical rupture, a new beginning. Protest camps are not simply mirror images of a social order that is already in place, but nor are they faraway utopias devoid of any relationship to the here and now. Indeed, in protest camps the tensions between antagonistic demands for a new beginning meet with the practical requirements of making things work in the present.

The constituent power of protest camps It is worthwhile dwelling a while on the notion of political association and constituent power that emanate from protest camps, even if they are set up in the most specific of single issue campaigns. The idea seems to be that people come together and share the resolution to live together under a new, partially autonomous framework. To highlight the difference we can deduce here between protest camps and other forms of social movements it is illustrative to read Arendt's (2006) concept of revolution and its political meaning. Arendt differentiates between the concept of power and the meaning of politics in modern constitutions. In the latter, politics is merely a matter of 'limited government', the safeguarding of individual and collective rights against government and rule – be it democratic or monarchical.

In her concept of power – in contrast – Arendt describes a collective phenomenon where there is no difference between rulers and rules. Power is potential (*potenza*), and by definition a collective phenomenon. Following Starhawk (1987) and Gordon (2010), we discussed 'power with' found in experimentation and innovation with organisational forms; as Gordon argues, it is found in voluntary associations of activists. In Chapter 4, we extended the notion of 'power with', describing how it can be specifically enhanced in the spatial and temporal territories of the protest camp.

In a sense, much social movement and protest activity aims at, and corresponds to, Arendt's concept of 'limited government'. Putting forward demands and requesting limits, social movements take the role of the ruled and appeal to government through protest, law and lobbying. Often, protest camps do precisely this: they put themselves in the way of building projects or they attempt to change government policy in some way. But protest camps also, importantly, point beyond this notion of politics as 'limited government'. In its constitutional capacity as a political space, a protest camp creates the possibility to overcome the very idea of a separation between rulers and ruled, at least within its claimed space, its re-created territory. A protest camp therefore can be understood as a 'new beginning', the political meaning that Arendt gives to revolutions. We have shown in the previous chapter how protest camps, often ironically and not entirely seriously, claim to constitute their own new republics. And although they do not issue passports, more often than not they start to operate as a social space, where people eat, sleep and care. Here, to some extent, there are attempts to pursue social reproduction in a total sense, including the provision of shelter, food, childcare, education, and so on. In this way, protest camps are at the same time constitutionally charged political spaces (where power is experienced as 'power with') and spaces that are constituted as social units (where power is related to managing social life). In this dual character, as a place that opens up possibilities of political autonomy *and* a place of social care, protest camps take up – sometimes directly and at other times implicitly – the long-running debates that cast a politics of individual autonomy as contradicting questions of care and social reproduction, as well as placing the politics of antagonism in contradiction to a collective responsibility for inclusivity. We suggest that the protest camp's dual role should be thought of as resulting in a set of dilemmas addressed more or less successfully in a *politics of commons*.

Protest camps and the commons

Protest camps face well-known dilemmas. As already discussed, there is a tension between utopian and heterotopian outlooks. But there are also tensions between individual autonomy on the one hand, and equality or social care on the other. As we have argued throughout this book, protest camps emerge with force from the end of the 1960s onwards as part of a trend towards more autonomy and more heterogeneous movements, notably described in the literature on new social movements. Protest camps emerge here; however, the form is neither that of the coffee house or salon of nineteenth-century Europe, considered so central to liberal democratic theory of the public sphere (see Habermas 1984), nor that of the utopian socialist communities of the same period (both of which, in different forms, have continued to exist since the eighteenth century). What we find instead is that protest camps are much more globally resonant forms of communal and nomadic living, of co-operative values and yearnings for relations beyond that of the ruler and ruled, the consumer and producer. *Equality*.

Protest camps, as we have argued, develop a set of infrastructures related to their aims both as places of autonomy and as social spaces of communality. Both developments come with a range of innovations and learning experiences by and for the people involved. In our view, infrastructures are important because they signify a relationship between things and people, where it is not only people that make things but also things that make people. Protest camps, in their operation, help form new subjectivities and, as such, contribute to a 'new beginning'. This is not to say that all camps call for revolutions. Rather, the 'new beginning' here is both experiment and experience. This is manifested in a range of learning processes, and in the development of new subjectivities and collectivities. Under certain conditions, a protest camp can be the catalyst for major political changes, and, in some instances, revolutionary uprisings. We discuss some consequences of the experimental and experiential revolutionary act that is protest camping in more detail as we now turn to revisit the findings from our infrastructural analysis.

Media and communication infrastructures Protest camps address critical issues that derive from their relationship to the outside world through what we call an ecological approach. In their relations to the outside, when protest camps speak and act as collectives, they tend to develop infrastructures that address the dilemmas inherent in these acts. For example, there is the very practical question of how to represent a diverse collective with varying opinions to a press and media from the outside world that expect leaders and unified positions. Protest camps show the power of opening up those dilemmas to broader debates and including journalists and other outsiders in these debates by way of permanent communication. Protest camps thus enable discussions among activists to address this dilemma, which frequently leads to some form of mainstream media policy being adopted and adapted at protest camps. At the same time, protest camps create the power to enforce their own standards on to the media (which has to adapt to protest camps' heterogeneity and refusal to speak with one voice) – we term this 'dual adaptation'.

Protest camps empower participants not only in this way but, more importantly, as they provide spaces in which participants may learn and pursue their own radical, camp-based media. As the rich and ongoing history of protest camp-based media shows, radical media plays a significant role in protest camps. It offers a means to escape the dilemma of media representation which comes when camps become sites of media interest. Moreover, it offers a platform to escape the confines of mainstream media representation, challenge official narratives, and expand the scope of representation using analogue and digital media. As shown by the protest camp media produced and the practice of production, protest camps have repeatedly been sites for the innovative use of technology; protest camps are places where people learn to use these technologies both theoretically and practically. It is therefore very apparent how the unique structures, objects and environments of protest camps shape subjectivities in the sense that protest camp media infrastructures play a role in forming media-savvy activists.

Action infrastructures In our discussion of action infrastructures, we began by noting that protest camps are actions in multiple ways. First, protest camps are the sites where the planning for protest takes place. Protest camps are 'base camps' for action. Protest camps are also places where people become 'active' or 'activate' their politics. Action, as we discussed, requires planning, training and skill-sharing. Protest camps offer people opportunities and outlets to tap into, develop and normalise the skills often required to take part in direct action. Lastly, protest camps are often protest actions in themselves. In such cases, the presence of the protest camp is itself antagonistic, a physical and direct intervention at the site of contestation. *

In considering action, one of the key dilemmas faced by many social movements is the question of violence. It sometimes splits movements and weakens resistance. Fundamentally, it boils down to a question similar to that facing communication: namely, how to define the relationship to the outside. In both practical and theoretical *Boundary.* terms we find a boundary here, defined by the state, which separates the realm of political action considered legitimate and accepted from the one that is not accepted and has to be repressed. While social movement activists, when they discuss violence, often find themselves on different sides of these borders, it is important to remember that the boundaries are not theirs in the first instance. Instead, these boundaries are drawn in legal and political discourse, and, more importantly, by the executive power (or we should say 'authority') itself.

For most people, the question of whether violent action is justified or not emerges out of a given situation. What we find so interesting about protest camps is that, in this context, they autonomously create a crucial boundary between the law of the land and its outside. By claiming a territory, often without the consent of authorities, the very act of establishing a protest camp is seen as violent from the perspective of the state. We argue that this changes the whole character of discussion over violence that happens in protest camps. The infrastructures of action in the camp are influenced by this autonomous setting. Within the camp, an ecology of action can emerge in which there is space for negotiations about and perspectives on what constitutes legitimate and legal action. As we discussed, protest camps cannot resolve decades-old debates about tactics. But their own materiality, the ways in which protesters are entangled with each other and with the objects and environments of their encampment, can make the more substantial questions of political violence and autonomous protest apparent to participants in ways that exceed the spatial–temporal experiences of confrontation in a demonstration or in other forms of direct action.

Governance infrastructures In questions of organisation and governance, the dilemma many social justice movements face is how to organise without undermining diversity and without introducing hierarchies and bureaucracies. Our discussion showed how important protest camps have been in addressing this question and allowing activists to experiment with new forms of organisation, and in particular partial organisation. The issue of organisation directly relates to questions of autonomy and commons. We argued that, since the 1970s, there has been a drive towards autonomy in many social justice movements across the world. This drive resulted from the experiences of previous policies and political action that focused primarily on addressing questions of social care by establishing increasingly forceful working-class organisation. In some countries, this led to the creation of socialist states that tended to focus mainly on the provision of care at the expense of autonomy of the individual. In systems that maintained capitalist production and liberal democracy, unions negotiated for better wages but did so in organisational forms that did little to enhance the autonomy of the workers in the workplace or within their political organisation. In the post-colonial world, the fallacy of development without autonomy came to the fore as well, as crude modernisation projects locked the post-colonial states into new dependencies and did little – in the end – to address either social welfare or autonomy of the people.

In a sense, then, the 1970s' new orientation of the left towards autonomy comes as no surprise; even if some are critical today of 'lifestyle anarchism' or 'artistic critique', we maintain that these interventions were crucial (if partly unsuccessful) against an onslaught of managerialist bureaucracy and organisation that continues to limit our autonomy. Equally, social movements have not, of course, totally abandoned ideas of social care since the 1970s. We would argue instead that these ideas are in a process of being reinvented in the bio-political notion of commons (Hardt and Negri 2009). Protest camps play an important role in this struggle for autonomy and commons because they allow participants to experience a dilemma that can be solved only in practice. The dilemma of democratic organisation or governance is addressed through partial organisation, whereby certain elements of organisation are employed but not all. We discussed the ways in which protest camps built on the experience of 'organic horizontality', which derives from antagonism and collective political dissent. In putting into practice and developing procedures such as horizontal decision-making, protest camps have attempted to preserve the organic horizontality experienced in expressions of antagonism (and more generally in moments of liminality). But rather than relying on procedure alone, they also develop a range of spatial practices aimed at enabling autonomy in the organisation of collective live. One central element, among others, is partial organisation through spatial practice, found in decentralisation. Thus protest camps develop a common practice as the foundation of their political commune which is based on a shared social reproduction. This forms the basis of the ability of protest camps to organise in a way that leads towards a reconciliation of the ideals and desires of autonomy and social care in a politics of the commons. Finally, however, further reflection is needed on the issue of how the social is reproduced and re-created in commons.

Re-creation infrastructures In our investigation of re-creational infrastructures we explored how protest camps are playing on and replicating very basic principles of human collectivity through infrastructures of shelter, food and care provision. While protest camps might be cast as 'nomadic' in the sense that their structures are ephemeral and generally architecturally unstable or impermanent, we warned against the essentialist duality evoked between notions of nomads and settled people. Rather, we noted the invention and reinvention (or various appropriations) of nomadic and tribal traditions. As notions of nomads and nomadic life travel transnationally, often via social movement literature and reflections, they often lose their contextualised histories. Instead, they are shaped into new mythologies that have become, in many instances, foundational to autonomous notions of community and commons. We see this in evocations from the origins of North American organised camping (Woodcraft Indians) to the Donga Tribe of the UK's 1990s anti-roads movement, to the drum circles of Occupy. These indigenous appropriations are often obscured in post-structuralist work as the conceptual 'nomad' or 'tribe' is lifted out of its imperial history. The post-structural nomad then becomes accustomed to re-reading histories of social movement activism without reference to the actual nomads or tribes that form part of the historical genealogy of organised communities, and hence organised camping. Tracing these processes would be a fascinating project.

Our analysis also emphasised the important role of exceptionality in enabling protest camps to tackle the bio-political juncture of autonomy and social care in the commons. The exceptionality of protest camps points not to an inherent character of a particular protest camp, but rather to the exceptionality of the organisational form and the way it is established through its infrastructures. This is partly because the exceptionality of the protest camp may best be conceived as contested, partial, and constantly challenged in ways that relate to its ephemeral and experimental character. In many ways, protest camps remain obviously connected to the status quo from which they aim to differ. In this sense, protest camps are likely to face the difficulties of accommodating newcomers and strangers. Questions of who is in and who can take part are permanently relevant. In a utopian settlement, or in an otherwise settled and closed intentional community, participation is often limited and highly regulated. From a political perspective, this constitutes a problem, since closure to the outside opens a Pandora's box of collective identities, nationalism or exceptionalism. While in one sense exceptionality is what allows the camp to territorially and culturally stake out its antagonism to the status quo, when turned into exceptionalism it can lead to camp failures and intense reproductions of nationalist and even fascist identities. As we discussed in our introduction on the history of organised camping, the re-creational infrastructures a camp provides, its unique temporal and spatial qualities, make it ripe for ideological training. In relation to protest camps, we see this form of more 'nationalist' or separatist exceptionalism produced when certain narrow notions of patriotism and activist identity are used to police and monitor a camp's borders and character.

Such potential similarity to the nation state is not accidental. Exceptionalism, regulating and limiting membership and creating an exclusive terrain, is precisely the approach through which nation states – or isolated alternative communes for that matter – propose to solve the dilemma of autonomy and social care: some autonomy and some care for some people. Needless to say, this 'solution' does little to actually solve anything. Indeed, protest camps often emerge precisely to take on the limits and failures of the state form. When protest camps use territorial exceptionality, we often see a conscious drive to open rather than close the borders, something that is also built into the very nature of the protest camp. There is an innate openness due to the fact that protests normally aim to increase support and numbers.

Moreover, protest camps' provisional architecture, their materiality that eschews bricks and mortar and employs tents and light-weight wood instead, prevents or at least hinders closure. As a result, most protest camps have to face the dilemma of autonomy and social care head on. It is because of this that we believe they occupy a special place in the grammar of social revolutionary practice. Of course, empirically speaking, some protest camps are more successful than others in working with and around the dilemma. The more inclusive a protest camp is, the more it must deal with dilemmas of autonomy and social care as it seeks to provide a homeplace for all its inhabitants. Some do attempt to close themselves off, sometimes verging on the reinvention of some sense of authentic community of campers, in a way repeating (both as tragedy and farce) the fallacy of nationalism. In other instances, protest camps might diffuse their boundaries in favour of an all-inclusive approach to such an extent that the antagonistic gesture towards the status quo becomes diluted. And perhaps most crucially, at times the re-creation of social space in common can lead to a denial of autonomy, or, conversely, the exercise of autonomy may become hollow because of a denial of care. We could call these developments the fallacies or pathologies of protest camps.

To win and to fail

The issue of failed camps, and perhaps pathologies of protest camps, is one that activists and the media often reflect upon. The questions about what 'it would mean to win' (Turbulence 2007) and what it means to lose are, of course, discussed more generally across social movements and not simply relevant to protest camps.

Protest camps may fail for a variety of reasons. And, of course, the failure of a protest camp might be read in different ways. So in this sense neither Tahrir Square nor the Spanish M15 movement would be considered, from our perspective, as failures, just because they might not have achieved all their political aims. Discussing the pathology of protest camps is not about measuring their success against a set of internal or external targets. Instead, we like to highlight some problematic dynamics that we as participants have witnessed but that are sometimes also widely reported. These have to do – more often than not – with the contentious struggle for (im)possible autonomy.

We are interested here, specifically with regards to protest camps, in some of the pitfalls and potentialities of this form. As we discussed earlier, protest camps are based on a dual promise: namely to provide autonomy, linked to an absence of 'power over' or violence, and to bring about the end of the division between rulers and ruled. The second promise relates to the 'care' of social inclusivity, the bio-political consideration to provide not simply autonomy but also new subjectivities co-produced in shared social reproduction. Both promises may and do fail in protest camps.

We discussed the centrality of antagonism for the constitution of protest camps, but we also indicated that antagonism that fails to remain inclusive in its ability to offer entry might turn into particularity, a culturally defined difference. Here, the criticism of a 'merely cultural' protest moves centre stage. Conversely, if social reproduction takes over, protest camps may start to engage primarily in social support work instead of focusing on their antagonistic questioning of the political process of the status quo. A danger is that the antagonistic political stance of the camp's original outlook remains only in name. This tension came about in Climate Camps and, more recently, in the Occupy movement.

Protest camps can also develop from their utopian practice into dystopian or perhaps pathological places; this happens as dilemmas that are more generally applicable to social movements become territorialised in protest camps. Just as much as the experience of direct democracy can be enhanced, so too can the 'dark sides of camping' emerge, something that is concisely described in reflections on the 2002 Strasbourg NoBorders camp (Schneider and Lang 2002). The 'dark sides' concern the potential pitfalls of attempts to organise autonomously as exemplified in endless meetings, and sometimes in the inability to make decisions. From our evidence presented in this book, it seems that when camps face dilemmas concerning individual and social care, their solutions vary widely, sometimes challenging and sometimes sustaining the status quo. Experimental and innovative techniques for re-creation based on combinations of existing practices are often imagined, and on occasion successfully deployed. Paying attention not only to action and governance but also to the processes of social reproduction that sustain ongoing protest is crucial to the advancement of social movement struggle and a fundamental part of alternative world-making.

A protest camp with specific campaign goals, and an antagonistic politics against the status quo, often encounters tensions around how to engage with people who inhabit the camp out of necessity (for free food and shelter), as well as those who see the camp as a place just to hang out or party. This is particularly an issue in urban camps, as was the case in many Occupy camps, but it also arises on a smaller scale even in remote locations. This brings about challenges as protesters cannot ignore matters of care and class, but at the same time they strive to remain focused and committed to their aims. Unique in their form as a site of both ongoing protest and daily living, protest camps (and similar place-based social movement forms) show us that these challenges are deeply entangled in environments, structures and objects (tents, kitchens, alcohol policies). In addition, they reveal to us that without re-creating our values and practices of both individual and collective autonomy, all we can win is a single campaign goal. The task of creating alternative worlds demands a co-operative approach to both antagonism and social care.

Different scales of violence and repression produce, and are caught up with, different protest camp practices and infrastructures. Sometimes camps are in a militarised confrontation of extreme violence and develop architectural as well as tactical responses to this. The Red Shirts' camp in Thailand, as well as the barricades in Oaxaca, might serve as an example here for a development that is politically necessary in the situation. Sometimes direct action camps also adopt militant tactics that are not necessarily for survival, or arising out of immediate threats of extreme violence, but are deemed the best strategy for achieving campaign aims and articulating an antagonism to the status quo. These practices can be transformative as participants enact collective autonomy in the face of repressive control. In some cases, however, when the possibility of violent state action is exaggerated and becomes the priority, it can produce forms of domination within the camp. This can create a pathology of bravado in which the defence of boundaries comes at the expense of care and collective autonomy, of giving attention to the differences that matter in creating conviviality and spaces of autonomy for everyone.

While protest camps face these internal challenges, at the same time there is a variety of ways in which they may win. While we could look at just the outcomes of camps as they end, as the tents are cleared and people go home, this gives us an incomplete picture. Sometimes a campaign goal has been won, nuclear weapons are removed, an airport or a pipeline is not built. Sometimes the battle is lost, the camp is evicted and the road is built. But whether the immediate target is 'won' or 'lost', as we have shown, protest camp experiences spill over between movements (Meyer and Whittier 1994). This spill-over can be seen as participants move on to new campaigns, their movement knowledge travelling and being translated into new contexts as they join new groups and encounter other activists at sites of exchange – whether later protest camps or the 'convergence spaces' of conferences, world social forums and counter-summits. This spill-over also happens with the infrastructures, as the materials and architectures of camping move from camp to camp. For example, the very tents and marquees of the HoriZone camp in Scotland in 2005 were used in NoBorders and Climate Camps in the UK throughout the second half of the decade.

In some cases, we even see protest campers develop protest camping 'careers'. For example, in the UK there are those who started off as Woodcraft Folk and then translated their experiences from one protest camp to another. The 2007 Climate Camp against Heathrow led to the establishment of a permanent 'intentional community', Grow Heathrow, which through its very presence and life on land destined to become a new runway combined the advance of the campaign goal and the formation of emancipatory forms of living.

In the final analysis, the joys and successes of protest camps, as well as their pathologies, do not necessarily correspond to the results of a particular campaign. In fact, protest camps might succeed in halting a certain building project or changing a policy and yet fail as a camp. If winning comes at the expense of activating an everyday politics of care and solidarity, if it makes the provision of autonomy impossible – does it succeed as a protest camp? While many protest camps might 'fail' to accomplish a specific campaign goal, they often succeed in myriad other ways. They instil experiences of autonomy and social care among their participants, activate politics and foster skills, knowledge and tactics that can spill over and inform other struggles and projects.

Overall, what remains when the tents are cleared and debriefs have been concluded is the presence of a range of dilemmas – in particular, over what it means to re-create daily life and maintain ongoing protest in ways that provide the individual and collective care we need, while still being able to carry antagonism forward. This problem lies at the heart of the attempt to build a politics of the commons. But reflection alone cannot navigate these dilemmas. It is at some point necessary in this quest to put the books away and join a protest camp. There can be no new answers to these questions without the experimental, collective experience of building alternative worlds together.

Protest camps research

This book brings alive the amazing worlds that are protest camps and calls for more critical and reflective attention to this phenomenon. Like protest and political action more generally, camps have become a universal occurrence. However, when speaking of protest camps, we must recognise how they differ from other social movement tactics, such as marches or strikes. Indeed, protest camps are much more than a passing tactic. To better understand protest camps as a unique genre of political action, we suggest that more research is done on them, continuing the ongoing debates and conversations brought together here. Protest camps offer a rich field of empirical study as they exist in all their different forms, but with striking parallels and similarities across transnational and trans-local contexts.

At the same time there is a broader sociological value in studying and comparing protest camps. This comes largely from recognising camps as a phenomenon that cuts across a wide variety of social movements, thus allowing for studies of how infrastructures, practices and strategies travel and are exchanged across movements and develop uniquely within specific movements and contexts. Protest camps raise important questions about the role and our understanding of autonomy and democracy. We argued that protest camps are places where people can experience organic horizontality in a political context, where attempts are made to translate these experiences into more permanent, and perhaps to some extent transferable, procedures and principles of organisation. The study of protest camps may therefore yield answers to some of the fundamental questions of sociology and social movements.

We feel that protest camps can be read as laboratories of the politics of the commons. We see that in current social movement practices there is a range of examples of such place-based laboratories, including social centres, neighbourhood organisations and newly founded autonomous universities, to name but a few. In these laboratories, people take matters into their own hands, pursuing a 'post-capitalist politics' that seeks to expand non-capitalist practices and to gain collective autonomy for them. However, beyond the important building works of post-capitalist politics, protest camps remain intrinsically wedded to the idea of antagonism and political action. As we have argued, it is from this constellation – as a laboratory of post-capitalist building works, as well as a tool of constituent political practice – that protest camps derive their specific relevance to a politics of the commons.

In this politics, our relationships with each other and with things are also actively recast. What we described as infrastructural analysis opens a path to study the materiality of the politics of the commons and a process to produce subjectivities. However, it also offers new assemblages of production where the duality of producer and consumer is re-created in multiple ways. At the same time, this analysis foregrounds the ways in which objects can become producers of our subjectivities. Infrastructures travel between camps, as do campers, and while we started tracing some of these journeys, we have certainly not exhausted the potential to make connections. We hope that our framework and the infrastructures identified can serve as a guide to study protest camps past, present and future.

What's missing? What next? When we began this book, our aim was to cover protest camps from every continent and as many nations and movements as possible. Early in the process of seeking out these stories, it quickly became apparent that while we might know of protest camps around the world, finding out enough about them to summarise their struggles and analyse their practices was in many cases not going to be possible. First, there are the obvious barriers of language and translation. Collectively, we speak only three languages fluently, and another few roughly. Without the time or funding to translate large bodies of archival materials or conduct multilingual interviews and focus groups, we quickly realised that our sample was becoming skewed towards Anglophone and German-language movements. So while there are many camps that have well-documented records and would have served as excellent case studies (No TAV in Italy, the Western Sahara, the Israeli housing protests, La ZAD in France to name only a few), we found ourselves only mentioning them in passing.

Another impediment to the kind of transnational sample we sought is the uneven documentation of different camps. The most common factor in how much material is available is the size of the camp, as well as how much international media coverage it received. It is therefore not surprising that Greenham Common is the subject of a number of books and articles, while the Puget Sound women's peace camp is documented in only a few sources. However, these discrepancies do not result from size alone. There are also differences in protesters' social and economic capital, access to documentary resources, and position in relation to broader networks that engage in documenting practices. These challenges highlight the need for more collaborative research and project networks that bring together scholars and activists working across different periods and national contexts. It also draws attention to the importance of preserving activist records, as well as of knowledge recuperation and oral history projects that seek to generate records of social movements using a variety of oral and written formats.

In the introduction, we discussed how this book takes place in the middle of an ongoing conversation. Over the past couple of years, as we began to write, present and chat to others about this work, we found that there were many people who shared our interest in protest camps and place-based social movement practices. Meeting in tents, at training sessions and by conference coffee tables, our research network has grown to include scholars from different countries, disciplines and stages in their careers. Together, we continue to work to create a welcoming and nurturing research environment, building some of the changes we want to see in university life. It is our hope that those reading this book will join in, and help us join up the ongoing discussions and debates about how we make and build alternative worlds together.

In the process of writing this book, we have been struck by all of the amazing stories our interest in protest camps has elicited. Whether after public talks or in everyday conversations, we find ourselves transforming from speaker to listener; from documenting these camps to bearing witness to others' memories of them. Throughout the process of writing this book, we found that in our quest to name and outline the protest camp as a recurrent, transnational phenomenon, we entered into a dynamic process. The meanings we were generating from existing accounts, testimonies and experiences were tempered and expanded by the anecdotes and reflections we collected from others. The protest camp became what Sara Ahmed refers to as a 'sticky object' to which experiences and affects adhere. In other words, as we have worked to make sense of the protest camp as a conceptual thing, 'the protest camp' has entered a process of becoming that thing.

The stories collected on our journey of making 'the protest camp' a conceptual thing have come from dedicated organisers, sympathetic visitors and arm's-length supporters, as well as from sceptics who do not see the point. There have been funny stories, sad stories, touching stories, short stories and long stories. But, most strikingly, and perhaps most often, there have been stories of transformation and discovery. Sometimes these are about a moment where the 'magic' of community was deeply sensed. Memories that capture a glimpse in time when another world felt possible. Yet also, of course, there were the dark stories. Stories of violence, both exhibited by the police and reproduced within the camp by protesters. These stories also stick, to ourselves and to our movements. They are the stories that demand – sometimes in shouts and at other times in whispers – that we care better for each other. They expose, via the collective act of encampment, how breakdowns and barriers are (re)produced in protesters' attempts to re-create communication, action, governance and everyday life.

It is through these kinds of story collections that this book writes its own genealogy. It is not a genealogy of linear chronology, direct inheritances or straightforward spill-overs. Rather, it reveals and revels in its crooked paths, its promiscuous infrastructures and practices. It shows us how camps can come to communicate with each other, whether via a travelling organiser, a pamphlet or a truck full of tent tat. Knowledge of practices and infrastructures both move and are exchanged in straightforward and unpredictable ways. Yet, as we go to press, eyes are on Turkey as another uprising grows from what was – and was not – a protest camp about a tree. The Taksim protesters choose to camp to protest the demolition of park area for a proposed shopping mall. After a violent eviction by the police, Turkish resistance soon grew. The issues quickly broadened to target neoliberal agendas and the repression of democracy. People camped, among other tactics, not only to claim freedom and care but to put them into practice. Soon after camps sprang up in solidarity, one was pitched in Berlin-Kreuzberg where many Turkish immigrants live. In this German neighbourhood, and all across the world to the uprisings in Brazil, protesters carried the slogan: 'Her yer Taksim, her yer direnis' ('Taksim is everywhere and everywhere is resistance').

From Tahrir Square to Syntagma Square, from the Puerta del Sol to the streets of Tel Aviv, from Occupy Wall Street to Occupy Gezi, and back through all the protest camps that came before, there is a yearning that resounds – a vision, an experiment, an attempt to make alternative worlds.

REFERENCES

a g.r.o.a.t (2010) 'Critiquing Climate Camp'. In Shift Magazine and Dysophia (eds) *Criticism without Critique: A climate camp reader*. Leeds: Dysophia, pp. 10–16. Available at http://dysophia.files.wordpress.com/2010/01/cca_reader.pdf (accessed 24 May 2013).

Adorno, T. (1991) *The Culture Industry: Selected essays on mass culture*. London: Routledge.

Agamben, G. (1998) *Homo Sacer: Sovereign power and bare life*. Stanford, CA: Stanford University Press.

Ahmed, S. (1998) *Differences that Matter: Feminist theory and postmodernism*. Cambridge and New York, NY: Cambridge University Press.

— (2004) *The Cultural Politics of Emotion*. New York, NY: Routledge.

Ahrne, G. and N. Brunsson (2011) 'Organization outside organizations: the significance of partial organization'. *Organization* 18(1): 83–104.

Alcadipani, R. and J. Hassard (2010) 'Actor–network theory, organizations and critique: towards a politics of organizing'. *Organization* 17(4): 419–35.

Alma (1983) 'The press'. *Outwrite*, January.

Arendt, H. (2006) *On Revolution*. New York, NY: Penguin Books.

Artivistic (2011) *Promiscuous Infrastructures*. Research residency at Centre des Arts Actuels Skol, Montreal, 27 June–20 August. Information available at http://skol.ca/en/programming/promiscuous-infrastructures-artivistic-at-skol/ (accessed 24 May 2013).

Atton, C. (2003) 'Reshaping social movement media for a new millennium'. *Social Movement Studies* 2(1): 3–15.

Baer, W. and K.-H. Dellwo (eds) (2012) *Lieber heute aktiv als morgen radioaktiv I: Die AKW Protestbewegung von Wyhl bis Brokdorf*. Berlin: Laika Verlag.

Barad, K. (2007) *Meeting the Universe Halfway: Quantum physics and the entanglement of matter and meaning*. Durham, NC: Duke University Press.

Bardini, T. (1997) 'Bridging the gulfs: from hypertext to cyberspace'. *Journal of Computer-Mediated Communication* 3(2). Available at http://jcmc.indiana.edu/vol3/issue2/bardini.html#Agents (accessed 24 May 2013).

Bauman, Z. (1992) *Intimations of Postmodernity*. London, New York, NY: Routledge.

BBC (2011) 'Egypt unrest'. BBC News [website], 11 February. Available at www.bbc.co.uk/news/world-12434787 (accessed 24 May 2013).

Benford, R. D. and S. A. Hunt (1992) 'Dramaturgy and social movements: the social construction and communication of power'. *Sociological Inquiry* 62(2): 36–55.

Bennett, J. (2010) *Vibrant Matter: A political ecology of things*. Durham, NC: Duke University Press.

Bey, H. (1991) *T.A.Z.: The temporary autonomous zone, ontological anarchy, poetic terrorism*. Brooklyn, NY: Autonomedia.

Blissett, L. (2002) 'Remembering Woomera'. Available at http://anti-popper.com/papers/remembering-woomera/ (accessed 24 May 2013).

Böhm, S., A. C. Dinerstein and A. Spicer (2010) '(Im)possibilities of autonomy: social movements in and beyond capital, the state and development'. *Social Movement Studies: Journal of Social, Cultural and Political Protest* 9(1): 17–35.

Boltanski, L. and E. Chiapello (2005) *The New Spirit of Capitalism*. London and New York, NY: Verso.

Bookchin, M. (1995) *Social Anarchism or Lifestyle Anarchism: An unbridgeable chasm*. Oakland, CA: AK Press.

Booth, M. (1999) 'Campe-toi! On the origins and definitions of camp'. In Cleto, F. (ed.) *Camp: Queer aesthetics and the performing subject – a reader*. Ann Arbor, MI: University of Michigan Press, pp. 66–79.

Bradshaw, F. and T. Thornhill (1983) 'Northern Ireland and Greenham Common: connections and contradictions'. *Spare Rib*, August.

Breines, W. (1989) *Community and Organization in the New Left, 1962–1968: The great refusal*. New Brunswick, NJ: Rutgers University Press.

Brodkin, K. (2007) *Making Democracy Matter: Identity and activism in Los Angeles*. New Brunswick, NJ: Rutgers University Press.

Brown, G. and H. Yaffe (2013). 'Nonstop against apartheid: practicing solidarity outside the South African embassy.' *Social Movement Studies* 12(2): 227–34. Available at: http://www.tandfonline.com/doi/abs/10.1080/14742837.2012.704355 (accessed 18 June 2013).

Butler, J. (1998) 'Merely cultural'. *New Left Review* 227: 33–44.

Calhoun, C. (1992) *Habermas and the Public Sphere*. Cambridge, MA: MIT Press.

Camp for Climate Action (2007) 'Revised Camp for Climate Action mainstream media access policy. How and why has the policy changed?' Camp for Climate Action [website], 14 August. Available at http://web.archive.org/web/20070927204549/http://www.climatecamp.org.uk/newpress.php (accessed 24 May 2013).

— (2010) 'Media access policy'. Camp for Climate Action [website]. Available at http://climatecamp.org.uk/press/media-access-policy (accessed 24 May 2013).

Carlson, R. (1986). In Eleanor Eells, *History of Organized Camping: The first 100 years*. Martinsville, IN: American Camp Assocation.

Carr, D. (2011) 'A protest's ink-stained fingers'. *The New York Times*, 9 October. Available at www.nytimes.com/2011/10/10/business/media/wall-street-protesters-have-ink-stained-fingers-media-equation.html (accessed 24 May 2013).

Castells, M. (1996) *The Rise of the Network Society*. Malden, MA: Blackwell Publishers.

Chase, R. T. (1998) 'Class resurrection: the Poor People's Campaign of 1968 and Resurrection City'. *Essays in History* 40(1). Available at www.essaysinhistory.com/articles/2012/116 (accessed 24 May 2013).

Chatterton, P. (2006) '"Give up activism" and change the world in unknown ways: or, learning to walk with others on uncommon ground'. *Antipode* 38(2): 259–81.

Cheek, L. W. (2012) 'In new office designs, room to roam and to think'. *The New York Times*, 17 March. Available at www.nytimes.com/2012/03/18/business/new-office-designs-offer-room-to-roam-and-to-think.html? pagewanted=all&_r=1& (accessed 24 May 2013).

Chesters, G. and I. Welsh (2004) 'Rebel colours: framing in global social movements.' *The Sociological Review* 52(3): 314–35.

— (2008) *Social Movements: The key concepts*. London: Routledge.

City Limits (1984) 'Greenham: a view from the stalls'. *City Limits*, 20–26 January. Review of the film *Carry Greenham Home*.

Cohen, G. A. (2009) *Why Not Socialism?* Princeton, NJ: Princeton University Press.

Collin, M. (2007) *The Time of the Rebels: Youth resistance movements and 21st century revolutions*. London: Serpent's Tail/Profile Books.

Cornell, A. (2011) *Oppose and Propose: Lessons from Movement for a New Society*. Oakland, CA: AK Press.

Costello, C. and A. D. Stanley (1985) 'Report from Seneca'. *Frontiers: A Journal of Women Studies* 8(2): 32–9.

Couldry, N. (1999) 'Disrupting the media frame at Greenham Common: a new chapter in the history of mediations?' *Media, Culture & Society* 21(3): 337–58.

— (2000) *The Place of Media Power: Pilgrims and witnesses of the media age*. London: Routledge.

— (2004) 'Theorising media as practice'. *Social Semiotics* 14(2): 115–32.

— (2012) *Media, Society, World: Social theory and digital media practice*. Cambridge: Polity.

CounterSpin Collective (2005) 'Media, movement(s) and public image(s): CounterSpinning in Scotland'. In Harvie, D., K. Milburn, B. Trott and D. Watts (eds) *Shut Them Down! The G8, Gleneagles 2005 and the movement of movements*. Leeds: Dissent!, pp. 321–33.

Cowan, G. (2002) 'Nomadology in architecture ephemerality, movement and collaboration'. MSc dissertation. University of Adelaide.

Cowan, R. (1983) *More Work for Mother: The ironies of household technology from the open hearth to the microwave*. New York: Basic Books.

Cowan, T. L. (unpublished) *Poetry's Bastard: The illegitimate genealogies, cultures and politics of spoken word performance in Canada*. Unpublished manuscript.

Cravey, A. J. (2010) 'Media geographies in the Oaxacan uprising: documenting the *People's Guelaguetza*'. *Aether: The Journal of Media Geography*, Fall 2010. Available at http://geogdata. csun.edu/~aether/pdf/volume_06/ cravey.pdf (accessed 24 May 2013).

Cremin, C. (2007) 'Living and really living: the gap year and the commodification of the contingent'. *Ephemera: Theory & Politics in Organization* 7(4): 526–42. Available at www.ephemerajournal.org/ contribution/living-and-really-living-gap-year-and-commodification-contingent (accessed 24 May 2013).

Cresswell, T. (1996) *In Place/Out of Place: Geography, ideology, and transgression*. Minneapolis, MN: University of Minnesota Press.

Crossley, N. (2003) 'Even newer social movements? Anti-corporate protests, capitalist crises and the remoralization of society'. *Organization* 10(2): 287–305.

— (2008) 'Social networks and student activism: on the politicising effect of campus connections'. *The Sociological Review* 56(1): 18–38.

Crown, S. (1979) *Hell No, We Won't Glow: Seabrook, April 1977: nonviolent occupation of a nuclear power site*. Pamphlet. London: Housmans.

Davies, C. (2012) 'Occupy London protesters to appeal against eviction ruling'. *The Guardian*, 18 January. Available at www.guardian.co.uk/ uk/2012/jan/18/occupy-london-protesters-appeal-eviction (accessed 24 May 2013).

Davis, M. (2000) *Fashioning a New World: A history of Woodcraft Folk*. Loughborough: Holyoake Books.

De Angelis, M. (2004) 'Separating the doing and the deed: capital and the continuous character of enclosures'. *Historical Materialism* 12(2): 57–87.

— (2007) *The Beginning of History: Value struggles and global capital*. London: Pluto Press.

de Jong, W., M. Shaw and N. Stammers (eds) (2005) *Global Activism, Global Media*. London: Pluto Press.

Debord, G. (1968) *The Society of the Spectacle*. New York: Zone Books.

della Porta, D., M. Andretta, L. Mosca and H. Reiter (eds) (2006) *Globalization from Below: Transnational activists and protest networks*. Minneapolis, MN: University of Minnesota Press.

Democracy Now! (2011) 'A guided tour of the protest encampment inside the Wisconsin State Capitol in Madison'. Video. Available at www.youtube. com/watch?v=pOv6S4aACx8 (accessed 24 May 2013).

Denham, D. and C.A.S.A. Collective (eds) (2008) *Teaching Rebellion: Stories from the grassroots mobilization in Oaxaca*. Oakland, CA: PM Press.

Diani, M. (1992) 'The concept of social movement'. *The Sociological Review* 40(1): 1–25.

Diken, B. and C. B. Laustsen (2005) 'Sea, sun, sex and the discontents of pleasure'. *Tourist Studies* 4(2): 99–114.

Do or Die (1997) 'A critique of Newbury'. *Do or Die* 6: 27–32. Available at www.eco-action.org/dod/no6/ newbury_critique.htm (accessed 24 May 2013).

— (1998) 'No escape from patriarchy: male dominance on site'. *Do or Die* 7: 10–13. Available at www.eco-action. org/dod/no7/10-13.html (accessed 24 May 2013).

— (1999) 'Comments on camps: out of site, out of mind?' *Do or Die* 8: 155–8. Available at www.eco-action. org/dod/no8/camps.html (accessed 24 May 2013).

Doherty, B. (1998) 'Opposition to road-building'. *Parliamentary Affairs* 51(3): 370–83.

Douglas, M. (1996) *Purity and Danger: Aan analysis of concepts of pollution and taboo*. London and New York, NY: Routledge.

Downey, G. L. (1986) 'Ideology and the clamshell identity: organizational dilemmas in the anti-nuclear power movement'. *Social Problems* 33(5): 357–73.

Downing, J. D. H. (2002) 'Independent Media Centers: a multi-local, multi-media challenge to global neo-liberalism'. In Raboy, M. (ed.) *Global Media Policy in the New Millennium*. Luton: University of Luton Press, pp. 215–32.

— (2003a) 'The IMC movement beyond "the West"'. In Opel, A. and D. Pomp-per (eds) *Representing Resistance: Media, civil disobedience, and the global justice movement*. Westport, CT: Praegar, pp. 241–58.

— (2003b) 'The Indymedia phenom-enon: space-place-democracy and the new Independent Media Centers'. In Lacroix, J.-G. and G. Tremblay (eds) *2001 Bogues: Globalisme et pluralisme*. Volume 2. Montreal, Canada: Les Presses de l'Université Laval, pp. 57–67.

— (2010) *Social Movement Media*. London: Sage Publications.

— T. Villarreal Ford, G. Gil and L. Stein (2001) *Radical Media: Rebellious communication and social movements*. Thousand Oaks, CA: Sage.

Duncombe, S. (ed.) (2002) *Cultural Resistance Reader*. London and New York, NY: Verso.

— (2007) *Dream: Re-imagining progres-sive politics in an age of fantasy*. New York, NY: New Press, distributed by W. W. Norton.

Economist (1994) 'The classless society'. *The Economist*, 19 February.

Eells, E. (1986) *History of Organized Camping: The first 100 years*. Martinsville, IN: American Camp Association.

Egan, E. M. (2006) *Commemorative History of the Minnehaha Free State and Four Oaks Spiritual Encampment*. Self-published zine. Available from Microcosm Publishing at http://microcosmpublishing.com/catalog/zines/1815/.

Ehrenreich, B. (2011) 'Throw them out with the trash: why homelessness is becoming an Occupy Wall Street issue'. TomDispatch [website], 23 October. Available at www.tomdispatch.com/blog/175457/ (accessed 24 May 2013).

Epstein, B. (2002) 'The politics of pre-figurative community'. In Duncombe, S. (ed.) *Cultural Resistance Reader*. London and New York, NY: Verso, pp. 333–46.

Escobar, A. (2004) 'Beyond the Third World: imperial globality, global coloniality and anti-globalisation social movements'. *Third World Quarterly* 25(1): 207–30.

Esteva, G. (2010) 'The Oaxaca commune and Mexico's coming insurrection'. *Antipode* 42(4): 978–93.

Evans, K. (1998) *Copse: The cartoon book of tree protesting*. Biddestone: Orange Dog Publications.

Eyerman, R. and A. Jamison (1998) *Music and Social Movements: Mobilizing traditions in the twentieth century*. Cambridge: Cambridge University Press.

Fager, C. E. (1969) *Uncertain Resurrection: Poor People's Campaign*. Grand Rapids, MI: W. B. Eerdmans Publishing Company.

Fairhall, D. (2006) *Common Ground: The story of Greenham*. London: IB Tauris.

Featherstone, D. (1997) 'Regaining the inhuman city: the "Pure Genius" land occupation'. *Soundings* 7(Autumn): 45–60. Available at www.amielandmelburn.org.uk/collections/soundings/index_frame.htm (accessed 24 May 2013).

Federici, S. (2004) *Caliban and the Witch: Women, the body and primitive accumulation*. Brooklyn, NY: Autonomedia.

Feigenbaum, A. (2007) 'Death of a dichotomy: tactical diversity and the politics of post-violence'. A review of Ward Churchill's *Pacifism as Pathology* (AK Press, 2007) and Peter Gelderloos' *How Nonviolence Protects the State* (South End Press, 2007). *Upping the Anti* 1(5). Available at http://uppingtheanti.org/journal/article/05-death-of-a-dichotomy (accessed 24 May 2013).

— (2008) 'Tactics and technology: creative resistance at the Greenham Common women's peace camp'. PhD thesis. McGill University, Montreal.

— (2010) '"Now I'm a happy dyke!": creating collective identity and queer community in Greenham women's songs'. *Journal of Popular Music* 22(4): 367–88.

— (2011) 'Promiscuous infrastructures: protest camps'. Canadian Centre for Architecture [website]. Available at www.cca.qc.ca/en/cca-recommends/1564-promiscuous-infrastructures (accessed 24 May 2013).

— (2013) 'Written in the mud: (proto) zine-making and autonomous media at the Greenham Common women's peace camp'. *Feminist Media Studies* 13(1): 1–13.

— P. McCurdy and F. Frenzel (2013) 'Towards a method for studying affect in (micro)politics: the Campfire Chats Project and the Occupy movement'. *Parallax* 19(2): 21–37.

Filip, J. (2011) 'Judge lets Occupy Fort Myers back into park'. Court House News. Available at www.courthouse

news.com/2011/11/23/41704.htm (accessed 24 May 2013).

Foley, G. (2001) 'Black Power in Redfern 1968–1972'. The Koori History Website. Available at http://kooriweb. org/foley/essays/essay_1.html (accessed 24 May 2013).

Foti, A. (2007) 'Pink, black, pirate: taking stock of Rostock: a new start for the European antiglobalization movement'. *Transform*. Available at http://transform.eipcp.net/correspondence/1182944688#redir (accessed 24 May 2013).

Foucault, M. (1967) 'Of other spaces, heterotopias'. Basis of a lecture given in March. Available at http://foucault.info/documents/hetero Topia/foucault.heteroTopia.en.html (accessed 24 May 2013).

Freedman, J. (1970) *Old News: Resurrection City*. New York, NY: Grossman Publishers.

Freeman, J. (1982) *The Tyranny of Structurelessness*. London: Dark Star. Available at www.jofreeman. com/joreen/tyranny.htm (accessed 24 May 2013).

Frenzel, F. (2009) *Politics in Motion. The mobilities of political tourists*. PhD thesis, Leeds Metropolitan University.

— (2011) 'Entlegende Ort in der Mitte der Gesellschaft die Geschichte der britischen Klimacamps'. In Brunnengräber, A. (ed.) *Zivilisierung des Klimaregimes: NGOs und soziale Bewegungen in der nationalen, europäischen und internationalen Klimapolitik*. Wiesbaden, Germany: VS Verlag für Sozialwissenschaften, pp. 163–86.

— (2013) 'The politics of mobility: some insights from the study of protest camps'. In Witzgall, S., G. Vogl and S. Kesselring (eds) *New Mobilities Regimes in Art and Social Sciences*. Farnham: Ashgate.

— A. Feigenbaum and P. McCurdy (forthcoming) 'A research framework for the study of protest camps'. *Sociological Review*.

— S. Böhm, P. Quinton, A. Spicer, S. Sullivan and Z. Young (2011) 'Comparing alternative media in north and south: the cases of IFIWatchnet and Indymedia in Africa'. *Environment and Planning A* 43(5): 1173–89.

Fuller, M. (2005) *Media Ecologies: Materialist energies in art and technoculture*. Cambridge, MA: MIT Press.

Gad, C. and C. Bruun Jensen (2009) 'On the consequences of post-ANT'. *Science, Technology & Human Values* 35(1): 55–80.

Gamson, W. and G. Wolfsfeld (1993) 'Movements and media as interacting systems'. *Annals of the American Academy of Political and Social Science* 528: 114–25.

Gerbaudo, P. (2012) *Tweets and the Streets: Social media and contemporary activism*. London: Pluto Press.

Geronimo (2012) *Fire and Flames: A History of the German autonomist movement*. Oakland, CA: PM Press.

Giddens, A. (1991) *Modernity and Self-identity: Self and society in the late modern age*. Palo Alto, CA: Stanford University Press.

Giesecke, H. (1981) *Vom Wandervogel bis zur Hitlerjugend: Jugendarbeit zwischen Politik und Pädagogik*. Munich: Juventa Verlag.

Gipfelsoli (2005) 'Counter Spin Collective – beginnings of some form of analysis'. Gipfelsoli [website], 20 November. Available at www. gipfelsoli.org/Home/Gleneagles_2005/859.html (accessed 24 May 2013).

Gitlin, T. (1980) *The Whole World is Watching: Mass media in the making and unmaking of the new left*. Berkeley, CA: University of California Press.

Goffman, E. (1959) *Presentation of Self in Everyday Life*. New York, NY: Anchor Books.

Gordon, A. (1997) *Ghostly Matters: Haunting and the sociological imagination*. Minneapolis, MN: University of Minnesota Press.

Gordon, U. (2008) *Anarchy Alive! Anti-authoritarian politics from practice to theory*. London: Pluto Press.

— (2010) 'Power and anarchy: in/equality + in/visibility in autonomous politics'. In Jun, N. J. and S. Wahl (eds) *New Perspectives on Anarchism*. Lanham, MD: Rowman & Littlefield, pp. 39–66.

Graeber, D. (2011) *Debt: The first 5,000 years*. Brooklyn, NY: Melville House.

Griffiths, J. (2000) *Pip Pip: A sideways look at time*. London: Flamingo.

— (2004) *A Sideways Look at Time*. London: Penguin Books, http://books.google.co.uk/books/about/A_Sideways_Look_at_Time.html?id=-_FbNDoZiNcC&redir_esc=y.

Grindon, G. (2007) 'The breath of the possible'. In Shukaitis, S., D. Graeber and E. Biddle (eds) (2007) *Constituent Imagination: Militant investigations, collective theorization*. Oakland, CA: AK Press, pp. 94–110.

Guattari, F. (2005) *The Three Ecologies*. London and New York, NY: Continuum.

Habermas, J. (1984) *The Theory of Communicative Action*. Boston, MA: Beacon Press.

Hailey, C. (2009) *Camps: A guide to 21st-century space*. Cambridge, MA: MIT Press.

Halvorsen, S. (2012) 'Beyond the network? Occupy London and the global movement'. *Social Movement Studies* 11(3–4): 427–33.

Hardt, M. and A. Negri (2000) *Empire*. Cambridge, MA: Harvard University Press.

— (2004) *Multitude: War and democracy in the age of empire*. New York, NY: Penguin Books.

— (2009) *Commonwealth*. Cambridge, MA: Harvard University Press.

Harford, B. and S. Hopkins (1984) *Greenham Common: Women at the wire*. London: Women's Press.

Harvey, R. (2010) 'The staying power of Thailand's red-shirts'. BBC Radio 4, 24 April. Available at http://news.bbc.co.uk/2/hi/programmes/from_our_own_correspondent/8640249.stm (accessed 24 May 2013).

Hassan, A. (1984) 'A black woman in the peace movement'. *Spare Rib*, May.

Heaney, M. T. and F. Rojas (2006) 'The place of framing: multiple audiences and antiwar protests near Fort Bragg'. *Qualitative Sociology* 29(4): 485–505.

Hedges, C. (2012) 'The cancer in Occupy'. Truthdig [website], 6 February. Available at www.truthdig.com/report/item/the_cancer_of_occupy_20120206/ (accessed 24 May 2013).

Hetherington, K. (1998) *Expressions of Identity: Space, performance, politics*. London: Sage Publications.

— (2000) *New Age Travellers: Vanloads of uproarious humanity*. London and New York, NY: Cassell.

Hodkinson, S. and P. Chatterton (2007) 'Autonomy in the city? Reflections on the social centres movement in the UK'. *City – Analysis of Urban Trends, Culture, Theory, Policy, Action* 10(3): 305–15.

Holloway, J. (2002) *Change the World without Taking Power: The meaning of revolution today*. London: Pluto Press.

hooks, b. (1990) *Yearning: Race, gender, and cultural politics*. Boston, MA: South End Press.

Hurl, C. (2004) 'Anti-globalization and "diversity of tactics"'. *Upping the Anti* 1. Available at http://uppingtheanti.org/journal/article/01-anti-globalization-and-diversity-of-tactics/ (accessed 24 May 2013).

Indymedia (2007) 'NUJ warns Climate Camp over restrictions on media'. Indymedia UK [website], 8 August. Available at www.indymedia.org.uk/en/2007/08/377840.html?c=on%20-%20comments (accessed 24 May 2013).

Invisible Committee (2009) *The Coming Insurrection*. Los Angeles, CA: Semiotext(e).

Ismail, S. (2012) 'The Egyptian revolution against the police'. *Social Research* 79(2): 435–62.

Jain, S. (1984) 'Standing up for trees: women's role in the Chipko movement'. *Women in Forestry*. Available at www.fao.org/docrep/R0465E/r0465e03.htm (accessed 24 May 2013).

Jasper, J. (1998) 'The emotions of protest: affective and reactive emotions in and around social movements'. *Sociological Forum* 13(3): 397–413.

Juris, J. (2008) *Networking Futures: The movements against corporate globalization*. Durham, NC: Duke University Press.

— (2012) 'Reflections on #Occupy Everywhere: social media, public space, and emerging logics of aggregation'. *American Ethnologist* 39: 259–79.

Kamel, N. (2012) 'Tahrir Square: the production of insurgent space and eighteen days of utopia'. *Progressive Planning* 191(Spring): 36–9. Available at www.plannersnetwork.org/wp-content/uploads/2012/04/PPMag_SP12_Kamel.pdf (accessed 24 May 2013).

Kanngieser, A. (2012) 'A sonic geography of voice: towards an affective politics'. *Progress in Human Geography* 36(3): 336–53.

Keraitim, S. and S. Mehrez (2012) 'Mulid al-Tahrir: semiotics of a revolution'. In Mehrez, S. (ed.) *Translating Egypt's Revolution: The language of Tahrir*. Cairo, Egypt: American University in Cairo Press, pp. 25–68.

Kinloch, J. (1985) 'Tens of thousands protest Star Wars in B.C.'. *Peace Magazine*, June. Available at www.peacemagazine.org/archive/v01n4p05.htm (accessed 24 May 2013).

Klandermans, B. (1994) 'Transient identities? Membership patterns in the Dutch peace movement'. In Larana, E., H. Johnston and J. R. Gusfield (eds) *New Social Movements: From ideology to identity*. Philadelphia, PA: Temple University Press, pp. 168–84.

Kneights, B. (2004) 'Baden-Powell, Robert Stephenson Smyth'. In Kimmel, M. and A. Aronson (eds) *Men and Masculinities: A social, cultural, and historical encyclopedia*. Santa Barbara, CA: ABC-CLIO, pp. 48–50.

Knell, Y. (2012) 'Egypt's revolution: 18 days in Tahrir Square'. BBC News [website], 25 January. Available at www.bbc.co.uk/news/world-middle-east-16716089 (accessed 24 May 2013).

Langlois, A. and F. Dubois (2005) *Autonomous Media: Activating resistance and dissent*. Montreal, Canada: Cumulus Press.

Latour, B. (2005) *Reassembling the Social*. Oxford: Oxford University Press.

Law, J. and J. Hassard (1999) *Actor Network Theory and After*. Oxford and Malden, MA: Blackwell Publishing.

Leed, E. (1991) *The Mind of the Traveler: From Gilgamesh to global tourism*. New York, NY: Basic Books.

Leidinger, C. (2011) 'Kontroverse Koalitionen im politischen Laboratorium Camp: antimilitaristisch – feministische Bündnisse und Bündisarbeit als kontingente, soziale Prozesse'. *Österreichische Zeitschrift für Politikwissenschaft* 3(4): 283–300.

Leontidou, L. (2007) 'Urban social movements: from the "right to the city" to transnational spatialities and flaneur activists'. *City – Analysis of Urban Trends, Culture, Theory, Policy, Action* 10(3): 259–68.

Lewis (2009) 'The Camp for Climate Action and the media: Part 1'. Indymedia UK [website], 21 April. Available at www.indymedia.org.uk/en/2009/04/428061.html (accessed 24 May 2013).

Loefgren, O. (1999) *On Holiday: A history of vacationing*. Berkeley, CA: University of California Press.

Lovink, G. (2011) *Networks without a Cause: A critique of social media*. Cambridge: Polity.

Mantler, G. (2010) '"The press did you in": the Poor People's Campaign and the mass media'. *The Sixties: A Journal of History, Politics and Culture* 3(1): 33–54.

McCurdy, P. (2008) 'Inside the media event: examining the media practices of Dissent! at the Hori-Zone eco-village at the 2005 G8 Gleneagles Summit'. *Communications: European Journal of Communication Research* 33(3): 293–311.

— (2009) '"I predict a riot" – mediation and political contention: Dissent!'s media practices at the 2005 Gleneagles G8 Summit'. PhD thesis. London School of Economics and Political Science. Available at http://etheses.lse.ac.uk/5/ (accessed 24 May 2013).

— (2010) 'Breaking the spiral of silence: unpacking the "media debate" within global justice movements. A case study of Dissent! and the 2005 Gleneagles G8 Summit'. *Interface: A Journal for and about Social Movements* 2(2): 42–67.

— (2011a) 'The fragility of Dissent!: Mediated resistance at the Gleneagles G8 Summit and the impact of the 7/7 London bombings'. *Culture, Language and Representation* 9: 99–116.

— (2011b) 'Theorizing "lay theories of media": a case study of the Dissent! network at the 2005 G8 Summit'. *International Journal of Communication* 5: 619–38.

— (2012) 'Social movements, protest and mainstream media'. *Sociology Compass* 6(3): 244–55.

McKay, G. (1998) *DiY Culture: Party and protest in Nineties Britain*. London and New York, NY: Verso.

Mehrez, S. (ed.) (2012) *Translating Egypt's Revolution: The language of Tahrir*. Cairo, Egypt: American University in Cairo Press.

Melucci, A. (1989) *Nomads of the Present: Social movements and individual needs in contemporary society*. London: Hutchinson Radius.

— (1996) *Challenging Codes: Collective action in the information age*. New York: Cambridge University Press.

Merrick (1996) *Battle for the Trees*. Leeds: Godhaven Ink.

Meyer, D. and N. Whittier (1994) 'Social movement spillover'. *Social Problems* 41(2): 277–98.

Mezzadra, S. and B. Neilson (2008) *Border as Method, or, the Multiplication of Labor*. Durham, NC: Duke University Press.

Mills, S. (2011) 'Be prepared: communism and the politics of scouting in 1950s Britain'. *Contemporary British History* 25(3): 429–50.

— (2012) '"An instruction in good citizenship": scouting and the historical geographies of citizenship education'. *Transactions of the Institute of British Geographers* 38(1): 120–34.

Montagna, N. (2007) 'The de-commodification of urban spaces and the occupied social centres in Italy'. *City – Analysis of Urban Trends, Culture, Theory, Policy, Action* 10(3): 295–304.

Moore, N. (2011) 'Eco/feminism and rewriting the ending of feminism: from the Chipko movement to Clayoquot Sound'. *Feminist Theory* 12(1): 3–21.

More, T. (1965) *Utopia*. London and New York, NY: Penguin Books.

— S. Duncombe (2012) *Open Utopia*. New York, NY: Minor Compositions.

N+1 (2011) *Occupy!: Scenes from occupied America*. London and New York, NY: Verso.

Nardi, B. A. and V. L. O'Day (1999) *Information Ecologies: Using technology with heart*. Cambridge, MA: MIT Press.

Nunes, R. (2005) 'The intercontinental youth camp as the unthought of the World Social Forum'. *Ephemera: Theory & Politics in Organization* 5(2): 277–96.

Offe, C. (1987) 'Challenging the boundaries of institutional politics: social movements since the 1960s'. In Maier, C. (ed.) *Changing Boundaries of the Political: Essays on the evolving balance between the state and society, public and private in Europe*. Cambridge: Cambridge University Press, pp. 63–105.

Offenburger, T. (1968) Transcript of an interview between Katherine Shannon and Thomas Offenburger conducted 2 July 1968 at Moorland-Spingarn Research Center, Howard University, Washington, DC.

Ostertag, B. (2006) *People's Movements, People's Press: The journalism of social justice movements*. Boston, MA: Beacon Press.

Participants of the Puget Sound Women's Peace Camp (1985) *We are Ordinary Women: A chronicle of the Puget Sound Women's Peace Camp*. New York, NY: Seal Press.

Pellagatti, M. (2012) 'Protests, livestreaming and lessons learned'. *The Huffington Post*, [website], 18 October. Available at www.huffingtonpost.com/michael-pellagatti/livestreaming-protests_b_1981210.html (accessed 24 May 2013).

Pickerill, J. (2003) 'Out in the open: Indymedia networks in Australia'. Paper presented at the Information, Communication and Society Symposium, Oxford University. Available at www.jennypickerill.info/Indymedia%20ics%20conference%20paper.pdf (accessed 24 May 2013).

— P. Chatterton (2006) 'Notes towards autonomous geographies: creation, resistance and self-management as survival tactics'. *Progress in Human Geography* 30(6): 730–46.

— K. Gillan and F. Webster (2011) 'Scales of activism: new media and transnational connections in anti-war movements'. In Cottle, S. and L. Lester (eds) *Transnational Protests and the Media*. New York, NY: Peter Lang Publishing.

Pusey, A. (2010) 'Social centres and the new cooperativism of the common'. *Affinities: A Journal of Radical Theory, Culture, and Action* 4(1). Available at http://affinitiesjournal.org/index.php/affinities/article/view/31 (accessed 24 May 2013).

Ramadan, A. (2013) 'From Tahrir to the world: the camp as a political public space'. *European Urban and Regional Studies* 20(1): 145–9. Available at http://eur.sagepub.com/content/20/1/145 (accessed 18 June 2013).

Raoof, R. (2011) 'About the media tent in Tahrir Square'. Retrieved from: http://ebfhr.blogspot.ie/2011/05/media-tent-in-tahrir-square.html (accessed 4 May).

Reed, T. V. (2005) *The Art of Protest: Culture and activism from the civil rights movement to the streets of Seattle*. Minneapolis, MN: University of Minnesota Press.

Ritchie, J. (1983) 'I meet the Greenham manhaters'. *The Sun*, 7 November.

Road Alert (1997) *Road Raging: Top tips for wrecking road building*. Available at www.eco-action.org/rr/ (accessed 24 May 2013).

Rojek, C. (1993) *Ways of Escape: Modern transformations in leisure and travel*. Basingstoke: Palgrave Macmillan.

Roseneil, S. (1995) *Disarming Patriarchy: Feminism and political action at Greenham*. Buckingham: Open University Press.

— (2000) *Common Women, Uncommon Practices: The queer feminisms of Greenham*. London and New York, NY: Cassell.

Ross, B. and T. Connor (2011) 'Occupy Wall Street: November 15th NYPD raid on Zuccotti Park, November 16th, and November 17th day of action'. *Daily News*, 15 November. Available at www.nydailynews.com/scribble#ixzz2UQsRfb6Ahttp://live.nydailynews.com/Event/Showdown_at_Zuccotti_Park_The_NYPDs_raid_on_Occupy_Wall_Street_NYC/18724990 (accessed 24 May 2013).

Rossiter, N. (2006) *Organized Networks: Media theory, creative labour, new institutions*. Amsterdam: Institute of Network Cultures.

Rossport Solidarity Camp (n.d.) '*Outside agitators' voices from across the water – reflections on resistance in Rossport*. Pamphlet.

Routledge, P. (1997) 'The imagineering of resistance: Pollock Free State and the practice of postmodern politics'. *Transactions of the Institute of British Geographers* 22(3): 359–76.

— (2000) '"Our resistance will be as transnational as capital": convergence space and strategy in globalising resistance'. *GeoJournal* 52(1): 25–33.

— (2003) 'Convergence space: process geographies of grassroots globalization networks'. *Transactions of the Institute of British Geographers* 28(3): 333–49.

— A. Cumbers and C. Nativel (2007)

'Grassrooting network imaginaries: relationality, power, and mutual solidarity in global justice networks'. *Environment and Planning A* 39(11): 2575–92.

Rucht, D. (2004) 'The quadruple "A": media strategies of protest movements since the 1960s'. In van de Donk, W., B. Loader, P. Nixon and D. Rucht (eds) *Cyberprotest: New media, citizens and social movements*. London and New York, NY: Routledge, pp. 29–56.

Sandoval, C. (2000) *Methodology of the Oppressed*. Theory out of Bounds, Volume 18. Minneapolis, MN: University of Minnesota Press.

Saunders, C. (2012) 'Reformism and radicalism in the Climate Camp in Britain: benign coexistence, tensions and prospects for bridging'. *Environmental Politics* 21(5): 829–46.

Schlembach, R., B. Lear and A. Bowman (2012) 'Science and ethics in the post-political era: strategies within the Camp for Climate Action'. *Environmental Politics* 21(5): 811–28.

Schneider, F. and S. Lang (2002) 'The dark side of camping'. Tactical Media Files [website]. Available at www.tacticalmediafiles.net/article.jsp?objectnumber=44087 (accessed 24 May 2013).

Scholl, C. (2012) *Two sides of a Barricade: (Dis)order and summit protests in Europe*. New York, NY: State University of New York Press.

Seel, B. (1997) 'Strategies of resistance at the Pollok Free State road protest camp'. *Environmental Politics* 6(4): 108–39.

Seller, A. (1985) 'Greenham – a concrete reality'. *Frontiers: A Journal of Women Studies* 8: 26–31.

Shift Magazine and Dysophia (eds) (2010) *Criticism without Critique: A climate camp reader*. Leeds: Dysophia. Available at http://dysophia.

files.wordpress.com/2010/01/cca_reader.pdf (accessed 24 May 2013).

Shiva, V. (1991) *Ecology and the Politics of Survival: Conflicts over natural resources in India*. New Delhi and London: United Nations University Press and Sage Publications.

Shouse, E. (2005) 'Feeling, emotion, affect'. *M/C Journal* 8(6). Available at http://journal.media-culture.org.au/0512/03-shouse.php (accessed 24 May 2013).

Shukaitis, S., D. Graeber and E. Biddle (eds) (2007) *Constituent Imagination: Militant investigations, collective theorization*. Oakland, CA: AK Press.

Silverstone, R. (1999) *Why Study the Media?* London: Sage Publications.

— (2007) *Media and Morality: On the rise of the mediapolis*. Cambridge: Polity.

SionPhoto (2007) 'News from the green zone...'. SionPhoto [website], 30 July. Available at http://sionphoto.blogs.com/sionphoto/2007/07/news-from-the-g.html (accessed 24 May 2013).

Sitrin, M. (ed.) (2006) *Horizontalism: Voices of popular power in Argentina*. Edinburgh and Oakland, CA: AK Press.

— D. Azzellini (2012) *Occupying Language*. New York, NY: Zuccotti Park Press.

Smith, M. B. (2006) '"The ego ideal of the good camper" and the nature of summer camp'. *Environmental History* 11(1): 70–101.

Snitow, A. (1985) 'Pictures for 10 million women'. *Frontiers: A Journal of Women Studies* 8(2): 45–9.

Snyder, S. (2006) *Past Tents: The way we camped*. Berkeley, CA: Heyday Books.

Sofia, Z. (2000) 'Container technologies'. *Hypatia* 15: 181–201.

Solnit, R. (2005) *Hope in the Dark: The untold history of people power*. Edinburgh: Canongate Books.

Starhawk (1987) *Truth or Dare: Encounters with power, authority, and mystery*. San Francisco, CA: Harper & Row.

— (2005a) 'Diary of a compost toilet queen'. In Harvie, D., K. Milburn, B. Trott and D. Watts (eds) *Shut them Down! The G8, Gleneagles 2005 and the movement of movements*. Leeds: Dissent!, pp. 185–202.

— (2005b) 'G8 2005 update #1'. Available at www.starhawk.org/activism/activism-writings/G8_2005_1.html (accessed 24 May 2013).

Stavrides, S. (2012) 'Squares in movement'. *South Atlantic Quarterly* 111(3): 585–96.

Stengers, I. (2005) 'Introductory notes on an ecology of practices'. *Cultural Studies Review* 11(1): 183–6.

Taffel, S. (2008) 'The three ecologies – Felix Guattari'. Media Ecologies and Digital Activism [website], 7 October. Available at http://mediaecologies.wordpress.com/2008/10/07/the-three-ecologies-felix-guattari/ (accessed 24 May 2013).

Tarrow, S. (1998) *Power and Movement: Social movements and contentious politics*. Cambridge: Cambridge University Press.

Tausig, B. and P. Doolan (2012) 'Music on the table'. *Sensate: A Journal for Experiments in Critical Media Practice*. Available at http://sensatejournal.com/2012/06/ben-tausig-peter-doolan-music-table/ (accessed 24 May 2013).

The Free Association (2010) 'Antagonism, neo-liberalism and movements: six impossible things before breakfast'. *Antipode* 42(4): 1019–33.

Thompson, A. K. (2012) 'Chris Hedges vs. CrimethInc. on violence: will we get the debate we deserve?' Truthout [website], 12 September. Available at http://truth-out.org/news/item/11471 (accessed 24 May 2013).

Treré, E. (2012) 'Social movements as information ecologies: exploring the coevolution of multiple internet technologies for activism'. *International Journal of Communication* 6: 2359–77.

Trocchi, A., G. Redwolf and P. Alamire (2005) 'Reinventing Dissent! An unabridged story of resistance'. In Harvie, D., K. Milburn, B. Trott and D. Watts (eds) *Shut them Down! The G8, Gleneagles 2005 and the movement of movements*. Leeds: Dissent!, pp. 61–100.

Tsomou, M., V. Tsianos and D. Papadopoulos (2011) 'Athen: Metropolitane Blockade, direkte Demokratie'. *Duisburger Institut für Sprach und Sozialforschung*. Available at http://www.diss-duisburg.de/2011/11/athen-metropolitane-blockade-direkte-demokratie/ (accessed 25 June 2013).

Turbulence (2007) 'Move into the light?' Turbulence [website], December. Available at http://turbulence.org.uk/turbulence-3/move-into-the-light/ (accessed 24 May 2013).

Turner, V. (1977) *The Ritual Process: Structure and anti-structure*. Ithaca, NY: Cornell University Press.

van de Donk, W., B. Loader, P. Nixon and D. Rucht (eds) (2004) *Cyberprotest: New media, citizens and social movements*. London and New York, NY: Routledge.

Van Deusen, D. and X. Massot of The Green Mountain Anarchist Collective (eds) (2010) *The Black Bloc Papers: An anthology of primary texts from the North American Anarchist Black Bloc 1999–2001. The Battle of Seattle (N30) through Quebec City (A20)*. Shawnee Mission, KS: Breaking Glass Press. Available at www.infoshop.org/amp/bgp/BlackBlockPapers2.pdf (accessed 24 May 2013).

Vidal, J. (2007) 'Climate camp's media mismanagement'. *Guardian*, 21 August. Available at www.guardian. co.uk/environment/blog/2007/aug/21/climatecamps mediamismanagme (accessed 24 May 2013).

Vollmer, J. (2007) 'Vom "Denkmal des mündigen Bürgers" zur Besetzungsromantik. Die Grenzen symbolischer Politik in der frühen Anti-AKW-Bewegung'. In Knoch, H. (ed.) *Bürgersinn mit Weltgefühl: Politische Kultur und solidarischer Protest in den sechziger und siebziger Jahren*. Göttingen, Germany: Wallstein Verlag, pp. 271–84.

Waterman, L. and G. Waterman (2002) *Yankee Rock and Ice: A history of climbing in the northeastern United States*. Mechanicsburg, PA: Stackpole Books.

Wiebenson, J. (1969) 'Planning and using Resurrection City'. *Journal of the American Institute of Planners* 35(6): 405–11.

Wolfson, T. (forthcoming) *The Cyber Left: Indymedia and the making of 21st century struggle*. Ithaca, NY: Cornell University Press.

Worthington, A. (2004) *Stonehenge: Celebration and subversion*. Loughborough: Alternative Albion.

Wright, A. N. (2007) 'Civil rights' "unfinished business": poverty, race, and the 1968 Poor People's Campaign'. PhD thesis. University of Texas. Available at https://repositories.lib.utexas.edu/bitstream/handle/2152/3230/wrighta71412.pdf (accessed 24 May 2013).

— (2008) 'Labour, leisure, poverty and protest: the 1968 Poor People's Campaign as a case study'. *Leisure Studies* 27(4): 443–58.

Young, I. M. (2005) *On Female Body Experience: 'Throwing like a girl' and other essays*. Oxford: Oxford University Press.

Zhao, D. (2001) *The Power of Tiananmen: State–society relations and the 1989 Beijing student movement*. Chicago, IL: University of Chicago Press.

INDEX

About Zed Books

Zed Books is a critical and dynamic publisher, committed to increasing awareness of important international issues and to promoting diversity, alternative voices and progressive social change. We publish on politics, development, gender, the environment and economics for a global audience of students, academics, activists and general readers. Run as a co-operative, Zed Books aims to operate in an ethical and environmentally sustainable way.

Find out more at:

www.zedbooks.co.uk

For up-to-date news, articles, reviews and events information visit:

http://zed-books.blogspot.com

To subscribe to the monthly Zed Books e-newsletter, send an email headed 'subscribe' to:

marketing@zedbooks.net

We can also be found on **Facebook**, **ZNet**, **Twitter** and **Library Thing**.